The Christian Sacraments of Initiation

Baptism
Confirmation
Eucharist

KENAN B. OSBORNE, O.F.M.

PAULIST PRESS
New York/Mahwah

The Publisher gratefully acknowleges the use of the translation of the passages on eucharist from D.J. Sheerin, *The Eucharist,* (Wilmington, Del: Michael Glazier, 1986) used by permission.

Scripture quotations in this book are from *The Jerusalem Bible.*

Library of Congress Cataloging-in-Publication Data

Osborne, Kenan B.
    The Christian Sacraments of initiation.

    Bibliography: p.
    1. Initiation rites—Religious aspects—Catholic
Church.   2. Sacraments—Catholic Church.   3. Catholic
Church—Doctrines.   I. Title.
BX2203.0785   1987   265'.1   87-6870
ISBN 0-8091-2886-1 (pbk.)

Published by Paulist Press
997 Macarthur Boulevard
Mahwah, New Jersey 07430

Printed and bound in the
United States of America

Contents

iii

Eucharist

Introduction

From the earliest period of the Christian era, the Church has celebrated the initiation of converts and neophytes into the community by a sacramental process which is seen as baptism–(confirmation)–eucharist. As one studies the various documents concerned with the baptismal rites of these early years, one sees that it was not only the ritual of baptism which the early Christians considered to be the initiation process, but also the sharing in the eucharistic meal. Baptism–eucharist is truly the sacrament of initiation into the Christian Church, and this baptismal–eucharistic process is clearly evident in the renewed rite of baptism in the Roman Catholic Church after Vatican II, particularly in the RCIA *(The Rite of Christian Initiation of Adults)*.

Confirmation is placed in brackets in the above description, and the reasons for this parenthetical approach will be clear when we begin the section on confirmation.

If the approach to the initiation into the Church is seen not merely as baptism, but also as baptism–eucharist, the implications for the ecumenical movement become somewhat acute, since there is often a recognition of one Church's baptism, but a refusal to welcome such baptized Christians to the eucharistic table. This, too, we will consider, once the picture of the sacraments has been presented. Moreover, the document presented by the World Council of Churches is entitled, not without deep theological reasons, ''Baptism, Eucharist and Ministry.''[1] There is not only a liturgical but also a theological connection between Church baptism, Church eucharist and Church ministry. Indeed, this document, which has been under study for decades, has wrestled with the inter-connection of these three ecclesial dimensions.

A similar situation can be seen in the Lutheran/Roman Catholic dialogues in the United States of America. In these documents, the Nicene Creed was the initial topic of discussion, which did not raise significant controverted questions. As a result, the second topic was one of the items in this creed: *One Baptism for the Remission of Sins.* This discussion on baptism led to the topic of eucharist, which became the third theme: *The Eucharist as Sacrifice.* Eucharist opened up the discussion to theme four: *Eucharist and Ministry.* But this moved the discussion to: *Papal Primacy and the Universal Church,* followed by *Teaching Authority and Infallibility in the Church.* Evidently, there is an inner dynamism which moves from baptism to eucharist to ministry. Not only is sacramental theology at stake here, but also ecclesiology.[2]

Both of these documents, in which Roman Catholics have had a great share as far as authorship is concerned, indicate one of the major themes of this present volume: namely, that one cannot talk of baptism without treating eucharist and ministry as well. The issue of ministry, however, is bracketed in this volume since it requires a volume all its own.

Without any doubt, the New Testament is the basic source for the study of baptism (confirmation) and eucharist. In the following pages much space will be given to the New Testament data. Since the turn of the century, Christian scholars have devoted considerable time and scholarship to the history of the sacraments. At no other period of Church history have the Church authorities and the Church theologians possessed such a clear view of the historical development of the Christian sacraments. Today we have insights into the sacraments which Augustine, Thomas Aquinas, Bonaventure, Scotus, Luther, Calvin, and Robert Bellarmine never had. For this reason, there are indeed new theological approaches to the sacraments in our present age, which help us transcend the limitations of the scholastic period, the reformation period and the post-reformation period.[3] Therefore, a great deal of time and weight will be given to the history of the sacraments in the pages which follow.

Of equal if not greater importance will be the emphasis on Jesus as the primordial sacrament, and the Church itself as the basic sacrament. The latter is presented to the Catholic world in the documents of Vatican II. The former is treated by eminent Catholic scholars in today's world. That Jesus and the Church would be considered sacraments is also quite new and affects one's total approach to the issue of sacramentality, a step which can only be welcomed by Catholic and Protestant alike.

Since the book is basically written from the viewpoint of the Latin Church, I will set out initially for each of the sacraments treated below the solemn teaching of the Roman Catholic Church. The fact that such a chapter comes first does not imply that the magisterium of the Church is above the Word of God, as expressed in the New Testament. Any and every solemn teaching of the Church must be based on and arise from the New Testament. Logically, then, it might seem that the initial chapters should be on the New Testament data rather than on the solemn teachings of the Church. Nonetheless, I feel that if these teachings are expressed from the outset, the reader will not suspect that there are any hidden cards. Rather, I hope to show that what the Church on very few occasions has proclaimed in a solemn way regarding baptism, confirmation and eucharist expresses the belief of the total Church as regards these sacraments, and not something which only Catholics, with their theological teaching, might be able to accept.

The Sacrament
of
Holy Baptism

Holy Baptism
A Selected Bibliography

Only volumes in English are presented here; in the footnotes references are made to materials in other languages.

Bausch, William J.

A New Look at the Sacraments, Mystic, Conn.: Twenty-Third Publications, 1983.

Bourgeois, Henri

On Becoming Christian: Christian Initiation and Its Sacraments, trans. Mary Groves, Mystic, Conn.: Twenty-Third Publications, 1984.

Deiss, Lucien, C.S.Sp.

Springtime of the Liturgy, trans. Matthew J. O'Connell, Collegeville, Minn.: The Liturgical Press, 1980.

Duggan, Robert, ed.

Conversion and the Catechumenate, New York: Paulist Press, 1984.

Dujarier, Michel

A History of the Catechumenate: The First Six Centuries, New York: William H. Sadlier, 1978.

————

The Rites of Christian Initiation: Historical and Pastoral Reflections, New York: William H. Sadlier, 1979.

Dunning, James B.	*New Wine: New Wineskins: Exploring the RCIA,* New York: William H. Sadlier, 1981.
Hatchett, Marion J.	*Commentary on the American Prayer Book,* New York: The Seabury Press, 1981.
	The Book of Common Prayer, New York: The Seabury Press, 1979.
Hovda, Robert, ed.	*Made Not Born: New Perspectives on Christian Initiation and the Catechumenate,*Notre Dame, Ind.: Univ. of Notre Dame Press, 1976.
Inter-Lutheran Commission on Worship	*Lutheran Book of Worship,* Minneapolis: Augsburg Publishing Co, 1979.
Johnson, Lawrence J., ed.	*Initiation and Conversion* (Presentations of 1984 Convention of FDLC) Collegeville, Minn.: The Liturgical Press, 1985.
Kavanagh, Aidan	*The Shape of Baptism: The Rite of Christian Initiation,* New York: Pueblo Publishing Co., 1978.
Kemp, Raymond B.	*A Journey in Faith: An Experience of the Catechumenate,* New York: William H. Sadlier, 1979.
Marsh, Thomas A.	*Gift of Community: Baptism and Confirmation,* Wilmington, Del.: Michael Glazier, 1984.
Mitchell, Leonel L.	*Praying Shapes Believing: A Theological Commentary on the Book of Common Prayer,* New York: Winston Press, 1985.
NCCB	*The Rites of the Catholic Church as Revised by the Second Vatican Council,* New York: Pueblo Publishing Co., 1976.

NCCB

Christian Initiation of Adults: A Commentary, Study Text 10, Washington, D.C.: USCC, 1985.

Neunheuser, Burkhard, OSB

Baptism and Confirmation, New York: Herder and Herder, 1964.

Reedy, William J., ed.

Becoming a Catholic Christian: A Symposium on Christian Initiation, New York: William H. Sadlier, 1978

Thurian, Max and Wainwright, Geoffrey, eds.

Baptism and Eucharist: Ecumenical Convergence in Celebration, Grand Rapids, Mich.: Wm. B. Eerdmans, 1983.

WCC

Baptism, Eucharist and Ministry, Geneva: WCC, 1982.

Wegman, Herman

Christian Worship in East and West, trans. Gordon W. Lathrop, New York: Pueblo Publishing Co., 1985.

E.C. Whitaker

The Baptismal Liturgy, London: SPCK, 1981.

———

Documents of the Baptismal Liturgy, London: SPCK, 1970.

1

Holy Baptism:
The Teaching of the
Roman Catholic Church

The following points must be considered as the teaching of the Roman Catholic Church, although they are as well the teaching of the Christian Church, Orthodox, Anglican and Protestant, for the most part.

1. HOLY BAPTISM IS A SACRAMENT

From Pentecost onward holy baptism has been an essential part of the Christian movement. We do not find it called a "sacrament" in the New Testament, but throughout the New Testament we find it to be the ritualized celebration in which one publicly expresses one's acceptance of Jesus as Lord and in which one believes that God accepts and forgives the individual baptized. As the terminology and theology of the Church developed, this ritual was called in the Greek-speaking world a "mystery," and slightly later, as Latin prevailed in the West, it was called "sacramentum." These two terms have remained constant throughout Christian history. Were one today to deny that baptism is a "mystery" or "sacrament" one would be outside the Christian framework and therefore heretical.

In the history of the Christian Church, particularly from the time of the Reformation onward, a small minority of Protestant churches have set aside the name "sacrament," and selected instead the name "ordinance." This was done not so much to deny the content of the term sacrament as applied to baptism, but to disassociate these small groups of Christians from the "seven-sacrament" theology of the Roman Church. It was and is not a case of denying specifically that baptism is a sacrament; rather, it is a case in which the non-biblical term "sacrament" was discarded, and a more biblically oriented term "ordinance" was selected. This was done, since in the New Testament we find that baptism and eucharist are the two rituals (sacraments) "ordered" by Jesus. We may be dealing here with a semantic problem, rather than an issue of heresy.[1]

Such a conclusion is further borne out by the recent document of the WCC, mentioned above. This document is often called the "Lima Document," since it stems, in its present form, from the WCC meeting at Lima. In this document baptism is theologically and liturgically seen as a constant for all Christian Churches and the term "sacrament" itself is used, though not in an abundant way. Since this is a document of consensus, involving even those Churches which prefer the term "ordinance," it would seem that the term "sacrament"—providing it does not entail a seven-sacrament theology—is acceptable to the entire Christian community.

2. BAPTISM IS THE "FIRST" OF THE SACRAMENTS

Whether a Church only accepts two sacraments (baptism and eucharist) or seven sacraments, all the Christian communities from New Testament times onward have maintained that baptism is to be received prior to eucharist, on the one hand, or prior to all six other sacraments, on the other hand. To deny this or to go against this constant practice would not be acceptable and would place one in an heretical situation.

I have placed the term "first" in quotation marks, since Vatican II has called the Church itself a sacrament, and even a basic sacrament.[3] In this approach to sacramental theology, the Church as sacrament is "first," not baptism. Moreover, current Roman Catholic theology on the sacraments (not expressed in Vatican II in any direct way) considers Jesus, in his humanity, a fundamental sacrament, indeed "the primordial sacrament."[4] In this approach to sacramental theology, Jesus is "first" to both the Church as sacrament and to any of the two or seven sacraments. However, even in this contemporary approach to sacramental theology, we are, as Christians, constrained to say that baptism precedes any and all other sacramental acts of the Church, such as eucharist, reconciliation, confirmation, etc.

3. BAPTISM WAS INSTITUTED BY JESUS

The belief that Christian baptism derives from Jesus has also been a constant teaching of all the Christian communities: Roman Catholic, Orthodox, Anglican and Protestant. Indeed, the Anglican and Protestant Churches have insisted that only baptism and eucharist were clearly instituted by Jesus and connected by him with the promise of grace. In Roman Catholic thought such a belief in the institution of baptism by Jesus has been a commonplace. The Catechism of Trent, and, in the United States, the derivative Baltimore Catechism, defined a sacrament as one "that was instituted by Christ to give grace." Once more, we have a teaching which would be heretical to deny.

Even though the "institution by Christ" has been constantly held by Roman Catholics, theologians have not been united in clarifying precisely when such an institution took place. Accordingly, there is no official teaching by the Church as to time and place when baptism was so instituted by Christ. *That* baptism was instituted by Christ is solemn Church teaching; *when* Jesus instituted baptism is a matter of theological opinion. Lercher, writing his theological textbook prior to Vatican II, enumerates five differing opinions suggested by reputable Catholic theologians on this matter. Lercher indicates his preference, but it is clear from the theological manuals that the time of institution is a matter of debate and therefore unsettled by any solemn Church teaching. The times which he enumerates are as follows:

a. On the occasion of Jesus' own baptism (St. Thomas).
b. On the occasion of Nicodemus' visit to Jesus (Estius).
c. Sometime after Jesus' baptism, either before or after the discussion with Nicodemus (Scotus, Suarez, Belser).
d. At the Last Supper (Aphraates). Lercher mentions that this opinion is somewhat unique.
e. At the Ascension, when Jesus sent his disciples out to make believers and to baptize (Alexander of Hales and Melchior Cano).[5]

Evidently, what is at stake here is not the precise occasion at which Jesus instituted baptism as a "sacrament." Rather, the issue of the Christian teaching is that baptism does not originate as a human institution, but that it comes from Jesus through revelation in one way or another. Baptism, then, is a matter of faith. It is not merely an historically and humanly established ritual. It is precisely in this area of God's work, not human work, in which the Church officially focuses our belief, and to go against this approach to baptism would indeed be heretical.

4. BAPTISM IS TO BE CELEBRATED WITH WATER

The baptism ritual has constantly throughout Christian tradition been celebrated with a washing in water. One would clearly be outside the Christian teaching if some other medium were used. Francisco a. P. Sola, S.J., in the theological textbook published on the very eve of Vatican II, mentions that a few have gone against this procedure of water baptism in the past. He mentions some Gnostic groups in early Church history and the Manichaeans who spiritualized baptism so much that natural water was eliminated. In the middle ages he indicates that some Cathari and Albigensians were similar in their approach to the baptismal ritual. Some groups have substituted a baptism by fire for a baptism in water. Here and there, other media have been promoted by splinter groups: oil with some water, saliva, wine, beer, etc. All of these the Christian community has judged unacceptable.[6]

The form of the washing has also been varied, and there is really no one way that must be used, that is, immersion in water, or pouring water over the head or forehead, or simply sprinkling with water. All three forms have, over the course of the Christian era, been used and approved by the Christian community, and are still in use today.

5. THE BAPTISMAL FORMULA MUST MENTION THE THREE DIVINE PERSONS

Theologians clearly present us with a baptismal formula which includes the "name of the Father and of the Son and of the Holy Spirit." In the Latin Church this invocation is preceded by the phrase: "I baptize you, in the name. . . ." In many of the Oriental Churches it is preceded by the phrase: "May you, servant of God, be baptized in the name. . . ." We also read in Acts that there may have been a baptism by Christians merely in the name of Jesus. Such a formula, documented by the New Testament, stands side by side with the formula we find at the end of Matthew's gospel, which mentions Father, Son and Spirit.

Over the centuries, certain other formulas have appeared, e.g., "in the name of the Trinity," or "in the names of the Father, Son, and Holy Spirit." Whenever the Christian teaching of the Trinity seemed to be compromised, such formulas were either declared heretical or ambiguous and therefore "suspect."[7]

Since trinitarian doctrine developed slowly during the first five centuries of the Church, one might ask what is the focus of this solemn teaching of the Church. The issue is, of course, not so much baptism, as it is a belief in the real, not simulated, incarnation of the Logos. Since the trinitarian doctrine of the Church developed precisely to vindicate the incarnation (this is the reason for the strong interconnection historically between the divinity of Jesus and the Trinity), baptism into Jesus would be seriously compromised if the trinitarian formula was ambiguous or incorrect. The centrality of Jesus in baptism is what is at stake in this insistence on a correct trinitarian formula.

The Council of Trent for its part refers to this trinitarian formula in the *Capitulum* (preliminary statement) on baptism and in the canons when it makes mention of a baptism administered by heretics who use the trinitarian formula and intend to do what the Church intends. However, it is not the focus of any of the solemn canons.

6. BAPTISM IS NECESSARY FOR SALVATION

In the widespread understanding of a sacrament as a ritual instituted by Christ "to give grace," the grace that is focused on is the grace of salvation. The Church's teaching underscores the intrinsic relationship between baptism on the one hand and the grace of salvation on the other. If the grace aspect were to be removed or denied, baptism would really no longer be a Christian sacrament. Grace and sacrament are two sides of the same coin.

When the known world of the Europeans was almost totally Christian, baptism and salvation as correlative were easily understandable. Those not yet baptized needed the preaching of the gospel, and for the medieval view, there were really only a few such unbaptized people: the Jews who lived a rather ghetto life in the European world, and the Islamic people against whom the Christians crusaded and attempted to missionize. When the Western hemisphere was discovered by the Europeans at the end of the fifteenth century, and the vast populations of the asiatic world were also discovered at about the same time, theologians faced a new problem. Since none of these people had ever heard of Jesus nor had the gospel proclaimed to them, did they all therefore go to hell, as all unbaptized should go? This opening of the European culture and the European theology to a world culture and a pluralistic religious scene was, in its time, a very challenging and revolutionizing situation. It was basically from this changed world view that the notion of a "votum baptismi" or a desire for baptism was theologically developed. The requirements of such a "desire" were disputed by theologians, some holding a rather narrow and well-defined group of truths, while others held that following one's conscience was sufficient.

The famous statement of Boniface VIII that there is no salvation outside the Church stems from this period of time. In the teaching of the Church on baptism as necessary for salvation, the main issue is not really with baptism, but with Jesus. The issue is christological. For Christians one must say that there is no salvation for anyone outside of Jesus Christ. This is the dominant and controlling idea behind the statement that baptism is necessary for salvation. Theoretically, then, baptism is necessary for all; practically, baptism as the acceptance of Jesus as the sole source of salvation has never happened. Baptism by blood (martyrdom for the sake of Jesus but prior to actual baptism) sufficed; and as mentioned some sort of "baptism by desire" was enough. It would lead us too far afield here to discuss this matter of the salvation of the unbaptized, but one might note that at Vatican II, in the Constitution on the Church, the most solemn of all the Vatican II documents, the bishops discuss the salvation of Catholics, Orthodox, Protestants, Jews, non-Christian believers, and even atheists. Clearly, there is still a large area of theological opinion involved. The main issue, however, remains: there is no salvation outside of Jesus Christ for any human being, and this mystery is celebrated in baptism; hence the necessary connection between baptism and salvation.

A secondary point that might be of interest to note is that theologians have not argued the case of the necessity of salvation on the basis of a doctrine on original sin. Rather, the case has been presented on the christological base: there is no salvation for anyone outside of Jesus Christ. To deny this would be clearly heretical.

7. BAPTISM IMPRINTS A CHARACTER ON THE SOUL

There is a long history to this teaching of the Church, a history which in a general way even precedes St. Augustine. Nor can one say that St. Augustine had a teaching on baptismal character. The theology of "character" developed long after Augustine. The Council of Trent states: "If anyone says that in three sacraments, namely, baptism, confirmation, and holy orders, a character is not imprinted on the soul— that is a kind of indelible spiritual sign whereby these sacraments cannot be repeated; let him be anathema." This teaching is a sort of summation by the bishops at the Council of Trent, and in language apropos to the theology of the time, of the centuries-long disputed issue on rebaptism (reconfirmation and reordination). We will enter into this history later on in more depth, but we need to say here that the council has indeed "defined" *that* there is a character. *What* that character might be was not defined. Actually, at the time of the Council of Trent theologians held to a variety of explanations, some as tenuous as that of the Dominican, Durandus. None of these opinions were disapproved and none were defined. The only issue which falls under the definition in the canon above is the fact of the existence of such a character.[8]

Again, one must look for the underlying issue, and the canon states it clearly: baptism is not to be repeated. Long battles had gone before Trent on the the issue of the rebaptism of those originally baptized by heretics. After long discussions, the Church solemnly came out on the side of no rebaptism.

8. ONE BAPTISM FOR THE REMISSION OF SINS

With clear reference to Ephesians 4:5, the early Church with great frequency referred to "one baptism." This is found in many of the early credal statements, e.g., the Coptic version of Hippolytus, the formula in St. Cyril of Jerusalem, or that in St. Epiphanius of Saliminia in Crete and in the "Nicene Creed."[9]

Clearly, two things are presented to us for our firm belief. First, baptism is not a diverse ritual, based on the person or the sect that administers the baptism. It is not Cephas or Apollo who baptizes, nor is it Paul himself; it is the Lord. Nor was it a Donatist baptism, an Arian baptism, an Orthodox baptism, a Protestant baptism, a Catholic baptism. Rather, there is one baptism, and this allows today the various Christian groups to accept the validity of each other's baptism.

Second, we are presented with the firm belief that baptism is related to the remission of sin and therefore with grace. Only God remits sin and only God bestows grace, and thus this is not a human ritual but one in which sacramentally God is at work. To deny these two aspects would clearly place one outside the Christian tradition.

9. BAPTISM AND ORIGINAL SIN

In the Decree on Original Sin, which the Council of Trent promulgated in 1546, a solemn mention of the connection between infant baptism and original sin was established. At the time of the Council of Trent there were some who denied the teaching on original sin or who had a variant view of what original sin meant. The Roman Catholic bishops at the Council wanted to clarify the stance of the Roman Church on this matter, since it was so vital to the theology of grace and sin itself.

In our own century, however, this particular teaching of the Church has not been perceived by highly respected Roman Catholic theologians as clear. In the 1930s and the 1940s a number of provocative articles were written on the issue of infants dying without baptism.[10] In the 1950s to the present theologians have reconsidered in a variety of ways the very meaning of original sin.[11] Today, the exact focus of this solemn teaching is not clear, and until the theological discussion of the various facets involved has become more unified, one must simply wait. This in no way means that the teaching should be discarded; rather, it means that the theological world, including the magisterium of bishops, needs to spend more time on the matter in order to clarify the issue. Factors which were not part of the discussion at Trent have arisen on this matter of original sin as well as salvation outside the Church; it is the insertion of this new material into the discussion which has complicated the matter at the present time.

*** *** ***

The above represents the solemn teaching of the Church on baptism. The issues discussed do not in anyway present a complete theology of baptism, but they specify certain aspects of such a theology which cannot be omitted or bypassed, without compromising in a serious way the Christian faith. Theologians have drawn together other aspects of baptism as well as the above to offer a more complete view of a theology of baptism. Such a "theology" includes the solemn teachings of the Church *and* a number of theological opinions which in no way are defined.

As far as definition by the Church is concerned, the Council of Trent has most solemnly declared the Church's position on baptism. In the following canons on baptism, drawn up by the bishops at the Council of Trent, some are pointedly directed to the sacrament of baptism; others are more concerned about sacramental theology generally, employing baptism as a case in point (e.g., no. 6, no. 8, no. 9 in which the relationship between faith and good works, here a sacrament, is fundamentally the key issue).[12]

THE COUNCIL OF TRENT, 1545–63

Canons on Baptism

687
(857)   1. If anyone says that the baptism of John had the same power as the baptism of Christ: let him be anathema.

688
(858)   2. If anyone says that true and natural water is not necessary in baptism, and therefore interprets metaphorically the words of our Lord Jesus Christ, "Unless a man be born again of water and the Holy Spirit" *(John 3:5)*: let him be anathema.

689
(859)   3. If anyone says that the Roman Church (which is the mother and teacher of all churches) does not have the true doctrine concerning the sacrament of baptism: let him be anathema.

690
(860)   4. If anyone says that baptism, even that given by heretics in the name of the Father, and of the Son, and of the Holy Spirit, with the intention of doing what the Church does, is not true baptism: let him be anathema.

691
(861)   5. If anyone says that baptism is optional, that is, not necessary for salvation: let him be anathema *(see 560)*.

692
(862)   6. If anyone says that a baptized person cannot lose grace even if he wants to, no matter how much he sins, unless he is unwilling to believe: let him be anathema *(see 572)*.

7. If anyone says that through baptism baptized persons become obliged merely to faith alone, and not to keeping the whole law of Christ: let him be anathema *(see 566)*.

693
(863)

8. If anyone says that baptized persons are freed from all the precepts of holy Church, either those that are contained in the Scriptures or those that are handed down by tradition, so that they are not bound to observe them unless of their own accord they wish to submit themselves to these precepts: let him be anathema.

694
(864)

9. If anyone says that the remembrance of the baptism which they have received ought to be so impressed on men that they be brought to understand that all vows taken after baptism are invalid by reason of the promise already made in baptism itself, as if these vows detracted from the faith they professed or from baptism itself: let him be anathema.

695
(865)

10. If anyone says that all the sins which are committed after baptism, are remitted or at least made venial by merely recalling and believing in the baptism once received: let him be anathema.

696
(866)

11. If anyone says that he who has denied the faith of Christ before infidels must, when he is converted to repentance, receive baptism again even when it was truly and rightly performed: let him be anathema.

697
(867)

12. If anyone says that no one is to be baptized except at the age at which Christ was baptized, or at the hour of death: let him be anathema.

698
(868)

13. If anyone says that because infants do not make an act of faith, they are not to be numbered among the faithful after they receive baptism and,

moreover, that they are to be rebaptized when they
come to the use of reason; or if anyone says that it
is better to omit the baptism of infants rather than
to baptize, merely in the faith of the Church, those
who do not believe by an act of their own: let him
be anathema.

14. If anyone says that when these baptized infants   700
grow up they are to be asked whether they wish to   (870)
ratify what their sponsors promised in their name at
baptism; and if they answer in the negative, they are
to be left to their own judgment, and that until they
come to their senses, they are not to be forced to a
Christian life by any punishment except that of
being kept away from the Eucharist and the reception of other sacraments: let him be anathema.

In the fifth session of the Council of Trent, June 17, 1546, the
bishops promulgated the following canon regarding original sin and its
connection with the sacrament of baptism. One must recall that, notwithstanding this canon, contemporary Catholic theologians in large
numbers have debated the very meaning of original sin, as was referred
to above.

If anyone says that this sin of Adam, which is one by origin,
and which is communicated to all men by propagation not by imitation, and which is in all men and proper to each, is taken away
either through the powers of human nature or through a remedy
other than the merit of the one mediator, our Lord Jesus Christ who
reconciled us to God in his blood, having become for us justice,
and sanctification, and redemption *(see I Cor. 1:30)*; or, if anyone
says that, through the sacrament of baptism rightly conferred in the
form of the Church, this merit of Christ Jesus is not applied to adults
and to infants alike: let him be anathema. Because "there is no other
name under heaven given to men by which we must be saved" *(Acts
4:12)*. Hence the words: "Behold the lamb of God, behold him who
takes away the sins of the world" *(see John 1:29)*. And: "All you
who have been baptized into Christ, have put on Christ" *(Gal.
3:27)*.

These solemn moments, in which the Church has professed in a
very articulate way its belief in baptism, are few, indeed. They are,

however, of great help to us in the twentieth century to see our way through the many aspects of baptismal theology. From a negative side, they are like beacons warning us of dangerous positions which earlier generations of Christians had to face, ponder and argue, and which they ultimately declared unacceptable on the basis of their New Testament faith. From a positive side, these teachings tell us that we have certain aspects of our baptismal theology, of which we can be, in faith, quite sure. Other aspects of our baptismal theology, which are more or less grounded on theological opinions, will be strengthened the more they interact with these foundational tenets. Metaphorically, we might say that we have a grid, bequeathed to us from former generations of the Christian community, which aids us to see more clearly into the mystery of holy baptism.

In the pages above we have nine summary statements on the one hand, and the full text of the canons of the Council of Trent on the other hand. In the theological manuals, which were so popular prior to Vatican II, the scholars made use of the "thesis method," i.e., statements based on the solemn Church teaching. The nine summary statements above follow in many ways this approach, but I have tried to underscore more clearly the "main issue involved" or "the basic teaching" which the Church has stated in such a solemn way. These nine statements, in many respects, seem to be acceptable not only to Roman Catholics, but also to other Christian Churches as well. They can do so, of course, only if they reflect clearly the very Word of God revealed to us in Jesus and articulated in the New Testament.

It is also clear, if one reads only the canons (or even the chapters) from the Council of Trent on the sacrament of baptism, that one does not have a complete "theology of baptism." To arrive at a comprehensive "theology of baptism" one needs historical data, liturgical data, opinions of various theologians, etc. In other words, a "theology of baptism" includes much more than merely New Testament data or the solemn teaching of the Church. There is a large area of historical variances and pluralism, of ritual variances and pluralism, and of theological opinions. This is found in all of the Christian Churches. If this area of "opinion" or "variances" or "pluralism" is not acknowledged, then Churches tend to absolutize areas which in no way represent "solemn teachings." The Roman Catholic Church, as is evident from the above, has been both circumspect and even reticent in formulating "solemn teachings." Practically speaking, this means that at times what is presented as "Church teaching" really includes a great deal of theological opinion and/or historical-liturgical one-sidedness. Hopefully, the above description of the solemn teachings of the Church presents a more sober and truthful accounting of the matter on the sacrament of holy baptism.[13]

With this in mind, let us now turn to an examination of the New Testament data on the sacrament of baptism.

Discussion Questions

1. What is the main issue behind each of the following Church statements?

   a. Holy baptism is a sacrament.

   b. Baptism is the "first" of the sacraments.

   c. Baptism was instituted by Jesus.

   d. Baptism is to be celebrated with water.

   e. The baptismal formula must mention the three divine Persons.

   f. Baptism is necessary for salvation.

   g. Baptism imprints a character on the soul.

   h. One baptism for the remission of sins.

   i. Baptism takes away original sin.

2. Using the documentation from the Council of Trent above, find each of those statements in the documents themselves.

3. Could an Anglican or a Lutheran, a Presbyterian or a Baptist agree with the nine statements above? If so, why, and if not, why not.

4. What do you as a Catholic find difficult with any of the above nine statements? Why?

5. What does a "solemn teaching of the Church" mean?

2

Holy Baptism and
the New Testament

The New Testament provides all Christians with the basis of a theology of the sacrament of baptism, and therefore the New Testament is truly the ecumenical starting point for baptismal discussion today. Indeed, there is presently a great deal of consensus among the Christian Churches on the meaning of baptism, and there is an ever-growing recognition of baptism performed outside one's own denomination among the Churches. Such mutual recognition is already a step in the Christian Churches' efforts to breach the scandal of a divided Christianity. Much of the literature developed by this ecumenical endeavor focuses on the history of the rite of baptism, or certain specific issues related to baptism, such as the question of infant baptism in the New Testament and the early Church. Another topic is the issue of infant or adult-only baptism in the Christian Churches.

What I would like to do in this and the following chapters is move the discussion off such specific questions, and relate baptism to the primordial sacramentality of Jesus and the Church itself. This is a fairly new and radical approach, at least in such terms as primordial sacramentality and derived sacramentality. Aidan Kavanagh helps us move in this direction when he writes:

> It must be remembered that the baptism of Christians was not jo-hannine but christic: it was a baptism not of water but of Holy Spirit. The water bath is a function of the Spirit. This means that pneumatic data concerning Christian baptism subordinate water data: the latter

are to be understood in terms of the former. This alters the usual approach adopted by scholars looking for evidence of initiatory ritualization in the New Testament.[1]

Kavanagh places Spirit data first and these govern the water data. This alters research. Since the Spirit is the Spirit of Jesus, I would like to reword the idea and say that Jesus as baptized is first and as such governs whatever might be said about the water-initiation, together with all the ritualization which developed out of this. This Jesus/Spirit governance is extremely helpful from an ecumenical standpoint, whereas debate over the New Testament evidence on infant baptism would not be so helpful.

On the following pages I have gathered the New Testament mainline thinking on baptism. These are all passages which the reader will have seen on innumerable occasions. What I would ask of the reader is that he or she consider them anew with the idea that Jesus in his humanness is the primordial sacrament; for Christians baptism is only a sacrament because Jesus is a sacrament and the Church is a sacrament. We begin, then, with probably the most central baptismal passage of all, namely, the account of Jesus' own baptism.

1. THE BAPTISM OF JESUS

Too often scholars who treat of baptism go immediately to the ritual of baptism as practiced in the early Church. In today's theological world, more and more emphasis is being placed on the baptism of Jesus himself as the focal point for an understanding of the Christian baptismal ritual. The baptism of Jesus was a key moment in his life, as portrayed by all four evangelists, and its significance needs to be ascertained more profoundly. To do this, let us consider, first of all, the text itself, and it is helpful to see these gospel texts in a "synoptic" way, that is, in a way which indicates the parallel passages in Mark, Matthew, Luke and John. Mark is placed first in this series, since his gospel seems to have been the first written one, and it also served as a basis for both the gospel of Matthew and that of Luke. One can see readily, in such an arrangement, the variations which both Matthew and Luke have brought to the Markan text. John's account is apparently of an independent nature; at least, one can say that his account is not based on the written material in Mark.

Mark
1:9-11

It was at this time that Jesus came from Nazareth in Galilee and was baptized in the Jordan by John.

No sooner had he come up out of the water than he saw the heavens torn apart and the Spirit like a dove descending on him. And a voice came from heaven, "You are my Son, the Beloved; my favor rests on you."

Matthew
3:13-17

Then Jesus appeared: he came from Galilee to the Jordan to be baptized by John. John tried to dissuade him. "It is I who need baptism from you," he said, "and yet you come to me!" But Jesus replied, "Leave it like this for the time being; it is fitting that we should in this way do all that righteousness demands." At this, John gave in to him.

As soon as Jesus was baptized he came up from the water, and suddenly the heavens opened and he saw the Spirit of God descending like a dove and coming down upon him. And a voice spoke from heaven, "This is my Son, the Beloved; my favor rests on him."

Luke
3:21-22

Now when all the people had been baptized,

and while Jesus after his own baptism was at prayer, heaven opened and the Holy Spirit descended on him in bodily shape, like a dove. And a voice came from heaven, "You are my Son, the Beloved; my favor rests on you."

John
1:29-34

The next day, seeing Jesus coming toward him, John said: "Look, there is the lamb of God that takes away the sin of the world. This is the one I spoke of when I said: A man is coming after me who ranks before me because he existed before me. I did not know him myself, and yet it was to reveal him to Israel that I came baptizing with water."

John also declared, "I saw the Spirit coming down on him from heaven like a dove and resting on him. I did not know him myself, but he who sent me to baptize with water had said to me, 'The man on whom you see the Spirit come down and rest is the one who is going to baptize with the Holy Spirit.' Yes, I have seen and I am the witness that he is the Chosen one of God."

We will take up the theological importance of this baptism later on; for the moment we might notice simply a few textual and contextual items. First of all, all four gospels mention the baptism; it is presumed by the Acts of the Apostles (1:22); it is mentioned in the Gospel of the Ebionites, although all our knowledge of this gospel derives from Epiphanius (*Adv. Haer.* 30, 13, 7-8); Jesus' baptism is likewise mentioned in the so-called Gospel according to the Hebrews, although our source for this is Jerome (*Contra Pelag.* 3, 2; *Comm. in Is.* 11, 2): Ignatius of Antioch makes reference to this baptism (*Ad Smyrn.* 1, 1); and Justin the Martyr does likewise (*Dial.* 88, 3-8; 103, 6). There seems to be little doubt that the baptism actually took place.

This is further substantiated by the way that the actual baptism of Jesus is accounted in the four gospels.

Mark: [Jesus] was baptized in the Jordan by John.

Matthew: A lengthy hesitation on the part of John the Baptist and a reassurance on the part of Jesus precedes the phrase ''as soon as Jesus was baptized.'' The baptism is not the main part of the sentence, but in a subordinate clause.

Luke: Literally a genitive absolute: ''When Jesus was baptized and while he was at prayer. . . .''

John: No mention at all of the actual baptism.

Evidently, and contemporary scripture scholars attest to this, there was some embarrassment to the early Christian community over the fact that John has baptized Jesus. After all, John had preached a baptism for the remission of sins, and Jesus was considered sinless. So the gradation from the bald statement that Mark so unabashedly makes, through the explanatory additions of Matthew to the silence of John bears witness to this embarrassment. Let us consider each of these accounts singly, in order to catch something of the author's intentions.

1. Mark's presentation of the baptism of Jesus is his opening statement. Mark includes no infancy narratives nor prologue; rather, he begins immediately with the baptism of Jesus and the subsequent public ministry of the Lord. The main purpose of the passage is to tell the readers who Jesus is. For the readers (listeners), there is no secret as to Jesus' identity (Mark's so-called messianic secret). The readers know from the start: ''You are my Son.'' In Mark, Jesus is the one who sees

the heavens opening; the vision belongs to Jesus alone. As we noted above, Mark is the only evangelist who unabashedly recounts that Jesus was baptized by John. Mark makes no qualifications nor explanations for this. Moreover, it is evident that the focus is not on John the Baptist nor on his baptism for the conversion from sin. In the baptism of Jesus we find only God's approbation and acknowledgement: "I am well pleased with you."

It should be noted that there is no mention of the messiah, and the pericope cannot be seen as a messianic consecration. Nor is there any mention of Jesus' own response or reaction. In Mark the focus remains on God's activity vis-à-vis Jesus.

2. Matthew, for his part, clearly utilizes Mark's basic text, but for Matthew the baptism is not the beginning of his gospel-account. A fairly lengthy infancy account precedes this section on John the Baptist and the baptism of Jesus. In that infancy account Matthew has already indicated to the readers who Jesus is. In chapter three, Matthew presents John the Baptist as announcing the kingdom of God, not merely repentance for sin (as in Mark). The Baptist's ministry is recounted in richer detail than in Mark, and the Matthaean message of the Baptist is urgent, decisive, striking hard against the mediocre approach of Jewish religiosity.

When Jesus enters the scene, Matthew indicates some embarrassment, for John's baptism was for the remission of sins as well as the kingdom. Jesus was, of course, without sin, and so Matthew introduces a conversation between John and Jesus, in which John protests and admits that Jesus should really baptize John and not vice versa. (One should remember that followers of the Baptist remained active through the time of Matthew and even that of the fourth evangelist, i.e., through 70 to 100 A.D.) Jesus' reply to John's protestations: "Let it be this way for now, for thus it is fitting for us to fulfill all justice," does not clearly indicate the reasons for which John should baptize Jesus. Nevertheless, the focus is thereby shifted from John to God and to Jesus.

In Matthew, God's words are not addressed to Jesus alone (as in Mark), but to all in a sweeping declaration: "This is my beloved Son." Likewise, God acknowledges Jesus: "In him I am well pleased." Again, one should not see in these words a messianic consecration, since there is no mention of messiah at all. The baptism, then, cannot be seen as a messianic consecratory act. Rather, the spotlight remains on God's acknowledgement of Jesus as his beloved Son. Just as the infancy narratives had told us who Jesus truly was and is (cf. Matthew's genealogy, the story of Joseph. the account of the magi), so, too, the baptism is portrayed as a divine acclamation that Jesus is the Son of God.

3. The account in the gospel of Luke varies considerably from both Mark and Matthew. Although some claim has been made that Luke had before him an independent source, not simply that found in Mark, biblical scholars today tend to discount this claim as somewhat extreme and unbased. Differences can be attributed to Luke's own intentions and style.[2]

Since only Jesus preaches the kingdom in Luke, John the Baptist is not a preacher of the kingdom, only of repentance. Moreover, in a way similar to Matthew, Luke has an infancy narrative which belongs to the structure of the gospel, and is not some later addition. The baptism of Jesus is not, then, the beginning of the gospel for Luke. Nonetheless, there are also good reasons to indicate that a substratum to Luke's gospel was a narrative account so that the baptism was for the substrate a beginning. The opening sentence of chapter three is indicative of this, since it is a very ornate periodic sentence: "In the fifteenth year of Tiberius Caesar's reign, when Pontius Pilate was governor of Judaea, Herod tetrarch of Galilee, his brother Philip tetrarch of the lands of Ituraea and Trachonitis, Lysanias tetrarch of Abilene, during the pontificate of Annas and Caiaphas, the word of God came to John, son of Zechariah, in the wilderness." This sentence is very much of a beginning sentence for something, even though it is not a beginning sentence for Luke's gospel. Some sort of substrate material is in evidence here.

In Luke, John preaches repentance for the forgiveness of sins, and in a way that is similar to Matthew's John presents a very harsh message. This section on John the Baptist, who is for Luke the last figure of the period of Israel (actually the first period is from creation to John the Baptist), a period dominated by the law and the prophets, concludes with a focus on Jesus, the beginning of a new period, the one "who is greater and who is coming."

In contrast to all the other three evangelists, Luke presents John the Baptist as a finished entity. He has been arrested and is in jail, when Jesus comes for baptism. There is in Luke a clean break between John and Jesus. Once John is imprisoned and effectively finished, Jesus is baptized, and clearly not by John himself.

At the baptism, Jesus is the center, and the entire baptism is placed in the context of prayer. Indeed, the actual baptism is simply referred to indirectly by a genitive absolute. Once more no mention is made of the messiah, preventing anyone from construing Luke's intent for this scene as a sort of messianic consecration. Rather, as Fitzmyer notes, "The main purpose, then, of the baptism scene in the Lucan Gospel is to announce the heavenly identification of Jesus as the 'Son' and (indirectly) as Yahweh's servant."[3]

4. John begins his section of Jesus' baptism with a clear presentation of who John really is: not the messiah, not Elijah, not a prophet, but a "voice in the desert," a herald of Jesus. The evangelist is not interested in John as a baptizer nor as a prophet, but only in John as the "first witness in the great trial of the Word."[4] John the Baptist describes his own baptism as preliminary, focusing on the one who is to come. In fact, the evangelist makes John rather effusive in what the Baptist says about Jesus: Jesus is the lamb of God, the pre-existent one, the one on whom the Spirit rests, God's chosen. As lamb, Jesus can be seen as (a) the apocalyptic lamb, i.e., the conquering lamb who puts an end to evil, which fits in well with apocalyptic literature generally, or (b) as the suffering servant of Deutero-Isaiah, which is the interpretation found in Jeremias, Cullmann, and Boismard, as well as the Eastern Fathers generally. Not until the Christian period does there appear to be any Jewish expectation of an eschatological suffering servant, much less a suffering messiah, and therefore John the Baptist would not have thought in these categories either, which is fairly much a post-resurrection reflection on the meaning of the life and death of Jesus. This leaves (c), namely that the lamb refers to the paschal lamb, which C.K. Barrett and the Western Fathers generally, among others, seem to favor. A reference to the paschal lamb might have been made by the evangelist but not by John the Baptist. Whatever interpretation of "lamb" which one adopts, it is important to realize that the focus is on Jesus and especially on Jesus as savior. His life, death and resurrection (the paschal mystery) is evoked by John's exclamation: "Behold, the lamb of God."

In line with the synoptics, the fourth evangelist describes Jesus as the one on whom the Spirit rests. Actually, John the Baptist alone claims to have seen the descent of the Spirit (in Mark and Matthew it is Jesus alone; in Luke it is everyone). However this is described, the presence of the Spirit marks Jesus as the chosen one. The choosing of this Jesus is God's action alone, and in this we see that baptism is not our own work, that is, our conversion or our repentance, but fundamentally the work of God.

John gives us a picture of the baptism as one fully transformed by the paschal mystery of Jesus, who is permeated by the Spirit, chosen by God, destroying evil, bringing new life. In all of this there is in the fourth gospel not one word about the actual baptism of Jesus, but we nonetheless have in his presentation all the deep theological elements of baptism, and it will be on these elements that a theology of baptism will be constructed by the early Christian communities. This theology, it must be noted, is not simply on the baptism of Jesus, but on the baptism which is seen from a post-resurrection vantage point.

To conclude this section on the baptism of Jesus, we have seen that the central aspect of the baptism in all four writers was not on John the Baptist nor his baptism, but on the identity of Jesus. Actually, the baptism as remission of sin is a secondary, yet important, aspect of these presentations. This presence of the remission of sins has caused some difficulty in interpretation over the centuries. Fitzmyer gives four possible answers which Christian scholars over the centuries have developed:

(a) Jesus, like all men and women, was himself conscious of sin. This view, however, goes against almost the entire Christian tradition from New Testament times onward (cf. Jn 8:46; 2 Cor 5:21; Heb 4:15; 7:26; 9:14).

(b) Jesus approves John the Baptist and all that he stood for by accepting his baptism. However, only Matthew's account might in any strong way support this interpretation.

(c) Jesus is portrayed as a "sort of disciple of John" through this baptism, which is seen as an initial connection with him. Although Conzelmann has raised strong objections to this approach, all four gospels could be seen in this way.

(d) Jesus' baptism by John is an anticipatory symbol of Jesus' submission to his suffering and death, a baptism which Luke mentions later in his own gospel (12:50). Fitzmyer finds this interpretation as the least likely.[5]

From a textual and contextual standpoint, the third approach (c) seems to be the most acceptable. One might also say that the baptism of Jesus by John is portrayed from a post-resurrectional standpoint and therefore already interpreted by later events. In this respect, the baptism of Jesus by John is *not* portrayed as a baptism of John applied to Jesus, hence remission of sins, but as a baptism of Jesus, the main focus, which profoundly transforms the very meaning of baptism into the acceptance by God through the Spirit. As Kavanagh has stated: the Spirit data governs the water data.

2. REFERENCES TO BAPTISM IN THE GOSPELS

Let us now consider the additional mentioning of baptism in the New Testament. Other than the opening passages on John the Baptist and the references to him (6:14ff.) and the baptism of Jesus recounted above, Mark's gospel makes only two other references to baptism:

Mk 10:38–39:   "You do not know what you are asking," Jesus said to them. "Can you drink the cup that I must drink or be baptized with the baptism with which I must be baptized?"

Mk 11:27–33:   They came to Jerusalem again, and as Jesus was walking in the Temple, the chief priests and the scribes and the elders came to him and they said to him, "What authority have you for acting like this? Or who gave you authority to do these things?" Jesus said to them: "I will ask you a question, only one; answer me and I will tell you my authority for acting like this. John's baptism—did it come from heaven or from man? Answer me that." And they argued it out this way among themselves: "If we say from heaven, he will say, 'Then why did you refuse to believe him?' But dare we say from man?" They had the people to fear, for everyone held that John was a real prophet. So their reply to Jesus was: "We do not know." And Jesus said to them, "Nor will I tell you my authority for acting like this."

In Matthew's gospel, other than the references to John the Baptist (11:2ff.; 14:3ff.) and the account of Jesus' own baptism, transcribed above, we have the following two passages:

Mt 21:23–27:   A restatement of Mark's passage, 11:27–33, without
              any substantial change.

Mt 28:18–20:   "Go, therefore, make disciples of all the nations;
              baptize them in the name of the Father and of the
              Son and of the Holy Spirit, and teach them to
              observe all the commands I gave you."

In the gospel of Luke, again with the references to John the Baptist
(7:18ff.; 9:7ff.) and to Jesus' own baptism on the one hand, we have
on the other hand merely two references:

Lk 12:50:   There is a baptism I must still receive, and how great
              is my distress till it is over!

Lk 20:1–8:   A restatement of Mark's passage, 11:27–33,
              recounted above, and with no substantial change.

In John's gospel, again with the same provisions as regards John
the Baptist and the baptism of Jesus himself, we have the following
baptismal references:

Jn 3:5:   "Unless one is born of water and the Spirit he
              cannot enter the kingdom of God." [Note: add to
              this verse the context of the entire conversation
              between Jesus and Nicodemus.]

Jn 4:2:   When Jesus heard that the Pharisees had found out
              that he was making and baptizing more disciples
              than John—though in fact it was his disciples who
              baptized, not Jesus himself—he left Judaea and went
              back to Galilee.

Jn 4:7–15:   The theme of water in the conversation with the
              Samaritan woman seems to have an acceptable
              reference to baptism.

Jn 7:38:   "If any man is thirsty, let him come to me. Let the
              man come and drink, who believes in me. As
              scripture says: 'From his breast shall flow fountains
              of living water.'" He was speaking of the Spirit,
              which those who believed in him were to receive.
              [Possible reference to baptism.]

Jn 9:1–41:   The story of the man born blind, the washing in the
                 pool of Siloam, and the restoration of sight.
                 Reference to baptism can be seen here.[6]

Jn 13:1–20:   The scene of the washing of the disciples' feet may
                 have a secondary symbolism connected with
                 baptism.[7]

Jn 19:24:   One of the soldiers pierced his side with a lance, and
                 immediately there came out blood and water.

One other series of statements are found in the four gospels which
have reference to Christian baptism, and these statements are the words
of John the Baptist when he makes reference to Jesus:

Matthew
3:11–12

"I baptize you in water for
repentance, but the one who
follows me is more powerful
than I am, and I am not fit to
carry his sandals; he will baptize
you with the Holy Spirit and
fire."

Mark
1:7–8

"Someone is following me,
someone who is more powerful
than I am, and I am not fit to
kneel down and undo the strap of
his sandals. I have baptized you
with water, but he will baptize
you with the Holy Spirit."

Luke
3:15–18

"I baptize you with water, but
someone is coming, someone
who is more powerful than I am,
and I am not fit to undo the strap
of his sandals; he will baptize
you with the Holy Spirit and
fire."

John
1:26–28

"I baptize you with water, but
there stands among you—
unknown to you—the one who is
coming after me; and I am not fit
to undo his sandal strap."

One should also confer Acts 13:25:

Before John ended his career he said, "I am not the one you imagine
me to be; that one is coming after me and I am not fit to undo his
sandal."

The association of Jesus' baptism and the Holy Spirit is not something we can leave to one side. Indeed, the Spirit data governs the water data, and the basic meaning of Jesus' baptism is the presence of the Spirit of God. We see this in the baptism of Jesus himself. Jesus was portrayed as anointed with the Spirit. We see this in the above references as well, in which the major gift of Jesus is the Spirit.

In the four gospels references to baptism are not abundant, and one would be hard-pressed to find a "theology of baptism" in these scattered and often occasional passages. There are, however, issues of fundamental importance for baptismal theology, but one must wait until the Acts and St. Paul to find this fleshed out in the New Testament data.

3. REFERENCES TO BAPTISM IN THE ACTS OF THE APOSTLES

Let us turn now to the Acts of the Apostles. In this document we gain some small insight into the communal activity and faith of an early Jesus community. We find that there is still missionizing going on, but we also find that there is a strong central core of the followers of Jesus. There are still strong ties to Judaism, but the Greek influence begins to make itself felt. It is a community in early growth and transition, with all the pains and doubts which this entails. Ministerial leadership has not yet settled into set forms; ritual life is being developed; even aberrations have begun to appear.[8]

We are not given a complete picture of early Christian life and belief, and as a consequence baptism is mentioned only in an occasional way. Still, there are strong overtones on the meaning of this ritual in these various passages. It seems wise to read through such passages first and only then attempt to summarize their theological issues. References to John the Baptist and his baptism will be omitted; only references to Christian baptism have been cited.

Acts 1:5:   "It is," he had said, "what you heard me speak
                   about: John baptized with water but you, not many
                   days from now, will be baptized with the Holy
                   Spirit."

Acts 2:37–41:   Hearing this, they were cut to the heart and said to
                   Peter and the apostles, "What must we do,
                   brothers?" "You must repent," Peter answered,

"and everyone of you must be baptized in the name of Jesus Christ for the forgiveness of your sins, and you will receive the gift of the Holy Spirit. The promise that was made is for you and your children, and for all those who are far away, and for all those whom the Lord our God will call to himself." He spoke to them for a long time using many arguments, and he urged them, "Save yourself from this perverse generation." They were convinced by his arguments, and they accepted what he said and were baptized. That very day about three thousand were added to their number.

Acts 4:4: [Indirect reference only] But many of those who had listened to their message became believers, the total number of whom had now risen to something like five thousand.

Acts 8:12–17: But when they believed Philip's preaching of the Good News about the kingdom of God and the name of Jesus Christ, they were baptized, both men and women, and even Simon himself became a believer. After his baptism Simon who went around constantly with Philip was astonished when he saw the wonders and great miracles that took place.

When the apostles in Jerusalem heard that Samaria had accepted the word of God, they sent Peter and John to them, and they went down there, and prayed for the Samaritans to receive the Holy Spirit, for as yet he had not come down on any of them; they had only been baptized in the name of the Lord Jesus. Then they laid hands on them and they received the Holy Spirit.

Acts 8:36–38: Further along the road they came to some water, and the eunuch said, "Look, there is some water here; is there anything to stop me from being baptized?" He ordered the chariot to stop; then Philip and the eunuch both went down into the water and Philip baptized him. But after they had come up out of the water again Philip was taken away by the Spirit of the Lord, and the eunuch never saw him again but went on his way rejoicing.

Note: v. 37 is a very ancient gloss which, though not original to Acts, provides an interesting, early baptismal profession of faith: "And Philip said: 'If you believe in your heart you can.' And he replied, 'I believe that Jesus is the Son of God.'"

Acts 9:17-19   Ananias entered the house and at once laid his hands on Saul and said: "Brother Saul, I have been sent by the Lord Jesus who appeared to you on your way here so that you may recover your sight and be filled with the Holy Spirit." Immediately it was as though scales fell away from Saul's eyes and he could see again. So, he was baptized there and then, and after taking some food he regained his strength.

Acts 22:12–16   [The second account in Acts of Paul's conversion] "Someone called Ananias, a devout follower of the Law and highly thought of by all the Jews living there, came to see me; he stood beside me and said, 'Brother Saul, receive your sight.' Instantly my sight came back and I was able to see him. Then he said, 'The God of our ancestors has chosen you to know his will, to see the Just One and hear his own voice speaking, because you are to be his witness before all mankind, testifying to what you have seen and heard. And now why delay? It is time you were baptized and had your sins washed away while invoking his name.'"

Note: In the third account of Paul's conversion narrated by the Acts of the Apostles, Acts 26:16-18, there is no reference to his baptism, nor is there any reference in Paul's own account of his conversion, found in Galatians 1:15-17.

Acts 10:44–48:   While Peter was still speaking, the Holy Spirit came down on all the listeners. Jewish believers who had accompanied Peter were all astonished that the gift of the Holy Spirit should be poured out on the pagans too, since they could hear them speaking strange languages and proclaiming the greatness of God. Peter himself then said, "Could anyone refuse the water of baptism to these people now they have received the Holy Spirit just as much as we have?" He then gave orders for them to be baptized in the name of Jesus Christ.

Acts 11:15–18:   "I [Peter] had scarcely begun to speak when the Holy Spirit came down on them in the same way as it came on us at the beginning, and I remembered that the Lord had said, 'John baptized with water, but you will be baptized with the Holy Spirit.' I realized then that God was giving them the identical thing he gave us when we believed in the Lord Jesus Christ, and who was I to stand in God's way? This account satisfied them, and they gave glory to God. 'God,' they said, 'can evidently grant even the pagans the repentance that leads to life.'"

Acts 16:14–15:   "She [Lydia] listened to us, and the Lord opened her heart to accept what Paul was saying. After she and her household had been baptized, she sent us an invitation: 'If you really think me a true believer in the Lord,' she said, 'come and stay with us.' And she would take no refusal."

Acts 16:29–34:   The jailer called for lights, then rushed in, threw himself trembling at the feet of Paul and Silas, and escorted them out, saying, "Sirs, what must I do to be saved?" They told him, "Become a believer in the Lord Jesus, and you will be saved, and your household too." Then they preached the word of the Lord to him and to all his family. Late as it was, he took them to wash their wounds, and was baptized then and there with all his household. Afterward he took them home and gave them a meal, and the whole family celebrated their conversion to belief in God.

Acts 18:7–8:   Then he [Paul] left the synagogue and moved to the house next door that belonged to a worshiper of God called Justus. Crispus, president of the synagogue, and his whole household, all became believers in the Lord. A great many Corinthians who had heard him became believers and were baptized.

> Note: The account of Apollos in Acts 18:24-28 implies that Apollos was baptized but it does not explicitly state this.

Acts 19:1-7:   While Apollos was in Corinth, Paul made his way overland as far as Ephesus, where he found a number of disciples. When he asked, "Did you receive the Holy Spirit when you became believers?" they answered, "No, we were never even told there was such a thing as a Holy Spirit." "Then how were you baptized?" he asked. "With John's baptism," they replied. "John's baptism," said Paul, "was a baptism of repentance; but he insisted that the people should believe in the one who was to come after him—in other words Jesus." When they heard this they were baptized in the name of the Lord Jesus, and the moment Paul had laid hands on them the Holy Spirit came down on them, and they began to speak with tongues and to prophesy. There were about twelve of these men.

Such are the direct references to baptism which occur in the Acts of the Apostles; indirect references generally refer to belief, a turning from something and a believing in the Lord Jesus. There are some points, however, which should be underscored, which derive from this material out of Acts:

1. There is no extended theological interpretation given to Christian baptism, such as we find in Paul's letters.

2. Baptism is associated with:
   (a) The Holy Spirit and his gifts
   (b) Salvation

(c) Belief in the Lord Jesus

(d) Belief in God (Acts 16:34) which in some ways is curious

(e) An entire household, which some scholars interpret to include small children

(f) Repentance of sin

(g) The preaching of the Good News, the Gospel

(h) Jew and Gentile alike

It is clear that for both the gospels and for the Acts of the Apostles the central idea or focus in baptism is Jesus, and all that Jesus has brought: salvation, the Holy Spirit, the possibility of repentance, etc. Were one to take Jesus from this picture of baptism in the early Church, there would be no baptism at all. We are dealing with Christian baptism, a baptism centralized around Jesus, and this clearly gives us a New Testament basis for understanding Jesus as the primordial sacrament.

In the gospels and in Acts, baptism is not a private matter, but one which involves the disciples of Jesus. In the earliest strata of the Christian community, there may not be a self-understanding by this community of itself as a "Church." But there clearly is a self-understanding of a community, centralized by Jesus. Baptism is, then, a community ritual, and this helps us to understand the Church itself as a basic community, the community of the baptized. It is on this footing that the Church as a basic sacrament finds its stability in the theological world, and thereby enters into the theology of sacraments.

Nonetheless, with only the gospels and Acts we do not have a very detailed theology of baptism. For such a theology, we must turn to the writings of St. Paul.

4. REFERENCES TO BAPTISM IN ST. PAUL

All of Paul's letters are addressed to Christian communities and consequently baptism is a self-understood datum. Still, what we are looking for are his deliberate references to baptism and above all his theological interpretation of baptism. There is something to be gained by going through his letters in chronological order which presents his own growth in understanding the mysteries of the Christian faith. The dates that are offered are those found in the *Introduction to the New Testament* by Feine-Behm-Kümmel,[9] and in this context are merely meant to indicate the general time of composition without making any defense for a particular given date, since the dating of each letter, as is well known, is open to question.

1 Thes (c. 50)	No explicit reference to baptism is made; perhaps an indirect reference can be found in 4:8: "In other words, anyone who objects is not objecting to a human authority, but to God who gives you his Holy Spirit."
2 Thes (c. 50/51)	Again no explicit reference to baptism is made. In both letters Paul evidently felt no constraint to underscore the meaning of baptism for the life of the Thessalonian Christian community.
1 Cor (c. 54/55)	
1:12–16:	What I mean are all these slogans that you have, like: "I am for Paul," "I am for Apollos," "I am for Cephas," "I am for Christ." Has Christ been parceled out? Was it Paul that was crucified for you? Were you baptized in the name of Paul? I am thankful that I never baptized any of you after Crispus and Gaius so none of you can say he was baptized in my name. Then there was the family of Stephanus, of course, that I baptized too, but no one else as far as I can remember.
6:11:	These are the sort of people some of you were once, but now you have been washed clean, and sanctified, and justified through the name of the Lord Jesus Christ and through the Spirit of our God.
6:19–20:	Your body, you know, is the temple of the Holy Spirit, who is in you since you received him from God. You are not your own property; you have been bought and paid for. That is why you should use your body for the glory of God.

Note: This line of thinking might also be
connected with 6:17: "But anyone who
is joined to the Lord is one spirit with
him."

10:1–5:   I want to remind you, brothers, how our
fathers were all guided by a cloud above them
and how they all passed through the sea. They
were all baptized into Moses in this cloud and
in this sea; all ate the same spiritual food and
all drank the same spiritual drink, since they all
drank from the spiritual rock that followed
them as they went, and that rock was Christ. In
spite of this, most of them failed to please God
and their corpses littered the desert.

Note: Joachim Jeremias sheds some light on
this rather dense passage. Jeremias is
discussing the Old Testament basis for
proselyte Jewish baptism, and the
difficulty that the followers of Rabbi
Hillel had in establishing such a basis.
For these Hillelites "the device
employed was to start with Num. 15:14:
'as ye do, so shall he [the stranger] do.'
This sentence the Hillelites interpreted
to mean that the proselyte should be
received within the Sinaitic Covenant as
the people of Israel once were at Sinai.
Thus they made the assumption that the
people of Israel at Sinai had been
baptized before their reception into the
Covenant. There is indeed no mention
of this in the Book of Exodus. But this
act of baptism was inferred from Ex.
24:8, where it is written 'Moses took
blood and sprinkled the people
therewith' for 'It is valid traditional
teaching that there is no sprinkling
without (previous) baptism.' Thus

scriptural proof was adduced for proselyte baptism. In this way originated the doctrine of the baptism of the generation of the desert wandering before the reception of salvation at Sinai. 1 Cor 10:1–2 shows us that this doctrine of the baptism of the desert generation, which is of fundamental importance for proselyte baptism, was already familiar to Paul, the pupil of the Hillelite Gamaliel I. He applied it to Christian baptism: as the Jewish theologians saw in this baptism of the desert generation the exemplar of proselyte baptism, so Paul saw in it the type of Christian baptism.''[10]

12:13:   In one Spirit we were all baptized, Jews as well as Greeks, slaves as well as citizens, and one Spirit was given us all to drink.

15:29:   If this were not true, what do people hope to gain by being baptized for the dead? If the dead are not ever going to be raised, why be baptized on their behalf?

Galatians (c. 53/55)
3:25–4:7:   Now that the time has come we are no longer under that guardian, and you are, all of you, sons of God through faith in Christ Jesus. All baptized in Christ, you have all clothed yourself in Christ, and there are no more distinctions between Jew and Greek, slave and free, male and female, but all of you are one in Christ Jesus. Merely by belonging to Christ you are the posterity of Abraham, the heirs he was promised.

Let me put this another way: an heir, even if he has actually inherited everything, is no different from a slave for as long as he remains a child. He is under the control of guardians and administrators until he reaches the age fixed by his father. Now before we came of age we were as good as slaves to the elemental principles of this world, but when the appointed time came, God sent his Son, born of a woman, born a subject of the Law, to redeem the subjects of the law and enable us to be adopted as sons. The proof that you are sons is that God has sent the Spirit of his Son into our hearts: the Spirit that cries, "Abba, Father," and it is this that makes you a son, you are not a slave any more; and if God has made you son, then he has made you heir.

6:15:   It does not matter if a person is circumcised or not; what matters is for him to become an altogether new creature.

It is clear that in stark contrast to the letters to the Thessalonians, the letter to the Galatians and the first letter to the Corinthians, written roughly around the same time, have begun to show a deepening theological interpretation of baptism on the part of Paul. Baptism in these letters is associated with the following:

1. The incarnation and redemption of Jesus, and so a christological centering is given to baptism.
2. The entire salvation history is alluded to, and baptism is seen as bringing the Christian into the fullness of salvation history.
3. The Spirit of God becomes so involved with the existence of the Christian that he or she becomes a "Temple of the Holy Spirit," and is so intimately related to Yahweh, that Yahweh can be addressed as "Abba," the very word that Jesus used to address Yahweh.
4. Baptism equalizes all people, so there can be no boasting of superiority because one is male or female, free or slave, Jew or Gentile. The dignity of the Christian arises from the life that is given to the baptized.
5. This life is a new creation; not only is sin washed away and holiness restored, but more than restoration takes place. Beyond this restoration there is a "new creation."

In the next letters Paul deepens this interpretation of baptism and really leads us to the depth of his thought.

2 Corinthians (c. 55/56)

1:21–22:

Remember that it is God himself who assures us all, and you, of our standing in Christ, and has anointed us, marking us with his seal and giving us the pledge, the Spirit, that we carry in our hearts.

Note: This passage possibly might refer to baptism, although it is unclear whether or not the anointing is meant to be understood metaphorically or realistically.

5:14–17:

And this is because the love of Christ overwhelms us when we reflect that if one man has died for all, then all men should be dead; and the reason he died for all was so that living men should live no longer for themselves, but for him who died and was raised to life for them.

From now onward, therefore, we do not judge anyone by the standards of the flesh. Even if we did once know Christ in the flesh, that is not how we know him now. And for anyone who is in Christ, there is a new creation; the old creation has gone, and now the new one is here. It is all God's work.

Romans (c. 55/56)

6:1–11:

Does it follow that we should remain in sin so as to let grace have greater scope? Of course not. We are dead to sin, so how can we continue to live in it? You have been taught that when we were baptized in Christ Jesus we were baptized in his death; in other words, when we were baptized we went into the tomb with him and joined him in death, so that as Christ was raised from the dead by the Father's glory, we, too, might live a new life.

If in union with Christ we have imitated his death, we shall also imitate him in his resurrection. We must realize that our former selves have been crucified with him to destroy this sinful body and to free us from the slavery of sin. When a man dies, of course he has finished with sin.

But we believe that having died with Christ we shall return to life with him; Christ, as we know, having been raised from the dead will never die again. Death has no power over him anymore. When he died he died once for all to sin; so his life now is life with God; and in that way too you must consider yourselves to be dead to sin but alive for God in Christ Jesus.

Paul here has taken an enormous step in conveying his understanding of the mystery of baptism. For the first time we hear the phrase: "We have been baptized into his death." And not only his death but his resurrection as well. This is not meant simply through some external symbolization, namely, a person's body descending totally under the water, the symbol of death, and the person's body coming back out of the water, the symbol of resurrection. Rather, there is a mystical union between the person being baptized and the very death-resurrection of Jesus. Moreover, this union with the death-resurrection of Jesus brings about the powerlessness of sin and in Paul's mind therefore the devil over the baptized Christian. Nor does he stop here; the union with the death-resurrection of Jesus not only marks the end of the power of sin, but it also brings about the new creation, the new life in Christ; just as Jesus himself did not rise merely to a continuation of life, but to a brand new life, the "risen life," so, too, the Christian does not merely have life without sin, but a wholly new kind of life which is for God and in Christ Jesus. Paul develops this line of thought even further in his subsequent letters but with the added notion that such a new life is a unifying life, unifying the baptized more strongly with one another, but above all more deeply unifying the believers with Christ, with the Spirit, and with the Father.

Colossians (c. 56/58
or 58/60, depending
on the place of
Paul's
imprisonment)

2:12–13:   You have been buried with him when you
                            were baptized; and by baptism too you have
                            been raised up with him through your belief in
                            the power of God who raised him from the
                            dead. You were dead, because you were
                            sinners and had not been circumcised; he has
                            brought you life with him, he has forgiven us
                            all our sins.

Ephesians (c. 61/63
if the letter is
genuinely Paul's;
80/100 if it is not
Paul's own)

2:4–6:   But God loved us with so much love that he
                            was generous with his mercy; when we were
                            dead through our sins, he brought us to life
                            with Christ—it is through grace that you have
                            been saved—and raised us up with him and
                            gave us a place with him in heaven in Christ
                            Jesus.

4:4–5:   There is one Body, one Spirit, just as you
                            were all called into one and the same hope
                            when you were called. There is one Lord, one
                            faith, one baptism, and one God who is Father
                            of all, over all, through all and within all.

5:25–26:   Husbands should love their wives just as
                            Christ loved the Church and sanctified himself
                            for her to make her holy. He made her clean
                            by washing her in water with a form of words,

so that when he took her to himself she should
be glorious, with no speck or wrinkle or
anything like that but holy and faultless.

Note: There are two passages in this letter
which speak of the ''seal'' and these
might possibly have reference to
baptism:

1:13–14: Now you, too, in him, have
heard the message of the truth
and the good news of your
salvation and have believed it;
and you, too, have been
stamped with the seal of the
Holy Spirit of the promise,
the pledge of our inheritance,
which brings freedom for
those whom God has taken
for his own, to make his glory
praised.

5:25–26: Otherwise you will only be
grieving the Holy Spirit of
God who has marked you
with his seal for you to be set
free when the day comes.

Only one additional note needs to be mentioned in this overview
of Paul's understanding of baptism. Union with Christ and becoming a
new creature is ''no mere individualistic experience for Christians, but
a corporate one, for through baptism a special union with all Christians
is formed.''[11] Salvation is, therefore, not a private enterprise, but one
that is worked out within a salvific community.

5. REFERENCES TO BAPTISM IN OTHER NEW TESTAMENT WRITINGS

Hebrews 6:1–2:   Let us leave behind us then all the elementary
teaching about Christ and concentrate on its
completion, without going over the fundamental

doctrines again: the turning away from dead actions and towards faith in God; the teaching about baptisms and the laying on of hands; the teaching about the resurrection of the dead and eternal judgment.

> *Note:* The plural "baptisms" is unique in the New Testament, and biblical authors mention that perhaps it includes Jewish proselyte baptism, the baptism of John the Baptist, and Christian baptism; or on the other hand it might refer to the threefold immersion, although this would be a very early indication of such a rite.

Hebrews 10:22:   So as we go in [to the sanctuary] let us be sincere in heart and filled with faith, our minds sprinkled and free from any trace of bad conscience and our bodies washed with pure water.

Titus 3:5:   It was for no reason except his own compassion that he saved us by means of the cleansing water of rebirth and by renewing us with the Holy Spirit which he has so generously poured over us through Jesus Christ our savior.

1 Peter 1:3–4:11:   It has been the opinion of most modern scholars since A. von Harnack that this section is a sermon given to Gentile Christians who have recently been baptized or at least materials which often were used in such baptismal exhortations have been incorporated into this section. The remainder of the letter, 4:12 to 5:11, seems to be addressed to Christians who took part in the baptismal liturgy. In general the thought of the author is this: Christian life is begun in baptism as an experience of regeneration. "From it, Peter draws his conclusions about the way the Christian is to conduct himself among pagan neighbors in the face of persecution. In baptism the Christian is regenerated to a new life through the very resurrection of Jesus. Baptism is not viewed

merely as a rite of initiation into the Christian community, but as a source communicating to the believer the life-giving power of the glorified Christ. But the corporate aspects of that regeneration are also emphasized, for by it one becomes part of God's people, a chosen race, a royal priesthood, a holy nation."[12]

Revelation: Some authors have attempted to see baptismal references in such verses as 7:2; 7:17; 21:6; 22:1–17; but there seems to be no conclusive evidence that baptism is intended. Even the advice to the faithful of Laodicea to buy white garments and a salve to allow them to see clearly (3:18) or the similar advice regarding unsoiled white clothing (3:4–5) cannot with any surety be allusions to baptism.

1 John 5:5–8:   Who can overcome the world? Only the man who believes that Jesus is the Son of God: Jesus Christ who came by water and blood; not with water only, but with water and blood; with the Spirit as another witness—since the Spirit is the truth—so that there are three witnesses, the Spirit, the water, and the blood, and all three of them agree.

Note: There is a possible reference to baptism here, but secondary.

If one simply added up all these New Testament references on baptism and presented them as the final, fundamental, immovable teaching of the Christian Church on baptism, there would still not be a complete picture of what baptism in the Christian community is all about. One could say, however, that these references are indeed "revelation," that is, the Word of God itself. Seen in this way, these references are profoundly important for the Christian life. A "total theology," however, goes beyond but not apart from these data. The "lived" experience of the Church enters into a "theology" of baptism, and this involves historical, liturgical and theological traditions. These, too, must be taken into account.

The reader notices that at the end of the section on the Acts, and again in the section on St. Paul, there were summarizing statements: namely, in Acts baptism is connected with . . . or in Paul baptism is connected with . . . As long as one stays on this firm ground while developing a theology of baptism (and eventually, as we shall see, a theology of confirmation), then one is on solid footing. Whenever the liturgical, historical, or ecclesiological ''lived'' experience of baptism (or confirmation) deviates from these solid New Testament bases, then the liturgical, historical, and ecclesiological variances easily become suspect. From an ecumenical perspective these New Testament guidelines provide the framework within which the Churches can discuss a theology of baptism. They also provide the parameters within which an Orthodox baptismal liturgy, a Roman Catholic one, a Lutheran one, an Anglican one, etc., can be developed and seen as true or not. In other words these New Testament positions provide the basis for a theology of baptism for all the Churches, but since they are of themselves not monolithic, they provide the amplitude for liturgical variances in baptismal ritual. For example, the question of total immersion or sprinkling finds both basis and variance in the New Testament data. The issue of infant and adult baptism or only adult baptism finds its basis in the same data and must be evaluated on this basis. In this latter case, it is the word ''only'' which needs to be established or not established. Does the New Testament allow for infant baptism or does it preclude it apodictically? The liturgical variance is not the issue; the rootage in the New Testament basis is the issue.

The New Testament, however, was not written in an historical vacuum, and baptism for the Christian community did not come from Jesus *de novo*. There is an historical *Sitz im Leben* for baptism, and the words of the New Testament which bring us the Word are meaningful only in this contextualized framework. Our next stage, then, is to consider the historical antecedents of Christian baptism.

6. HISTORICAL ANTECEDENTS TO CHRISTIAN BAPTISM

Jesus' own baptism was in many respects John's baptism, and John was baptizing long before Jesus came on the scene. If we ask where the very idea of baptism might have come from, we must look in three areas of baptismal significance in the Mid-Eastern life around the time of Jesus, namely:

(a) Hellenistic washings at the time of Jesus;

(b) Jewish proselyte baptism;

(c) the baptism performed by John the Baptist.

These three areas provide us with the context of Christian baptism, but none of them provide the focus for Christian baptism. This focus remains, as stated above, Jesus himself. Let us look at each of these contextual factors in some detail.

A. HELLENISTIC WASHINGS

At the time of Jesus, that is from the end of the B.C. and the beginning of the A.D. eras, washings among the people of the Middle East were fairly common. These were non-religious in nature. However, as one finds in many cultures, some washings were given a religious meaning. Already in the Old Testament we find instances of religious washings. In Leviticus 11–15 there are rules concerning the clean and the unclean. Cleaning often involves a washing. A similar situation is found in Numbers 19. Particularly Numbers 19:17–22 presents us with a washing that is both a cleansing from defilement and sin and a reunion to the community.

R. Fuller and J. Jeremias note that in later Old Testament theology there is the notion that the beginning of the messianic age would recapitulate the experiences of the exodus period, which included a passing through the reed sea, or water.[13] A connection between a washing and eschatology is thus established.

Qumran attests to religious washings, not in any initiating way, but in a cleansing way. In fact, the Essenes separated themselves from other Jews in a number of ways, one of which was that of religious washings. It is still argued whether these kinds of religious washings had any influence on John the Baptist and therefore on Christian baptism. Evidence for such a linkage appears sparse.

Cleansing from sin in a communal setting marks many of these religious washings and does provide at least the larger context in which both John's and Christian baptism take on meaning. However, only a general contextualization can be ascertained, not a clear or immediate connection. Let us turn now to something more specific in Jewish history.

B. JEWISH PROSELYTE BAPTISM

Because of the silence of the entire Old Testament, of Philo and of Josephus, scholars at one time tended to downplay Jewish proselyte baptism prior to the Christian era and thereby discount any influence of such a Jewish practice on Christian baptism. More contemporary scholarship, however, tempers this view. The discussions of the divergent schools of Hillel and Shamai, whose teaching influence was strongest in the last decades of the first century before Christ, indicate that the question of the impurity of Gentiles was a much discussed issue. According to Jeremias, basing himself on rabbinic data concerning Simeon, the son of Kamithos, who was high priest in the year 17-18 A.D., the school of Hillel was dominant. Gentiles, according to this school, were legally impure. According to this line of argumentation, the impurity of the Gentile necessitates a bath of purification when the Gentile converts to Judaism. Further substantiation for this comes from a redating of portions of the Testament of Levi, due to findings of fragments of the document in Qumran. It would seem that this Testament originated well into the period before Christ, and in this document (14:6) there is mention of "unlawful purifications." Jeremias continues his case by pointing up the following factors similar to both Jewish proselyte baptism and Christian baptism:

1. The name "baptism" and its derivates: nowhere in non-Jewish Hellenism do these Greek words take on a technical ritualistic meaning; only among Greek speaking Jews docs "to baptize," etc., do this. This would indicate that the origin of the name is Jewish.
2. The use of the middle voice, "to wash oneself," is bad Greek but good Jewish-Greek because of the semitic undertones.
3. D. Daube in 1956 analyzed an early rabbinic "Baptismal Catechism" and "finds a pattern of instruction," (a) testing motives for conversion; (b) instruction on the commandments; (c) on the duty of charity; (d) on penalties; (e) on rewards and the world to come. In Christian documents we find the "Two Ways" of the *Didache;* the emphasis on charity in 1 Peter; the question of punishment and eschatological retribution in Hebrews 6:2.

4. In both Jewish proselyte baptism and Christian baptism there is complete immersion; flowing water is preferred; there is a confession of sins.

5. In Jewish theology the proselyte was like a newborn child and the conversion to Judaism gave rise to a wholly new life and new creation. This new creation meant forgiveness of sin. To express this newness there is even the Jewish custom of a change of name.

Cautiously, Jeremias concludes that all of the correspondences cannot simply be chance. There is, indeed, some influence from Jewish proselyte baptism on Christian baptism.[14]

Raphael Schulte takes a somewhat reserved approach to this question, but points out a very important aspect, namely, that washings were common for Jewish people throughout the Old Testament times, and that these washings took on a cultic form as regards legal impurity. In post-exilic times such ritualized washings were multiplied and unfortunately took on the characteristic of a good work as a fulfillment of the law. The washings of the Essenes are well-known, although it cannot be said with any certitude that there was a ritualistic initiatory washing. However, proselyte baptism did indeed have the mark of an initiatory ritualistic washing.[15]

Rudolf Schnackenburg notes that from the middle of the second century B.C. down to 300 A.D., there was both in Palestine and Syria a widespread practice of baptism among divergent sects.[16] All of this indicates that baptisms of any kind, including Christian baptisms, have their roots in the Near Eastern custom of washings. Such washings were on occasion transformed into ritualistic washings with multi-dimensional significations, one of which was an initiatory signification. John the Baptist picked up this form of ritualistic washing and gave it a new significance, as also did Jesus, and from him the entire Christian mystery of baptism, with all the transformative elements that the Christ-event bequeathed to it, began to develop.

C. THE BAPTISM OF JOHN THE BAPTIST

Although John the Baptist, in many ways, fits into the pattern of Near Eastern baptismal activity, there are a number of characteristics which indicate the difference between his religious activity and that of others.

1. John did not present himself to the public as a member of the established Jewish priesthood, even though he was the son of Zechariah, himself a priest, nor did he present himself as a scribe or a representative of any particular religious movement of the time.

2. The New Testament makes it clear that he had a very definite sense of personal identity: he was the immediate and final precursor of the imminent coming of the kingdom of God. Whereas Jesus will proclaim that the kingdom of God is come, John proclaimed that the kingdom *was coming* (in Matthew).

3. He associated his message of conversion as preparation for this immediate coming of the kingdom with his baptism, so that his baptism took on the significance of radical religious conversion and a turning away from sin.

4. John preached and offered his baptism, not to a small in-group, but to all of Israel. Proselyte baptism had been for Gentiles who wished to convert to Judaism; John's baptism was for Jews, but not for some select group of Jews.

5. The baptism of John was administered once only; it was not a washing that was repeated often, and baptism was meant to prepare Jewish people so that they would be ready to be in a true sense of the term the eschatological people of God.

6. So effective was the religious movement which John began that he himself was simply entitled "The Baptist," in marked distinction to any other leader who used a washing or baptism as a religious ritual. This esteem of the "Baptist" lasted into the early part of the second century A.D., with its inevitable fall into sectarianism.

7. Jesus himself had the highest regard for John the Baptist. From the ranks of the disciples of John, Jesus drew his own first followers. On this matter the Johannine account is highly singular while the synoptic accounts seem to be more reliable. Not only that, but Jesus, according to Matthew 11:12ff., sees John's activity as the beginning of the new age, and if this is historically accurate, this is a high encomium indeed. Luke, on the other hand, in 16:16, seems to keep John the Baptist in the Old Testament time, with Jesus as the true beginner of the new aeon. The more difficult reading, that of Matthew, seems to be the more ancient reading.

8. It also seems that Jesus himself baptized, for the protestation in John 4:2, namely that Jesus himself did not baptize, but only his own disciples, seems to be a defensive ploy, aimed at avoiding any equating

of John and Jesus. Nonetheless, it would seem that Jesus too was a baptizer and was so without embarrassment, a fact that explains why so quickly after the resurrection-appearances the disciples of Jesus began baptizing. It was a normal procedure for Jesus and his disciples.[17]

Because of the many connections between John's baptism and Christian baptism, it is only fair to say that Christian baptism had its roots in the baptism of John. Jesus took over a rite, common enough in the Palestine of his day, and transformed it into an initiatory rite with his own characteristics. The actual baptisms performed by Jesus and his disciples during the lifetime of Jesus involved repentance, conversion, and profession that the kingdom of God was already taking place. With the death and resurrection of Jesus, however, Christian baptism took on an even greater meaning, that is, *it became transformed into something more*. It is likewise interesting to note that the baptisms administered by Jesus and his disciples did not have the meaning that one was being incorporated into a "Church." None of the disciples understood such baptisms in this way, since the notion of "Church" as opposed to the Jewish religion developed only gradually *after* Jesus' death and resurrection. For them, incorporation into the kingdom was far more important.

It is important to note that the semitic peoples *took over* the human phenomenon of washing and under certain circumstances gave it a ritualistic and religious meaning. John, too, *took over* a ritualistic washing and gave it under certain circumstances a new religious meaning. Jesus, in turn, *took over* a religious washing and again under certain circumstances provided it with a new meaning. The Christian community, after the death and resurrection of Jesus, *took over* the practice of baptism, but because of the death and resurrection of Jesus, this baptism gained new meaning. There is clearly at work here a process of transignification, and it is unwise to apply transignification only to the eucharist and not see it involved in the other Christian sacraments as well. A basic ritual under new contexts takes on new meanings for those who participate in that ritual.

7. NEW TESTAMENT CHRISTIAN BAPTISM

To end this chapter, let us consider several issues which involve New Testament studies, namely, baptism as a "sacrament," baptism of infants, baptism and regeneration, baptism and the mystery of Jesus.

The New Testament does not speak of baptism as a sacrament; indeed, the early Christians would not understand us with our theology of sacrament. Only gradually did the Greek terms, *mysterion* and *symbolon,* and the Latin term, *sacramentum,* come to refer to liturgical actions. Actually, the first clear reference is found in Athanasius (295–373), but beginnings of this classification can already be found in Clement of Alexandria, Origen, Tertullian, and Hippolytus. It is in this linguistic development that some influence from the Hellenistic mystery cults can be seen. The initiation into these mystery cults, called a *muesis,* gave rise to the Christian *naming* of baptism as *mysterion.* Let us be clear: Christian baptism as an act, and a liturgical act at that, already was practiced; the naming of this act as *mysterion* came second. In the Greek culture such a name, *mysterion,* had many non-Christian implications, some of which were utilized by the Greek Fathers of the Church to explain what baptism was all about. The same thing happened with the Latin Fathers, particularly Tertullian. *Sacramentum* among the Latin culture had meanings apart from baptism, such as "oath" and "consecration." Tertullian took over these meanings and began to apply them to the liturgy of baptism. Nonetheless, the grounding for baptism was always seen in the great mystery, the Christ-event. In other words, although "foreign" Hellenistic elements began to appear in patristic writings, the controlling factor remained the life-death-resurrection of Jesus.

The New Testament, in its totality, does not offer a complete theology of baptism, with all the careful distinctions and nuances which later became involved with the question of baptism. For instance, it is not totally clear from the New Testament data that the imparting of the Holy Spirit was necessarily connected with baptism; indeed, there seem to be instances when the Holy Spirit is imparted to Christians even though there is no baptism, such as we note in the case of the apostles, whose own baptism can by no means be verified. Moreover, Acts 10:44, speaks of the household of Cornelius which received the Spirit prior to baptism.

Another hesitation as to the extent of baptism in the New Testament is the question of infant baptism. This topic has been rather exhaustively treated by K. Aland, M. Barth, O. Cullmann and J. Jeremias.[18] It would seem that the New Testament data would be open to the possibility that some children and perhaps infants were baptized, but that on other occasions they were not. At any rate, baptism of children had nothing to do, as far as the New Testament was concerned, with the question of original sin. "The apparent reason," Raymond Brown notes, "is to bring a whole family into the church—a sense of solidarity."[19]

More importantly, one might ask what the New Testament data indicates as far as the relationship between salvation and baptism, and of course the famous statement in John 3:5 comes to mind: "Unless one is begotten of water and the Spirit, he cannot enter the kingdom of God." Commenting on this passage Rudolf Schnackenburg writes:

> Nonetheless, it remains a fact that it is not the water baptism (as an external rite and requirement) which is the proper viewpoint [of the passage], but rather the "begetting from the spirit," and consequently that fundamental salvation event, which for the early church (according to the institution of the Lord) was indeed bound to the sacrament of baptism. For this reason the teaching of Jesus as regards Nicodemus was not directly focused on baptism, but on the new creation through the spirit of God.[20]

To belong to God, to be immersed in his Spirit, and to be united to Jesus Christ—these do not happen simply because a man or woman is born in a natural way; these things happen because of a new creation, and it is this new creation that the external ritual of baptism celebrates, but as one can see the response of this grace of new creation is faith, and at times the New Testament places the saving-event in an individual's life more in the dimension of faith rather than in the dimension of baptism. To cite Raymond Brown once more: "Thus, even in the more developed works of NT theology baptism must share with faith and preaching the role of regeneration."[21]

Far more radical and significant is the New Testament understanding of *one* baptism. To read into the New Testament an understanding of such oneness, as though it implied a oneness of ritual and a oneness of formula does poor service to the profundity of the New Testament understanding of this oneness, for this oneness is Jesus himself. We are baptized into the one Lord. This underscores the radical christological foundation of baptism. It is the unity in the Christ-event, his earthly life, his death, and his risen life, that makes Christians one.

8. SUMMARY OF NEW TESTAMENT INSIGHTS INTO BAPTISM

Based on all the above, we might summarize the New Testament insights on baptism in the following way, with the proviso that only the major points are mentioned.

1. Jesus is presented as the center of baptism. The gospels and the later letters of Paul emphasize this.

2. Baptism is associated clearly with the Spirit. To say that there is, for Christians, a baptism of water and only later a baptism of the Spirit counters all that the New Testament says.

3. Baptism is presented in its connection to salvation history. There is an historical revelation of God's remission of sins and his bestowal of forgiving love.

4. Baptism is presented as a communal activity, involving the followers of Jesus. It is not a private affair, nor is it a family affair. Even if there might be some admission of infants to baptism in the New Testament, such baptisms are almost wholly overshadowed by adult baptism. Thus, the celebration is not of a child into a family, but of a person into the Jesus community.

5. Baptism renders meaningless any claim to preeminence due to gender, social class or ethnic background.

6. Baptism is a profoundly religious event, both in the life of Jesus and in the lives of his followers. Faith is involved, and this means a response to an antecedent gift of God: his call to repentance and to life. Baptism, therefore, is a moment of grace, a moment of gift, not a good work nor a keeping of a commandment.

7. Negatively, baptism is not compared to circumcision, nor is it seen as a Christian substitute for circumcision. Therefore, the theology of circumcision does not play a role in developing the theology of baptism.

8. Negatively, again, original sin is not mentioned at all in the New Testament insights into baptism. Therefore, original sin cannot be seen as a constitutive factor for a theology of baptism.

The New Testament clearly indicates that baptism is much more than a rite. In the life of Jesus himself, it is presented as an extremely significant event, revelatory of who Jesus himself is. In the entire New Testament the central aspect of baptism is its relationship to Jesus, and in Paul this becomes even a mystic relationship into the life, death, and resurrection of Jesus. It is this Jesus-relationship which grounds the current theological interest in Jesus as the primordial sacrament. We will deal with this more in detail later on.

The New Testament has absolutely no indication of another stage in Christian initiation which would come between baptism on the one hand and eucharist on the other. Baptism opens the door to the eucharistic banquet. This lack of any intermediary situation indicates, as we will see, first, a strong connection between baptism and eucharist, and, second, a theological anomoly to the contemporary practice of a Church recognizing another Christian community's baptism but refusing eucharistic hospitality. Again, we will deal with this problem later on, but it should be noted here that the New Testament provides no evidence for such a disruption and even more rejects such a disruption.

We are fortunate today to possess fine historical studies on the sacrament of baptism, both from a theological and from a liturgical point of view.[22] We are equally fortunate to have the revised rituals which stem from the Second Vatican Council, and which bring together for our times the New Testament data on baptism, particularly, as also the historical richness of this sacrament.[23] Over and over again, we see the profound christological base of baptism, not merely in theory but in the actual liturgical celebration of Jesus himself in baptism. This presence of Jesus in baptism is essentially connected with the presence of Jesus in the eucharist so that once again the link between baptism and eucharist is manifest. To clarify this even further, let us turn our attention to some areas in the history of this sacrament which were both foundational for the understanding of the sacrament and illustrative of the baptism-eucharist linkage.

Discussion Questions

1. Point out all the similarities between the baptism of Jesus accounts presented by the four evangelists. Point out all the discrepancies. Why are the common issues important? Why are the differing issues also important?

2. What does Paul mean by being baptized into the life, death and resurrection of Jesus?

3. What is the role of the Spirit in baptism as presented by the New Testament writers?

4. What are the main differences between the baptism of John and Christian baptism?

5. What do the main New Testament issues on baptism, summarized at the end of the chapter, mean for an understanding of baptism today?

Holy Baptism and
the Early Church

Scholars have, since the turn of the century, produced a number of studies, both in book form and in monograph form, on the history of the sacrament of baptism. Early source material has been collected and studied in great detail. This has helped both the theologian and the liturgist to an enormous degree, and has aided the work in all the Christian Churches to rethink and restructure baptismal rituals.[1]

The revised ritual of baptism in the Catholic Church is no exception to this: the revised ritual gives ample evidence of its dependence on early sources. The advantage of an historical understanding of the sacrament of baptism is that it allows a more profound theological understanding of the sacrament to manifest itself in the present form. Previously, the baptismal ritual was understood from a fairly narrow scholastic framework, which in the history of baptism is only one and not even necessarily the best approach to baptism.

The following pages do not intend to represent the history of baptism which other scholars have done in a deeper and more solid way. Rather, I wish to highlight those areas which have had a major influence on the formation of our baptismal ritual and baptismal theology over the years.

1. THE DIDACHE

The dating of this very early source is still debated. Audet places it around 70 A.D. and others place it just after 100 A.D. There are other attempts to date the work as well. Still, it gives us a window into the church

life of the Christian community very shortly after the apostolic period.
The following is the section in the *Didache* which deals with baptism:

> Baptize as follows: after first explaining all these points baptize in
> the name of the Father and of the Son and of the Holy Spirit, in
> running water. But if you have no running water, baptize in other
> water; and if you cannot in cold, then in warm. But if you have
> neither, pour water on the head three times in the name of the Father
> and of the Son and of the Holy Spirit. And before baptism, let the
> baptizer and the one that is to be baptized and others who are able,
> first fast; but you shall ask the one that is to be baptized to fast one
> or two (days?) before.[2]

According to this text, we see that the normal way of baptizing
was by immersion in running water, i.e., a stream, river or a sea. Baptism by sprinkling or infusion was also an approved way of baptizing,
if it was necessary. The formula in the name of the Father and of the
Son and of the Holy Spirit is standard. It was Jewish practice to fast,
and evidently the fasting preceding baptism has come from this Jewish
influence. This also helps us to see the antiquity of this document.

2. THE FIRST APOLOGY OF JUSTIN

Around 160 Justin of Rome wrote what is called the *First Apology*,
a defense of the Christian position, written for the Emperor Antoninus
Pius. In careful wording, even in vague expression, Justin describes the
baptismal ritual as he would have experienced it in the Roman community. What is noteworthy here is that the initiation is not only the
water-bath, of baptism, but also the eucharist.

> I will also relate to you the manner in which we dedicate ourselves
> to God, when we have been made new through Christ, lest if we
> omit this we seem to be unfair in the explanation we are making. As
> many as are persuaded and believe that what we teach and say is
> true, and undertake to be able to live accordingly, are instructed to
> pray and to entreat God with fasting for the remission of their sins
> that are past, we praying and fasting with them. Then they are
> brought by us where there is water, and are regenerated in the same
> manner in which we ourselves were regenerated. For in the name of
> God the Father and Lord of the universe, and of the Savior Jesus
> Christ, and of the Holy Spirit, they then receive the washing with

water. . . . And for this we have learned from the Apostles this reason. Since at our first birth we were born without our knowledge
and our choice by our parents' coming together and were brought
up in bad habits and wicked training, in order that we may not remain the children of necessity and of ignorance, and may obtain in
the water the remission of sins formerly committed, there is pronounced over him who chooses to be born again, and has repented
of his sins, the name of God the Father and Lord of the universe,
he who leads to the laver the person that is to be washed calling him
by this name alone. And this washing is called illumination, because they who learn these things are illuminated spiritually. But
also in the name of Jesus Christ, who was crucified under Pontius
Pilate, and in the name of the Holy Spirit, who through the prophets
foretold all things about Jesus, he who is illuminated is washed.[3]

In this account by Justin we see that there is a strong spiritual com-
ponent in the catechumenate, which is not only a time of teaching, but
also a time of prayer and fasting. The community prays and fasts with
those to be baptized, which underscores the social or communal aspect
of this ritual. The trinitarian formula, somewhat clarified, is employed,
and Justin offers a brief theological consideration of the reason for this
threefold invocation. In describing the actual water-bath, the notion of
prayer is once more highlighted. With the water-bath completed, the
eucharist then follows. The connection between baptism and eucharist—a connection which will remain constant in the history of this sacrament—is important both for an understanding of Christian initiation,
and for an understanding of what baptism is all about.

3. THE APOSTOLIC TRADITION OF HIPPOLYTUS

This document is dated around 215 A.D. It stems from Rome, and
the author Hippolytus was a scholar and fairly conservative individual.
What he describes, then, is certainly nothing which is radical or non-
traditional. The picture which he gives us is undoubtedly that of the
early third century in Rome, but also of the late second century as well.
This work was extremely popular in the early Church, particularly in
the East, and it was the basis for many manuals or Church Orders of
later years. It truly became a major source for the liturgy in the early
Church. The section on baptism is reprinted in full below since it presents us with a good view of the early catechumenate (16 to 19), the

immediate preparation for the water-bath (20) and the actual baptism (21 to 22). Immediately following (23) is a description of the eucharistic celebration which then took place. Once more there is this connection between baptism and eucharist as the initiation process for catechumens into the Christian Church.

16. New converts to the faith, who are to be admitted as hearers of the word, shall first be brought to the teachers before the people assemble. And they shall be examined as to their reason for embracing the faith, and they who bring them shall testify that they are competent to hear the word. Inquiry shall then be made as to the nature of their life; whether a man has a wife or is a slave. If he is a slave of a believer and he has his master's permission, then let him be received; but if his master does not give him good character, let him be rejected. If his master is a heathen, let the slave be taught to please his master, that the word be not blasphemed. If a man has a wife or a woman a husband, let the man be instructed to content himself with his wife and the woman to content herself with her husband. But if a man is unmarried, let him be instructed to abstain from impurity, either by lawfully marrying a wife or else by remaining as he is. [There follows a lengthy section on various trades and occupations which are incompatible with Christian baptism.]

17. Let catechumens spend three years as hearers of the word. But if a man is zealous and perseveres well in the work, it is not the time but the character that is decisive.

18. When the teacher finishes his instruction, the catechumens shall pray by themselves, apart from the believers. And all women, whether believers or catechumens, shall stand for their prayers by themselves in a separate part of the church.

And when [the catechumens] finish their prayers, they must not give the kiss of peace, for their kiss is not yet pure. Only believers shall salute one another, but men with men and women with women; a man shall not salute a woman. . . .

19. At the close of their prayer, when their instructor lays his hand upon the catechumens, he shall pray and dismiss them; whoever gives the instruction is to do this, whether a cleric or layman.

If a catechumen should be arrested for the name of the Lord, let him not hesitate about bearing his testimony; for if it should happen that they treat him shamefully and kill him, he will be justified, for he has been baptized in his own blood.

20. They who are to be set apart for baptism shall be chosen after their lives have been examined: whether they have lived soberly, whether they have honoured the widows, whether they have visited the sick, whether they have been active in well-doing. When their sponsors have testified that they have done these things, then let them hear the gospel. Then, from the time that they are separated from the other catechumens, hands shall be laid upon them daily in exorcism and, as the day of their baptism draws near, the bishop himself shall exorcise each one of them that he may be personally assured of their purity. . . .

Then those who are set apart for baptism shall be instructed to bathe and free themselves from impurity and wash themselves on Thursday. If a woman is menstruous, she shall be set aside and baptized on some other day.

They who are to be baptized shall fast on Friday, and on Saturday the bishop shall assemble them and command them to kneel in prayer. And, laying his hands on them, he shall exorcise all evil spirits to flee away and never return; when he has done this he shall breathe in their faces, seal their foreheads, ears and noses and raise them up. They shall spend all that night in vigil, listening to reading and instruction.

They who are to be baptized shall bring with them no other vessels, than the one each will bring for the eucharist. . . .

21. At cockcrow prayer shall be made over the water. The stream shall flow through the baptismal tank or pour into it from above when there is no scarcity of water; but if there is a scarcity, whether constant or sudden, then use whatever water you can find.

They shall remove their clothing. And first baptize the little ones; if they can speak for themselves, they shall do so; if not, their parents or other relatives shall speak for them. Then baptize the men, and last of all the women; they must first loosen their hair and put aside any gold or silver ornaments that they were wearing: let no one take any alien thing down to the water with them.

At the hour set for the baptism the bishop shall give thanks over oil and put it into a vessel: this is called the "oil of thanksgiving." And he shall take other oil and exorcise it: this is called "the oil of exorcism." A deacon shall bring the oil of exorcism, and shall stand at the presbyter's left hand; and another deacon shall take the oil of thanksgiving, and shall stand at the presbyter's right hand. Then the presbyter, taking hold of each of those about to be baptized, shall command him to renounce, saying:

I renounce thee, Satan, and all thy servants and all thy works.

And when he has renounced all these, the presbyter shall anoint him with the oil of exorcism, saying: "Let all spirits depart far from thee."

Then, after these things, let him give over to the presbyter, who baptizes, and let the candidates stand in the water, naked, a deacon going with them likewise. And when he who is being baptized goes down into the water, he who baptizes him, putting his hand on him, shall say thus:

Dost thou believe in God, the Father Almighty?

And he who is being baptized shall say: I believe.

Then, holding his hand placed on his head he shall baptize him once and then he shall say: Dost thou believe in Christ Jesus, the Son of God, who was born of the Holy Ghost of the Virgin Mary, and was crucified under Pontius Pilate, and was dead and buried, and rose again the third day, alive from the dead, and ascended into heaven, and sat at the right hand of the Father, and will come to judge the quick and the dead?

And when he says, "I believe," he is baptized again. And again he shall say: Dost thou believe in the Holy Ghost and the holy church and the resurrection of the flesh?

He who is being baptized shall say accordingly: "I believe," and so he is baptized a third time.

And afterward, when he has come up [out of the water], he is anointed by the presbyter with the oil of thanksgiving, the presbyter saying: I anoint thee with holy oil in the name of Jesus Christ. And so each one, after drying himself, is immediately clothed, and then is brought into the church.

22. Then the bishop, laying his hand upon them, shall pray, saying:

O Lord God, who hast made them worthy to obtain remission of sins through the laver of regeneration of the Holy Spirit, send into them thy grace, that they may serve thee according to thy will; for thine is the glory to the Father and the Son with the Holy Spirit in the holy church, both now and world without end. Amen.

Then, pouring the oil of thanksgiving from his hand and putting it on his forehead, he shall say: I anoint thee with holy oil in the Lord, the Father Almighty and Christ Jesus and the Holy Ghost. And signing them on the forehead he shall say: The Lord be with thee; and he who is signed shall say: And with thy spirit. And so he shall do to each one. And immediately thereafter they shall join in prayer with all the people, but they shall not pray with the faithful until all these things are completed. And at the close of their prayer they shall give the kiss of peace.

23. [There follows immediately in the text a description of the eucharist, indicating most strongly the connection between baptism and eucharist.][4]

This section from Hippolytus, lengthy though it is, is very instructive since it indicates an enormous development of the baptismal ritual from New Testament times down to the late 200s. One can certainly speak of an accumulation of symbolism and an institutional development as well. Some points which deserve our attention are the following:

1. There has developed a recognized group of teachers, primarily lay people, and of catechumens. The "order of catechumen" exists in fact if not in name.

2. The catechumenate is generally three years, with a program of both instruction and prayer. The early Church did not see the preparation time as a "convert class." There was indeed some instruction, undoubtedly bible stories, but also a religious or prayer aspect which was vital for the spiritual growth of those considering Christianity.

3. As in the account by Justin, the focus is on adults. Even though some children might, at this time, have been baptized, the far and wide majority of those baptized were adults, and both the ritual and the theology of baptism was focused on the adult.

4. An understanding of the "baptism by blood" has been inchoatively worked out.

5. The appearance of sponsors, which later developed into godparents, also indicates the extent of the investigation into the lives of those to be baptized as also the institutional character of the baptismal process.

6. The role of pre-baptismal exorcisms and laying on of hands had become a part of the baptismal process.

7. For the actual water-bath, the eminent role of the "episkopos" is clearly defined, even though his activity prior to the water-bath is negligible. The "episkopos" is indeed *the* liturgical presider.

8. Old Testament ideas on legal purity (e.g., the menstruous woman) have influenced the ritual, and the pre-baptismal washings might also stem from this Jewish background.

9. Baptism is to occur on the sabbath (Saturday) with all night vigils and prayers.

10. There is breathing on the faces and a sealing of forehead, ears and nose. The drama of the ritual is clearly evident, and for a basically illiterate civilization, such dramatic actions were highly important.

11. The fasting, already mentioned in the *Didache,* continues on and is made even more specific.

12. The people are to be baptized naked. This nudity remains a standard procedure for many decades after, both in the East and the West.

13. The children are to be baptized first. Evidently, at this time there was some baptism of children, but the rule really was baptism as an adult.

14. After the children, the men were baptized and then the women. Both men and women were completely naked, and the jewelry which the women might wear was to be removed. Later, deacons will assist the men and deaconesses will assist the women in the water-bath itself.

15. Oil is blessed. The blessing is done by the "episkopos." There are two kinds of oil: the oil of exorcism and the oil of thanksgiving.

16. Presbyters and deacons have assigned roles in the liturgy.

17. There is a threefold renunciation of Satan, perhaps modeled on the threefold invocation of God in the actual baptism. There is also threefold immersion, and a threefold credal statement.

18. There is a post-baptismal laying on of hands by the episkopos, as well as a post-baptismal anointing. For Hippolytus this is all part of "baptism" and in no way could be construed as "confirmation." Indeed, the entire ritual is called "baptism" which includes all the other ceremonies and rituals beyond the mere immersion in water.

19. The kiss of peace (denied to the catechumenate) and the stylized form "The Lord be with you . . . And with your spirit" has been liturgically established.

20. The role of the community is less participatory than it seems to be in the description by Justin. The community through prayer and at the kiss of peace are actively participants in the ritual.

21. Finally, there is a welcoming (initiation) of the new group of baptized into the eucharistic celebration, with the peculiar gathering together of bread, water, milk and honey as well as the eucharistic cup.

Other early witnesses to this process of initiation could be cited: *The Acts of Judas Thomas,* both in the Syriac and the Greek versions; *The Acts of Xanthippe and Polyxena;* St. John Chrysostom in the second of the *Eight Baptismal Catecheses;* Theodore of Mopsuestia in his *Instructions to Candidates for Baptism; Homily 21* of Narsai; Dionysius the Areopagite in chapter two of *On the Ecclesiastical Hierarchy.* James of Edessa is also attributed with a description of baptism, although the attribution is not all that justified. In all of these early documents the link between baptism and eucharist is clearly stated. Baptism is meant to bring the outsider not only into the Christian community, but also in a most explicit way into the eucharistic community.

Even when adult baptism ceased to be the rule, and infant baptism became standard, the water-bath was followed by eucharist, with the infant receiving a drop of the consecrated wine. This is still part of the Eastern Church's rituals, and it lasted in the West until the cup was taken from the laity in the early middle ages. When the consecrated bread became the only form for eucharistic reception open to the laity, the eucharistic aspect of the baptismal liturgy in the West was dropped. This separated baptismal liturgy from eucharist was, unfortunately, the basis on which the great medieval theologians, St. Thomas Aquinas, St. Bonaventure, etc., developed their theologies of baptism, a non-eucharistic baptism. This kind of baptismal theology was also the basis for the presentation of baptism at the Council of Trent. After Vatican II, the scholars who developed the new baptismal ritual for the Roman Catholic Church, have reincorporated the connection of baptism-eucharist into the RCIA. Once again, we are beginning to see that the sacrament of initiation, clearly in the case of an adult, is "baptism-eucharist."

4. RITUALS OF THE EASTERN CHURCHES

In the Eastern Churches we find rather elaborate and extremely meaningful ceremonies of baptism. The main lines of the ritual are the same as in the West: the pre-baptismal renunciation of Satan; at times pre-baptismal anointings; instructions; affirmation of faith in Jesus; the water-bath; post-baptismal anointings, clothing, laying on of hands. Eucharist follows.

In *The Barberini Euchologion* we find a very dramatic renunciation of Satan and an affirmation of Jesus:

> *And after the Amen, the candidate is stripped and his shoes removed, and the priest turns him to the west. The candidate's hands being raised, the priest says thrice:*
> I renounce Satan, and all his works and all his service and all his angels and all his pomp.
> *And the candidate or his sponsor answers each time.*
> *And again the priest asks, saying:* Have ye renounced Satan?
> *And he replies:* We have renounced.
> *And the priest says:* Then blow upon him.
> _ *And the priest turns him to the east, his hands being lowered, and says:*
> And I adhere to Christ, and I believe in one God, the Father Almighty, *and the rest.*
> *And when the priest has spoken thrice, again he asks them:*
> And have ye adhered to Christ?
> *And they answer:* We have adhered.
> *And the priest says:* Worship him.[5]

Although this is a somewhat late example of baptismal liturgy in the East, it is indicative of dramatic ritualization and symbolization. It sets the tone for an understanding of the Eastern Churches' baptismal theology and practice. One turns to the West, the abode of Satan; one holds out hands to repel Satan; one renounces Satan in a dramatic way by blowing on him. This is the evil and dark side, the sinful side of life. One turns to the East, from which the sun rises. The hands are lowered in humble acceptance, both of Jesus and of the creed. The presence of Jesus is recognized, accepted and responded to by worship. We find here, not so much a Satan/God axis, but rather a Satan/Jesus axis. It is the incarnate God in Jesus which is center stage. "Have you adhered to Christ?" "We have adhered." "Worship him."

Creation/incarnation/eucharist/eschaton—this is the fullness of the mystery in the Eastern Church. Baptism shares in this mystery of creation, mystery of incarnation, mystery of eucharist and mystery of eschaton. Let us consider, briefly, the rootage of this rather spiritual, even mystical view, of the *economia.*

The theology and ritual of holy baptism is profoundly indebted to Clement of Alexandria. Clement employs a number of theological and symbolical terms: charisma or gift of grace, enlightenment, perfection, a washing, a second birth, but above all he sees baptism as the gift of God's grace. Faith on the part of the community and the one to be baptized is indeed important, as also the amount of human activity involved, but the activity of the Holy Spirit and the gifts of grace are primary. This view clearly helped the Eastern Churches develop the notion of mystery, quite different than the Western approach through the term sacrament. This also provided a solid basis for the Eastern Churches' rituals for baptism in which the mysterious working of the Holy Spirit is symbolized ritually in many ways and through many lengthy prayers.

Origen, too, played an enormous role in setting the foundation of Eastern ritual and theology. In the area of baptism, his use of typology, symbol and mystery are paramount. Through these notions, Origen developed the theology of baptism, so that one saw baptism within salvation history. For Origen, baptism is no isolated act, but one among many that stems from creation to Christ and from Christ to the Church, and from the Church to the eschaton. The salvation history emphasis, the ecclesiological emphasis, the eschatological emphasis, and above all the Jesus-Spirit emphasis were foundational to Origen's approach and left his mark on Eastern theology and liturgy.

Building on all this was St. Cyril of Jerusalem in his *Mystagogical Catecheses* for the baptized. Imitation of the life, death and resurrection of Jesus plays a central role in his thought. The "Paschal Mystery" which is really the "Jesus Mystery" lies at the heart of his approach. One could readily say that there is a theology of baptism in Cyril's works, but there is also a spirituality of baptism as well, a spirituality which is christological to the core.

Gregory of Nyssa and John Chrysostom continue this way of thinking to a strong degree. The presence of the Holy Spirit and God's grace (Clement) working in salvation history (Origen) bursts into superabundance in the mystery of Jesus (Cyril). This mystery is one of holiness and of power, so that the waters of baptism are filled with this holiness and power but are also, just as Jesus himself, holy-giving and power-giving. The insights which Cyril of Alexandria describes so eloquently in his *Commentary on St. John* are clearly in the thrust of Jesus as not only holy himself but holy-making.

This deep spiritual, even mystical element goes far beyond a mere theologizing on baptism, and the Eastern ritualization of baptism reflects again and again this theo-mystical basis, established by the Eastern theo-mystical theologians.

The *Barberini Euchologium,* which is of fairly late vintage, picks up the dramatic element, but let us listen to Cyril of Jerusalem in his *Mystagogical Catecheses:*[6]

MYSTAGOGICAL CATECHESIS I

2. First you entered the antechamber of the bapistery and faced towards the west. On the command to stretch out your hand, you renounced Satan as though he were there in person. . . .

4. You were told, however, to address him as personally present, and with arm outstretched to say: "I renounce you, Satan." Allow me to explain the reason for your facing west, for you should know it. Because the west is the region of visible darkness, Satan, who is himself darkness, has his empire in darkness; that is the significance of your looking steadily towards the west while you renounce that gloomy Prince of night. . . .

5. Then in a second phrase you are taught to say, "and all your works." All sin is "the work of Satan"; and sin too, you must renounce, since he who has escaped from a tyrant has also cast off the tyrant's livery. . . .

6. Next you say, "and all his pomp." The pomp of the Devil is the craze for the theatre, the horse races in the circus, the wild-beast hunts and all such vanity. . . .

8. After this you say, "and all your service." The service of the Devil is prayer in the temple of idols, the honoring of lifeless images, the lighting of lamps or the burning of incense by springs or streams. . . .

9. When you renounce Satan, trampling underfoot every covenant with him, then you annul that ancient "league with Hell," and God's paradise opens before you. . . .

11. That was what was done in the outer chamber.

MYSTAGOGICAL CATECHESIS II

2. Immediately, then, upon entering [the inner chamber], you removed your tunics. This was a figure of the "stripping off of the

old man with his deeds." Having stripped, you were naked, in this also imitating Christ, who was naked on the cross. . . .

3. Then, when stripped, you were anointed with exorcised olive oil from the topmost hairs of your head to the soles of your feet, and became partakers of the good olive tree, Jesus Christ. Cuttings from the wild olive tree, you were grafted into the good olive tree and became partakers of the fatness of the true olive tree. . . .

4. After this you were conducted to the sacred pool of divine Baptism, as Christ passed from the cross to the sepulchre. . . . You were asked, one by one, whether you believed in the name of the Father and of the Son and of the Holy Spirit; you made that saving confession, and then you dipped thrice under the water and thrice rose up again, therein mystically signifying Christ's three days' burial.

MYSTAGOGICAL CATECHESIS III

1. . . . Similarly for you, after you had ascended from the sacred streams, there was an anointing with chrism, the antitype of that with which Christ was anointed, that is, of the Holy Spirit. . . .

4. You were anointed first upon the forehead to rid you of the shame which the first human transgressor bore about with him everywhere. . . . Then upon the ears, to receive ears, quick to hear the divine mysteries. . . . Then upon the nostrils, that scenting the divine oil, you may say: "We are the incense offered by Christ to God, in the case of those who are on the way to salvation." Then on the breast, that "putting on the breastplate of justice you may be able to withstand the wiles of the Devil.". . .

5. Once privileged to receive the holy Chrism, you are called Christians and have a name that bespeaks your new birth. Before admission to Baptism you were not strictly entitled to this name but were like people on the way towards being Christians.

The lengthy prayers which we find in these rituals of the Eastern Churches are so vital a part of the sacramental activity. We Westerners tend to move quickly to the actual pouring on of water (the matter) and the saying of the formula (the form) that we fail to see that the prayer aspect is central. Earlier on we quoted Kavanagh as saying that the water is subordinate to the Spirit, and it is precisely this exaltation of the Spirit that we find so strongly emphasized in the Eastern liturgies.

There is no magic in the water nor in the words; the efficacy is in the presence of the Spirit of God, the Spirit of Jesus in the entire action.

So, too, in the Eastern understanding of the eucharist. It is not the bread and wine (the matter) nor the formula (the correct words) which are center-stage; it is the calling of the Spirit, the *paraklesis*. Jesus is truly present in the eucharist because of the activity of God's Holy Spirit, not because of the activity of the priest.

5. RITUALS IN THE WESTERN CHURCHES

Around 600 the Western Churches begin to see a change in the baptismal process. More and more children are being baptized, and there are many reasons for this. First of all, the teaching on original sin, which began to develop after the time of St. Augustine, seemed to imply that an infant who died without baptism would go to hell (limbo is a later development). Parents were naturally concerned.

Secondly, the Christian faith had become the only faith. This is difficult for us today to imagine, but in certain areas everyone was Christian. There really was no question of growing into maturity and deciding whether one might want to choose Christianity or not. The culture was thoroughly Christianized. Some Jews lived on, but in ghettos. On the outskirts of the European world were a few Islamic tribes, who were to be converted or whose power was to be destroyed. In an atmosphere in which the very air is Christian, with no religious pluralism, baptism of infants became more and more the natural flow. As mentioned above, the eucharist remained a part of such baptism with the infant receiving a few drops of the consecrated wine.

The ritual of baptism remained geared toward the adult, rather than the child, in its format, but adult baptisms were few and far between. Personal faith was indeed quite explicit in this sacrament, as St. Bonaventure says: "There is in this sacrament a more explicit profession of faith than in any other sacrament."[7] This explicitness of faith, which of course the child could not make, became for some the "faith of the Church." To quote Thomas: "The personal faith of those who present the child for baptism is not necessary . . . but only the faith of the Church militant."[8]

Separated from eucharist, baptism emphasized the destruction of original sin; it makes us like Christ in the sense that we receive the *habitus* of faith, hope and charity. The character is imprinted in our souls;

we are conformed to Christ's passion, resurrection and ascension. The connection with the passion and death of Jesus, so common to the scholastic theologians, indicates that baptism, as with all the sacraments, is there for a remedy, a *virtus reparans* to assist us in our sick and sinful condition.[9]

Bonaventure notes that baptism is not a sacrament of the individual person, but a sacrament of the Church, and therefore he stresses the communal and social nature of the sacrament. In baptism the faith of the Church is clearly present, but alongside of this is the *pactio divina,* the promise on the part of God through Jesus that he will grace the baptized in the church. We enter into one of the major areas of discussion on baptism which the scholastic theologians participated in: namely, the question of the subjective side and the objective side of faith and sacrament. In infant baptism, in which the child cannot make a statement of personal faith, the faith of the Church plays a role, but it is still subjective, in the sense that it stands on the human side of the relationship. God's activity is that which is beyond our control, and therefore totally objective. In Western theology this subjective-objective concern tended to focus the theological discussion, and it became one of the main points of rupture in the reformation era.

This chapter was not intended as a complete history of the sacrament of baptism; rather, it was meant to provide some of the major historical moments which have molded and enriched both the theology of baptism and the liturgical celebration of baptism. In the wake of the reformation a sort of stagnation on both of these aspects set in in all of the Western Churches. The defensive posture disallowed creativity, and the lack of any solid historical knowledge on the development of baptism precluded such creativity. Scholasticism, reformation theology, and Catholic counter-reformation theology all suffered from a narrowness of vision and approach, for which they cannot be totally faulted.

6. SUMMARY OF HISTORICAL SURVEY

The above historical survey highlights only certain points concerning baptism, but these selected issues could be summarized as follows:

1. Baptism as a Christian ritual began in a very simple form and only gradually developed into a more elaborate form. This can be seen

in comparing the section from the *Didache,* that from Justin, and that from Hippolytus.

2. Jesus remains central to this elaboration process, as also the presence of the Spirit and the communal aspect of baptism.

3. Baptism and eucharist remain almost constitutively interconnected: in the East down to the present time, in the West down to the withdrawal of the eucharistic cup from the laity.

4. Baptism remains an adult ritual, until the teaching of original sin and the mono-Christian culture take over. Gradually, both in the East and the West (the East, however, without a teaching on original sin) infant baptism becomes normative.

5. A baptismal preparation takes on a more elaborate form. This is called the "catechumenate," and a fairly lengthy and detailed catechumenate is developed, but not in any monolithic way. Variations abound.

6. More and more ministries become involved in this catechumenate and baptismal process. Some of these ministries are basically lay (sponsors, teachers); others are basically clerical (episcopal presidency, then presbyteral presidency, the roles of deacons and deaconesses).

7. As the rite develops clerical roles take over almost completely.

8. Scholasticism and subsequently the Council of Trent theologized on a non-eucharistic baptism. This kind of baptismal theology tended to be, in the West, commonplace until the renewal of the baptismal ritual after Vatican II and until the renewal of interest in baptismal theology in contemporary ecumenical theology.

Today, we have the benefit of solid New Testament studies, including a critical edition of the New Testament itself. We have the benefit of solid Aramaic background to the New Testament. We have the benefit of critical editions of the Fathers of the Church and solid historical data on the history of the theology and liturgy of baptism. It is no wonder, then, that the Western Churches are moving beyond the sixteenth century positions and that the Eastern and Western Churches are sharing more extensively their appreciation of baptism.

One of these benefits has been a reclaiming of the union between baptism and eucharist as the sacrament of initiation in the Christian Church. The historical material just considered was meant to solidify this union of baptism-eucharist. Any non-eucharistic treatment of baptism is bound to falter; any non-baptismal treatment of eucharist is equally lame. With this in mind, let us now move to the contemporary baptismal scene.

Discussion Questions

1. Compare the text from the *Didache* and that from Justin. What details are similar? What details are different?

2. The *Apostolic Tradition* of Hippolytus was a major document in the early Church, both in the East and in the West. What details in this document are particularly important for an understanding of baptism today? Why are they so important for today?

3. In your view, what are the three most important aspects of Clement's *Mystagogical Catecheses?* Be prepared to explain why you think they are important.

4. What does the term "a non-eucharistic baptism" mean? How did baptism become separated so strongly from the eucharist?

4

Holy Baptism and Contemporary Theology

In contemporary sacramental theology, with its emphasis on Jesus as the primordial sacrament and the Church as the basic sacrament, one would have to say that the only reason, theologically, that baptism is a sacrament is that baptism has an intrinsic and foundational relationship to the humanness of Jesus on the one hand and to the Church on the other hand. If this were not the case, then such terms as "primordial" and "basic" would have no meaning.

This emphasis clearly goes beyond the definition of a sacrament, so commonplace in Roman Catholic theology: namely, an external sign, instituted by Christ to give grace. In this definition, no mention is made of either Jesus as the primordial sacrament nor of the Church as the basic sacrament. In other words, baptism is a sacrament not simply because Jesus instituted it, but more profoundly because Jesus himself is the very meaning of baptism.

This is all rather new in Roman Catholic thought, and as of now rather untouched by Protestant theologians. Vatican II did in its documents refer to the Church as the basic sacrament. It did not refer to Jesus as the primordial sacrament, although the theological base for the Church as a sacrament is indeed Jesus as the primordial sacrament. In other words, even with the statements of Vatican II, we are still in the area of theological opinion, and not in the area of "official and solemnly declared" teaching of the Church.

Officially, however, the Church has utilized this approach in some of the official documents which have recently been issued. In the Vatican II document, *Presbyterorum Ordines,* the method is to discuss Jesus as priest, then the Church as priestly, and only then the ordained priest.[1] In the document, *Ordo Paenitentiae,* the introductory section, the *Praenotanda,* speaks first of Jesus as reconciler, then of the Church as a reconciling event, and only then of the sacrament of reconciliation.[2] In these instances the Church gives us a lead as to the methodology we should consider in dealing with the sacraments: namely, Jesus, Church and then individual sacrament. This methodology brings out the primordiality of Jesus and the basic sacramental quality of the Church.

Let us follow this lead of the Church and investigate more deeply the interconnection between Jesus, Church and baptism. We will not only utilize the methodological elements, but attempt to delve into the deeper theological issues involved. The attempt remains on the tentative level, since this kind of theologizing is still rather new in the Roman Church.

1. JESUS THE PRIMORDIAL SACRAMENT OF BAPTISM

We now turn to an issue which can only be described as "contemporary" or "current." Jesus as a sacrament was not a topic for the early Fathers of the Church. The documents of the Second Vatican Council do cite St. Cyprian on a number of occasions, but it is clear that the bishops are stretching to find a patristic basis for this idea of Jesus as the primordial sacrament. Nor did the great scholastic theologians such as St. Thomas or St. Bonaventure write on Jesus as the primordial sacrament. Luther and Calvin did not take this approach either, nor did the Catholic theologians of the post-reformation period such as Robert Bellarmine or Suarez. "Jesus as the primordial sacrament" is clearly a twentieth century approach to the issue of sacraments.

Contemporary authors such as Karl Rahner and Edward Schillebeeckx did much to develop an understanding of Jesus as the primordial sacrament and the Church as a basic sacrament. Their writings on these subjects remain even today as excellent theological descriptions of the issues involved. These two writers as well as others who have dealt with the topic have remained within the general area of Jesus as the primordial sacrament and the Church as the basic sacrament. There has been only the slightest movement to describe how either Jesus or the Church is the "basic sacrament" for the individual sacraments. In other words, in what way can we say today that Jesus is the "primordial sacrament" of baptism? In what way can we say that the Church is the "basic sacrament" for baptism? These are the questions which we are looking at here.

If Jesus is the primordial sacrament of baptism and the Church is the basic sacrament for baptism, then baptism itself is not the "first" sacrament, as we noted above. Rather, Jesus in his humanity is the "first" sacrament. This is precisely what "primordial" means: Jesus enjoys a position of "primacy" of "firstness." Likewise, if the Church is a "basic" sacrament, then the Church, *qua* sacrament, is more basic than the rite of baptism, i.e., the individual celebration of the sacrament of baptism.

This is all rather new territory, and as such should be seen as "theological opinion." Even though the Church, through the magisterium of the Second Vatican Council, did instruct us to teach that the Church is the basic sacrament, the bishops did not present this teaching as a solemn teaching of the Church. The bishops utilized the theological approach of Jesus as primordial sacrament and Church as basic sacrament to disclose for our day and age the mystery of the Church, the primary focus of these conciliar statements.

In the following pages, it will be argued that Jesus, in his humanity, is *the* baptized, that is, Jesus is in himself what baptism is all about. When one hears the word "baptism," one thinks immediately of "water," or of "original sin," or of "entrance into the Church." However, if Jesus is the primordial sacrament of baptism, then when one says baptism, the first thought one should have is "Jesus," not water, original sin, or entrance into the Church. By and large, Christians, both Protestant and Catholic, do not think this way. Water, original sin, etc., are indeed the first thoughts which come to mind. If one is ever going to see Jesus as the primordial sacrament of baptism, an extensive effort toward a new catechesis must be made.

In order to accomplish this, let us consider the actual baptism of Jesus, not so much from a textual or contextual biblical approach, as from a theological approach. This means that we will consider the baptism of Jesus from the standpoint of its "meaning" within the framework of sacramental theology. We have already noted that Jesus' baptism was a very integral part of the early Church's kerygma. All four gospels have an accounting of the baptism in one way or another, and the Acts of the Apostles make it central for an "apostle." The actual baptism of Jesus, however, receives its greatest description in the gospel of Mark, not only because he forthrightly talks about Jesus' baptism, but because it is the opening section of his entire gospel. Indeed, the very first words of his gospel are: "The beginning of the good news of Jesus Christ" (1:1). Such a statement almost passes without note, and the reader might too quickly hurry on to the subsequent portrayal of John the Baptist. However, further meditation on this simple statement does raise some prominent issues. What does the author mean by "beginning"? Clearly he is not saying that this is the beginning page of his book, similar to the way that some writers attach a final *finis* at the end of their writings. Mark is clearly not writing an *incipium* on page one of his gospel and a *finis* on the final folio. If it is not a statement that the book begins here, then what is the beginning of which Mark speaks? It can really be no other than the very first things that Mark takes up, namely, the portrayal of John the Baptist and the account of the baptism of Jesus himself. In these events Mark sees the beginning of the good news of Jesus Christ. How different this is from both Luke and Matthew who trace the origins of Jesus into a conception-birth episode on the one hand, and a genealogical table on the other. Both of these evangelists are talking about the beginnings of Jesus, historically, physically, and above all with the virgin birth motif, the spiritual beginning of the Lord as well. John, in his prologue, traces the beginning of Jesus back to the Word: "At the beginning, the Word was with God" (Jn 1:1). In Mark we find none of this: no infancy narrative, no genealogy, no virgin birth; and yet here is "the beginning of the good news."

One other item of interest in this simple opening statement is the fact that there is, in Greek, no definite article prior to the noun "beginning." Literally translated, the sentence would read: "Beginning of good news . . ." We find the same situation with the opening sentence of the gospel of John, namely, no article before the noun. Again, literally translated, that opening sentence would read: "At the beginning was the Word." This also holds for the commencement of the book of Genesis, which has as its opening word in Hebrew: *be-reshith,* which literally translates as well into: "at beginning," not "at the beginning." The omission of the article is simply a semitic way of stating the emphasis of the matter; in English we might write these phrases as: "At *the* beginning . . ." or "*the* beginning . . ."[3] In other words, these authors are not dealing with just any beginning but they wish to address themselves to an *absolute* beginning: in Genesis, a beginning so absolute that, prior to it, everything is meaningless *(tohu wabohu)* except God; in John, the very beginning of the Word is in God, nowhere else. When we come to Mark, he is saying that in the baptism of Jesus we have an absolute beginning of Jesus himself, and therefore of good news, since the Jesus-event *is* the good news.

Christian Schütz invites us to consider this "beginning" quality even more profoundly. He writes:

> Mark dares to meet both the uniqueness and the mystery of Jesus' baptism, insofar as he portrays it in the light of a beginning *(arche)*. To this goal the original powers (of creation) are conjoined with the baptism: water, Spirit, voice, i.e., the Word (cf. Gn. 1:2). Insofar as these elements separate and/or unite do they establish the mystery of the untouched and unspent origin of pure, creative beginning.[4]

In this way we are speaking not simply of a beginning, but *the* beginning of the good news, and this beginning is an event: the baptism of Jesus. Such a beginning is made quite clear in Mark's gospel, so that the readership has no doubt as to what constitutes the very origin of Jesus: "You are my Son, the Beloved" in 1:11 corresponds to the statement in 15:39: "In truth this man was a Son of God." For the readers of the gospel, there is no messianic secret. They know from the introduction that Jesus is God's Son. Only when the introductory section is over, and the body of the gospel starts (Mk 1:14ff.) do the actors (not the readers) get caught up in the messianic secret.

Thus we have in this opening scene a statement that there is something of an absolute beginning in the event described, a climactic statement on the entire baptismal event in the words of God: "You are my beloved Son . . ." Although in Matthew's gospel this is stated impersonally, namely, "This is my beloved Son," Mark construes this in a direct communication between Jesus and the Father through his use of "You."

As a creator, God does not simply create generically. Rather, he creates individuals who respond to the word "you." In fact, part of the creative act of God is the bringing into existence of this very "you." Paul Tillich addresses this question when he talks about the "shock of non-being."

This "shock of non-being" opens up a totally new dimension for man. He experiences the threatening fact that he is *ex nihilo.* At that central point in the depth of his being, where man gathers together all the facets of his being, he experiences the loneliness of his ego. His entire "what" and his entire "what-should-be" stands over against *ex nihilo,* and therefore he asks a question: the question of being itself. The answer was not at hand in the dimension of object, for the objects themselves were all possibilities, but none were demanding. They, too, could or could not be. The answer was not at hand in the dimension of the subject; the subject, too, could or could not be. Hence the question of another dimension that is beyond subject-object. This is the dimension of the ultimate, the *Esse Ipsum.* . . . This is not to be construed as though man has two types of being: man has only one type of *being,* that is, *ex Deo.* An essence *ex nihilo* is no essence at all. Tillich can therefore say: "God is the dimension of the ultimate in being and meaning, present in and absent from everything that is."[5]

In Tillich's concept of God's creativity and human finite creatureliness, we see that were one to remove God, the Ground of all being, finite being would cease to exist. "At the very limits of the finite form (the essence) is correlatively and necessarily the Ground of all being. It is a presence that is needed continually as long as there is a 'what.' It is a presence and power as long as there is a 'what-should-be' in the dynamism of man's freedom to actualize his possibilities."[6]

The "you are" of Mark's gospel brings us face to face with this beginning: Tillich's Ground of all being, a beginning which is *ex nihilo,* in a negative sense, but *ex Deo* in its positive sense. It is the presence of the divine in Jesus, that establishes the very beginning of what Jesus is all about.

Mark hints at this since he seems to be saying, and this is the high point of the entire episode, that at the very origin, the very beginning of Jesus is the presence of God. One cannot understand Jesus unless one understands this relationship between the humanness of Jesus and the presence of the divine, and it is this presence of God incarnate that is *the* beginning of salvation, good news, redemption, sanctification. Beyond this absolute beginning there is no other originating source. Jesus is not simply a savior of men and women, he is *the* savior beyond whom there is no other. Jesus is not simply a lord, a messiah to all men and women; he is *the* lord, *the* messiah, beyond whom there is no other.

It is interesting to note that the infancy narratives, particularly in the virgin birth motif, are, theologically, expressing the same great mystery: at the very origin of Jesus is the presence of the Spirit, i.e., God himself. Jesus is totally unintelligible without this presence of God.[7]

The baptismal liturgies developed in the early Church and continuing in existence in some fashion or another down to the present time have employed a variety of symbolic actions: a washing, an anointing, a laying on of hands, to name only the most striking. Special words were used to describe such an event as baptism: a rebirth, an enlightenment, a new creation, a new life, people becoming the temple of the Spirit. All of these and so many more are trying to point to and to speak about what is at the very heart of baptism: the presence of God to an individual. As rebirth, baptism does not focus simply on the birthing, but on the birthing *to* some thing: new life with God. As enlightenment, baptism does not focus simply on the process of coming to knowledge, but knowledge of something: an awareness of the presence of God. All the exorcisms, and this is so evident in the more dramatic ones of the early liturgies such as we find in Cyril of Jerusalem, the Apostolic Constitutions, and the Byzantine Euchologion, highlight that there is a change of presence: the presence of evil, Satan, is ceremoniously ejected, and the holy presence of God is celebrated.

Of all men and woman, no one, and so we believe in our Christian faith, has ever been more intimately united to the presence of God than the humanness of Jesus, and it is this anointing of God's presence in and through the humanness of Jesus, it is this thorough washing of the humanness of Jesus, that symbolically in his own baptism on the one hand, but in the reality of his being, on the other, indicates the presence of God so immensely in the humanness of Jesus. Indeed we can rightfully say that Jesus was baptized in the Jordan, but the baptism was deeper than any immersion in water; it is the immersion of Jesus into God's own self. He is not only baptized, but as Schütz remarks he truly is *the* baptized. Schütz notes that Jesus was surely one of the strangest people to be baptized by John. In contrast to everyone else he had no reason and no purpose for such a baptism, but this lack of meaning has a very eminent position:

> Jesus is, namely, the only one, who in the proper and original sense is baptized. What happens to him, is baptism in a pure, full and completed sense. This baptism has within itself its own purpose,

reason and finality, and indeed in such a way that the baptism creates and brings it about only in the event, in the doing of it itself.
The baptism tolerates no borrowed object; every extraneous means,
bases or purposes disappear. Jesus cannot nor has he need to pro-
duce anything in this situation. He lets all sufficiency rest in the
occurrence itself. He is baptized with his entire nature and being;
in it he gives himself, not simply something of himself, e.g., sins,
as the others do. He keeps nothing of himself back.[8]

What reason did Jesus have to undergo the Johannine baptism?
The customary purpose of John's baptism was conversion and forgiveness of sins, but this is meaningless in the case of Jesus. Indeed, we
have in the baptism of Jesus total unreasonableness, total lack of purpose and goal. There was no reason for him to be baptized; otherwise,
the baptism would not be *the* beginning, since behind such a baptism,
there would have been reasons and purposes, and the baptism would
have been the result of such purposes, and consequently a culmination
and not a beginning. A beginning has within itself its own why, its own
purpose, its own meaning; and so, too, the baptism of Jesus has within
it its own why, its own purpose, its own meaning. We do not ask questions behind a beginning; rather, we begin with the beginning.

As mentioned by Schütz above, Jesus is baptized with his entire
human being; it is not something accidental, something superfluous,
something external which is baptized. No, it is Jesus himself who is
baptized, and this in the fullest and most proper and original sense. The
mystery of Jesus' baptism tells us something about the very locus in
which Jesus' humanness began to be. The baptism of Jesus tells us
something about the beginning of his very incarnate life.

Dietrich Wiederkehr expresses this relationship as follows:
"Moreover, the relationship between God and Jesus consists not in
some static unity or essential oneness, but it perfects itself in an actual
imparting of the Spirit; it is, consequently, not so much a community
but a communication."[9] The human ontological "I" of Jesus and the
"Thou" of the triune God are different but with the incarnation they
are inseparable. The mystery of this lies in the search for the identity
of Jesus. "Who do men say that I am?" The deeper one understands
this man Jesus, the closer one comes to this originating communication
of God's Spirit. Jesus cannot be understood except in his relationship
to God. As long as God is saying to him: "You are . . ." Jesus is, and

he *is* only because of the communication of God's Spirit. This is what primordially the baptism of Jesus is all about: the communication of the Spirit of God so that Jesus begins to be.

This line of thought regarding baptism truly revolutionizes our entire understanding of the matter of baptism, for if we pay more than simple lip service to the idea that Jesus alone is really *the* baptized in its deepest and fullest and most genuine sense, then it is clear at once that the very understanding of baptism far surpasses all that is usually included in some treatise on the sacrament of baptism. It is Jesus' very being (here, his human, created being) that is baptized; even more, this baptized humanness of Jesus is what baptism is all about. Consider for a moment some of the implications of this truly profound way of thinking:

(a) When I am in the presence of Jesus, I am in the presence of *the* baptized, in the presence of what baptism most fully means.

(b) Jesus is truly seen as the original sacrament insofar as he is the original baptism, the *Urtaufe*.

(c) All other "baptisms" are secondary and derivative from him as *the* baptized.

(d) If he is fundamentally and basically and most fully *the* baptized, and therefore baptism itself has its most comprehensive reality in Jesus, then the statement in the creed, namely, "We believe . . . in *one* baptism," takes on a much deeper meaning, since even though there have been literally millions of baptisms over the Christian centuries, there is radically only *one* baptism, the Lord himself as *the* baptized.

2. THE CHURCH AS THE BASIC SACRAMENT OF BAPTISM

The documents of Vatican II speak of the Church as a basic sacrament. In other words, the sacramentality of the Church is part of the ordinary magisterium of the Church. Since none of the documents of the Vatican Council were promulgated as infallible statements, these documents are, consequently, not considered the "solemn teaching of the Church," but they are the directives of the magisterium for our present age. To speak of the Church as a basic sacrament is, then, not simply a theological opinion, held by a few scholars. Rather, it is presented to the entire Roman Catholic Church as one of the major approaches to the Church for our times.

There has been a considerable amount of literature on the Church as a basic sacrament, but there has been almost no literature on the Church as a basic sacrament for the individual sacraments. In this sense, then, what follows is clearly theological opinion and not the teaching of the Church. This distinction must be kept in mind in a very strong way: the Church as a basic sacrament is Church teaching; the Church as a basic sacrament of baptism is a matter of theological speculation.

The Church is not only a locus for baptizing individuals, but the Church itself is a baptized people of God. The Church not only baptizes, but the Church is radically a baptized Church, and this means more than simply its individual members are baptized. It means, rather, that just as with Jesus baptism speaks of an intimate, deep relationship between his humanness and God, so, too, the baptized Church speaks about the real presence of *the* baptized one within the Church. Once again, the emphasis falls on presence and on relationship, and what is so tremendously important about the Church is the presence of the Lord within it. All talk about models of the Church, useful as these might be, pale when one realizes that central to the Church, beyond all its functioning and structures, is that the Church is a locus of the presence of God and Christ. The Church is Church only if and to the extent that it brings to presence Christ and his Spirit. But note the word "presence." Let us consider the notion of presence, namely that it is an event in which a depth of presence is offered and accepted on the part of one side, and a depth of presence is offered and accepted on the part of another. This mutual offering and accepting is, from our human standpoint, an experience, for we experience presence, and since the initiator and prime agent within this presence in the Church is Christ and God, this experience, at least inchoatively, is a *religious* experience. Just as Jesus is *the* baptized, because of the presence of God to his entire, created humanness, so, too, the Church is baptized because of the real presence of Jesus (and therefore the total Godhead) in and to the community. Because all Christians, and here rank, sex, age, social status, ethnic background have no meaning whatsoever, share in the presence of the *one* Lord, who is *the* baptized one, so we all share in *one* baptism. In the Lima document of the World Council of Churches, one reads of the multiple meaning of baptism as the sign of new life through Jesus

Christ: baptism means participating in the life, death and resurrection of Jesus Christ; it means conversion, pardoning and cleansing; it means the gift of the Spirit; it means incorporation into the Body of Christ; it means the presence of the kingdom of God. In dealing with incorporation into the Body of Christ, we read: "Through baptism, Christians are brought into union with Christ, with each other and with the Church of every time and place. Our common baptism, which unites us to Christ in faith, is thus a basic bond of unity."[10] This is clearly the meaning of what Christians profess when they say: we believe in one baptism.

Although this document, in its section on baptism, tends mostly to concentrate on the sacrament of baptism and its proper understanding and practice, it does make note of this one baptism. Perhaps something more extensive might be said on this matter, namely that the baptizing and baptized Church is a sacrament, indeed a fundamental sacrament, in and through this very dimension of baptism. If we ask those familiar questions, however, namely "Of what is the Church a sacrament?" and "For whom is it a sacrament?" with specific reference to the baptismal aspect in mind, we might formulate our replies as follows. The Church, in its baptismal character, is a sacrament of *the* baptized one, namely Jesus, and all that being *the* baptized means in him. This presence of God in the humanness of Jesus, which is at the core of his being *the* baptized, is a reconciling, justifying, saving presence. By being a sacrament of that presence, the Church in its baptismal character is a sacrament for all men and women of this same presence of God, reconciling, justifying, saving, as incarnated in the Lord himself. It is the real presence of Jesus, sacramentally evidenced, that lies at the heart of the baptized Church. R. Schulte words the position as follows: "The dynamic dimension of the Church as the baptized conversion-community participates ultimately in the basic character of the being of the incarnate Word of God."[11]

3. THE RITUAL CELEBRATION OF BAPTISM

When we turn to the individual celebration of the sacrament of baptism, we notice, first of all, that most of the literature on the subject deals with the New Testament data, first as this touches on the mystery of baptism, i.e., its connection with the very life, death and resurrection of the Lord, and, second, on the rite of baptism as evidenced in the primitive sources. The historical studies on baptism attempt to piece together the varying rites that appear from the second century on to the thirteenth century, both in the East and in the West. Out of all this material there are, then, some theological considerations on such topics as infant baptism, the character of baptism, the relationship between baptism and confirmation, etc. Even in contemporary ecumenical literature the emphasis in such discussions is on the rite of baptism and its accepted meaning by the various Churches. In other words, the bulk of literature available to us today concentrates on the rite of baptism, so that when the word "baptism" is mentioned, one almost automatically thinks of the rite of baptism. If, however, Jesus is seen as *the* baptized, i.e., the full meaning of baptism is found exclusively in his human nature and its relationship to the godhead, then what is needful today is to expand our notion of "baptism" so that we do not concentrate so heavily on the rite of baptism. With this precaution in mind, let us move on to the rite of baptism.

The first thing I want to say about the celebration of a baptism is that it must be seen in the context of prayer, or, even more sharply expressed, the baptizing event is itself a prayer-event. Not for nothing did the early Fathers see baptism as a mystery and spoke of it as "mysterion." If prayer is the very warp and woof of a baptismal celebration, there will be on the part of the Christian people of God a profound expression of wonder and amazement, which is the center of all prayer. This wonder and amazement is, however, a reaction to something else, namely God's own mysterious action. His action is primordial; the prayer-action of the Church is secondary and reactive. The community is celebrating the presence of grace, which is totally to be understood as gift, God's own free giving of himself to a concrete historical individual. The community is celebrating a *relationship* between God (as also Christ) and a given human person, since God's gift is primarily not some *thing* but his very self, and the giving of a self to another self and the mutual return of self to self is always a relationship. God's gift of himself is in, through, and with his incarnate Son, so that in baptism we have also a relationship between a given person and Jesus. In this sense there is something eucharistic about baptism, just as there is something baptismal about eucharist. For a very long period in the history of the Christian Church—in the West Nathan D. Mitchell notes that it was the Roman custom up to the twelfth century—the baptism-eucharist axis formed the rite of initiation into the Church.[12] This interconnection between baptism and eucharist needs much more attention than it generally receives.

A prayer-event, God's action of self-giving, the presence of the incarnate Lord form the foundation of the baptismal event, but, over the centuries, stress has been placed on baptism as initiation. K. Stendahl somewhat summarized the issue as follows:

> I would take my point of departure in the fact that baptism in the New Testament and in the early church is always an act of *initiation,* and that this fact should be the point of departure. Such an act is capable of many interpretations, but the force of initiation is primary. One cannot understand baptism by combining the elements of purification with the elements of death/resurrection, with the elements of regeneration, with the elements of receiving the Spirit, with the incorporation in the Body of Christ, etc. One must begin with the fact that in all cases the practice of baptism is the rite by which initiation takes place.[13]

With an understanding of Jesus as *the* baptized, some modifications in this position might have to be made. Still, initiation is a factor to be considered. Initiation, however, is not a beginning *de novo;* it is not a creation. The volume on baptism, *Made Not Born,* indicates not only that we are indeed not born Christians but become so after birth, but also that baptism is based to some degree on birth. Something which is already existing is realigned, reconstituted, rerelationed, transformed by an initiation. Moreover, in the case of baptism, it is not a part of the human person, one's mind, one's will, one's soul (if we think in a body-soul mentality), one's body, that is baptized; it is the total person. I say, "I am baptized," not "I have a soul that is baptized," etc. Baptism affects my entire being and in its most radical depths. Nor does baptism make me more human, in the sense of some accretion; rather, baptism speaks about all that humanness means. By this I do not want to say that there is any intrinsic, necessary, essential relationship between being a human person, on the one hand, and baptism on the other; I fully espouse the Scotistic principle of God's absolute power *(de potentia Dei absoluta),* which denecessitates everything created. The relationship between being human and baptism arises only from God's ordered power *(de potentia Dei ordinata).* God could have arranged the entire plan of human history, including salvation history, in whatever way he might have willed. Still, since baptism is, as we believe, the way that God has wished to make both manifest and real his own saving power, he is in and through baptism alerting us as to what human life ultimately should mean and does mean.

Thus, the sacraments *celebrate what God has been doing and is continuing to do*. By conception and birth God is already related to each individual in the sense of that continuing creation mentioned above. By baptism the very reason why God so creates is made explicit: he has created each man and woman specifically and ultimately for one particular reason: his own glory. He has created each man and woman to share in the redemptive love of his Son. He has created each man and woman with a basic predestination to eternal life with him, and the Christian Church has consistently rejected any and all attempts toward a dual predestination, namely that some are from the very beginning of their existence predestined to heaven, while others also from that very beginning are predestined to hell. It is a truism that Christ has redeemed us, and consequently we live *now* in a redeemed world. It is likewise a truism that the end-time has started, so that we are *now* in this end-time. It is furthermore a truism that the kingdom of God is currently at hand, so that *now* we are surrounded by and live in the kingdom. To quote Schulte once again:

> What the human person *now is, what he on the basis of the power and freedom that has been given to him can and should now* form of himself (cf. Col. 3), this is precisely to be read from the way in which God *now* (unexpectedly new) is revealed (cf. for this "now" especially Eph. 3, 10 within the context of the letter), from the way in which God *now* works in the human person; and this means: this is to be read from what the human person is and will become through the baptismal event.[14]

In this baptismal event, then, we are celebrating to a very serious degree that eschatological aspect which is both the "already" aspect, as well as the "but also" aspect of this same eschatological texture of salvation history.

But is there not something new which occurs in baptism? Here the notion of *transformation* comes into play. Human existence is a process and in each movement of that process a transformation takes place, whether for the better or the worse. From this aspect the baptismal event is a transformation for the better. In its more careful and clearer celebrations, a person deliberately joins a visible, eschatological community, namely the Church, and the people of God in this Church deliberately welcome this person into its midst. A new set of relationships between the people of God on the one hand and an individual human being on the other is being celebrated. Also, the individual in the baptismal-event professes, in personal freedom, his or her confession of the Lordship of Jesus and all that this implies. Just as an individual comes to a deeper faith in and through the entire baptismal event, so too God, in a biblical sense of the term faith, is more present to that person as a faithful God. Just as the individual person in and through the baptismal event enters into a more loving relationship with Christ and God, so, too, God is present to that person in a more loving way. And just as human life, even in its weakest moment, is still a life which can only be understood as sharing in some degree in the very life of God, since he is professed as life from life, so too the individual person in and through the baptismal event shares more deeply and consequently in a new way in the very life of God. It is the newness in this transformative process of human life that is the *initium* underlying the initiation aspect of a baptism.

All of the above scarcely makes sense if we understand grace as ultimately a thing, a quality, inhering in the soul. Such a theology in the past has indicated that at baptism we do indeed receive such qualities, more specifically defined as "habitus," through the infusion of faith, hope and charity. A non-baptized person does not have these qualities; a baptized person, including those who have at least the *votum baptismi*, has them. In this kind of natural/supernatural theology, the old and the new are easily distinguished, but if grace is seen ultimately not as a thing but as a relationship between God and the human, and if grace is really God himself, giving himself to an individual, then the "old" and the "new" need to be theologically considered on a different basis. P. Fransen, who in today's theology has probably written on grace more than any other contemporary Catholic theologian, has recently written the following guideline, in the introductory section of an essay, in which he establishes the methodology that will govern all that he wants to say about grace:

> Our method rests on an important principle of interpretation which can be considered from different aspects. If God wishes to "save" a creature, he will save it in the same way as he had created it. In

this sense Francis de Sales could say: "The more grace divinizes us, the more it humanizes us." This formulation is a more powerful form of speech than the classical axiom: grace builds on nature (gratia supponit naturam), which emphasizes too much the distinction between nature and grace. Salvation, which realizes itself through grace, must clarify and intensify our human existence. If grace disturbs anything, then it disturbs only that which threatens our human existence: evil and sin. Expressed in another way: the more intensive is our humanization, the more radical is our divinization; and the more total our divinization is, the more profound is our humanization.[15]

If there is this coordination between humanization and divinization, which Fransen refers to, then baptism which has always been seen as a great moment of divinization is, as well, a profound moment of humanization. The greatness, however, can be seen in only one area: the more intimate relationship between God (Christ) on the one hand, and the individual person on the other. Such a relationship, if it is to have any meaning at all, requires that God be truly present to the individual in and through the baptismal event, and that Christ be truly present to the individual in and through the baptismal event, so that we have here in baptism a *real presence* of the Lord. This Lord is present as *the* baptized, and his presence precisely as *the* baptized is constitutive of what the rite of baptism is and, from a theological viewpoint, indicates once again that Jesus is the primordial sacrament, without whom in a constitutive way baptism, as well as any of the other sacraments, would be meaningless *qua* sacrament.

Although this may appear as a new theological approach, the New Testament itself with its emphasis on the baptism of Jesus indicates strongly that this is the correct approach to baptism. Jesus as the primordial sacrament of baptism (and for all the sacraments) points out that christology lies at the base of both ecclesiology and sacramentology. Ecumenically, discussions on Jesus might be more helpful than the current discussions on sacraments and Church polity. K. Stofft notes:

Christology is now taking priority in theological dialogue. As such, Christology may become the major Christian contribution to the religious life of humanity. Within a strictly Christian framework, an examination of christology would have major bearing on the unity

Christians seek in "conciliar fellowship." It should become the basis for discussion on "evangelism," and aid in determining resolutions to such current problems as women's ordination, the recognition and development of ministries, the clarification of the role of Baptism, and the subsequent rights and responsibilities of the baptized within the faith-life of the Christian community.[16]

The deeper we study the primordiality of the sacrament of Jesus' humanness and the way it relates to such sacraments as baptism, the closer, so it seems, will the presently divided Christian Churches find their true unity in the Lord himself. The above chapters are offered merely to indicate a way that a christologically centered theology of baptism might aid in this process.

Baptism has never been a source of major controversy between the various mainline churches of the West, although certain aspects of a given baptismal rite were controversial, insofar as they appeared to be "good works" or "superstitions." Marion Hatchett provides an overview of the baptismal ritual in the Anglican Church from the 1549 Prayer Book onward.[17] One of the important aspects of this Anglican tradition, which at first blush might seem secondary, is the insistence on the term "Holy Baptism." This phrase emphasizes the role of God and the sanctity of the event, far more than the simple term "baptism." Holy Baptism is seen as "full initiation by water and the Holy Spirit into Christ's Body the Church. The bond which God establishes in Baptism is indissoluble."[18]

The second Lutheran-Catholic dialogue focused on baptism, and the convergence between the Lutheran and the Roman Catholics on this matter was extensive. Indeed, there is general consensus on a theology of this sacrament. In the Lutheran *Manual on the Liturgy,* care has been taken to provide an historical background of baptism, as it has developed within the Christian community.[19] Of particular importance is the issue of the baptism of infants, an issue which needs to be handled not in an indiscriminate way, but with careful responsibility.

In this *Manual on the Liturgy* we read: "Baptism is thus the beginning of the Christian life and the foundation on which the life in Christ is built. It is done once and is not repeated, lest doubt be cast on what God has done in this sacrament of adoption."[20]

One could read these contemporary documents from the Anglican and Lutheran traditions, as well as those from the Roman Catholic tra-

dition, and find extensive areas of agreement, not only in the ritualization, but also in the theological underpinnings. The history of this
sacrament, which has been so carefully researched in the last decades,
has helped all three traditions. What is still needed in all of these is an
explicit connection with the primordial sacrament, Jesus Christ. Hopefully, the above chapters on baptism will contribute some insights on
this matter to all three of these traditions.

Discussion Questions

1. What does the phrase "Jesus as the primordial sacrament of baptism" mean?
2. In what ways is the Church a basic sacrament of baptism?
3. How is the "new ritual of baptism christocentric?
4. What is "divinization"?

5

The New Ritual of Baptism and Jesus as the Primordial Sacrament

After the Second Vatican Council had concluded its sessions, commissions were set up to renew each of the sacramental rituals. The renewal of the sacrament of baptism was one of the most extensive and intensive undertakings, and in 1972 the new rite for adults, entitled the *Rite of Christian Initiation of Adults,* was promulgated. This is generally referred to in English as the RCIA. The rite for the baptism of children, in its renewed form, had been promulgated in 1969. The RCIA, however, has been the rite which has engendered many theological and liturgical commentaries, a great deal of adult education in parishes and even in dioceses, and in many ways provided a renewed "theology" of baptism. The document is lengthy and together with the renewed rite of children's baptism must be seen as part of the Church's magisterium, or official teaching.[1]

The RCIA is meant for those who have never been baptized and who now wish to be baptized into the Christian faith in the Roman Catholic Church. If someone is already baptized, but wants to transfer to the Roman Catholic Church, the RCIA is not the procedure to be followed. Rather, there is another ritual, namely, the *Rite of Receiving Baptized Christians into the Full Communion of the Catholic Church.*[2] In paragraph five of this document we read: "Any treatment of the candidates as though they were catechumens is to be absolutely avoided." In other words, the RCIA is clearly meant for those who are *not* baptized, and should not be used for those transferring to the Roman Catholic Church.

Secondly, the RCIA is seen as a "journey."[3] There is a series of stages or steps which candidates must go through, and these take a fairly long time. There is first of all a preliminary stage of inquiry into the meaning of Jesus' message and into the Church. If a person is serious then the document outlines three phases:

a. the point of initial conversion, at which a person is accepted as a catechumen by the Church;
b. the maturing of this faith, over a period of perhaps three years;
c. the final preparation for the reception of the sacraments of baptism, confirmation and eucharist.

This journey begins, as the document notes, when a person hears the preaching of the "mystery of Christ." Jesus is at the beginning or at the center of this "journey of faith." During the journey a person strengthens his or her faith in Jesus.

This journey concludes with the reception not simply of baptism, but of baptism-confirmation-eucharist. Once again, we see that the sacrament of initiation is not simply baptism, but rather baptism-confirmation-eucharist. Recall, here, that this is presented as "official Church teaching."

A complete commentary on the RCIA is not intended here. Rather, we will focus on those aspects of the document which help us see more clearly the "theology" of baptism, at least in its main aspects, as presented formally by the Church for today's world.

1. *The centrality of Jesus:* Although the document does not consistently make Jesus the center, it does do so in a much more intensive way than previous rituals on baptism. Were one to go through the entire document and note all the times that Jesus/Christ is mentioned, one would be quite surprised at the emphasis. The adult conversion is not so much a conversion to "belief in God" as it is a "belief in the mystery of Jesus." During the lengthy catechumenate (perhaps even three years) those in this RCIA journey are brought ever more fully into a prayerful understanding of the gospel, that is, of the mystery of Jesus. In the final period of illumination and purification, one is purified of all that is not "of Christ" and illumined by the "Spirit of Jesus" (170; 178).

Of great value in all of this are the prayers for each of these stages. Such phrases as "light of Christ," "leadership of Christ," "follow Christ," etc., abound in the prayers of accepting someone into the catechumenate. The people of God and the sponsors are asked to testify if the proposed catechumens "have chosen Christ as Lord," and if they are ready to help them "come to know and follow Christ."

The catechumens are traced with the sign of the cross, that is, the "sign of Christ's own love and his triumph." The priest prays that "Christ will be your strength. Learn now to know and follow him" (84–85).

After the welcoming into the Church of Christ, the gospels are read and a homily is given. The book of the gospels is given to the new catechumens: "Receive the Gospel, the good news of Jesus Christ, the Son of God." In the following prayers for the catechumens the Church prays that God will "reveal his Christ to them more and more," that they "may come to reflect the image of Christ" (93–95).

In the reception of the catechumen, the RCIA in many ways presents us with a picture of Jesus as central, although not in any over-extensive way.

2. *The catechumen already has faith:* In nos. 9, 10, 75, 82, we hear about the "faith" of the catechumen. This clearly accords with the traditional teaching of the Church. As an adult, there is no "limbo," which is presented as a "place" only for infants and those who have never matured into adults. Adults, in the traditional teaching of the Church, go either to heaven or to hell. Therefore, adults are seen as either having "faith" or denying "faith."

In the case of adult baptism, therefore, "faith" is not given for the first time. The effect of baptism, to speak theologically, is not the *habitus* of faith. The new RCIA clearly underscores this faith of the catechumen. He or she already believes in God and in the journey through the catechumenate comes to an ever deepening faith in Jesus. The "limbo" teaching also meant that there was an adult acceptance of sanctifying grace. Since there is no "limbo adultorum," adults accepted God and grace and went to heaven or rejected God and grace and went to hell. No intermediate situation was envisioned. This is clearly the theological insight of the "limbo" position. It is this insight which is continued by the RCIA. Baptism does not give an adult sanctifying grace for the first time, and therefore does not take away original sin from an adult. Long before baptism, adults had received grace and accordingly had been purified of "original sin." We noted above that in contemporary Roman Catholic theology, theologians of impeccable credentials were involved in a renewed study of the very meaning of "original sin." The RCIA does not touch on "original sin" in its theological presentation of baptism.

3. *The catechumen is a part of the Church:* The RCIA states very clearly that from the reception of the person into the catechumenate onward, such a person is "joined to the Church" and is a "part of the household of Christ" (18). As such they are encouraged to take part in the liturgy of the word, in blessings and sacramentals. If they marry, they follow the new ritual of marriage for Catholics, and if buried, they are buried in a Christian cemetery (18).

This status of the catechumen "in the Church" accords well with the practices of the early Church, which considered catechumens part of the ecclesial community and awarded them all the assistance which the Church might offer. However, this positioning of the catechumen "in the Church" tempers the theological position that baptism makes one a member of the Church. Baptism welcomes one into the eucharistic community of the Church. In the preliminary section of the new rite, it does say that "through baptism men and women are incorporated into Christ" (2), and again we read: "Baptism is the sacrament by which men and women are incorporated into the Church" (4). Evidently, there is still some theological discussion necessary as to the way in which one can say that a catechumen is already part of the Church, and that baptism is the way in which one is incorporated into the Church. Some nuancing and clarification remains to be done.

4. *The Church as integral part of the baptismal process:* There is much in the RCIA which strengthens the approach that the Church is the basic sacrament and particularly the basic sacrament of baptism. The constant stress in the ritual is on the activity of the Christian community. If one decides to be baptized into the Church, it is not a one-way street. The Church not only accepts the candidate, but selects, supports, evaluates, and encourages the candidate. We read of sponsors, parents, relatives, friends, neighbors and even the whole local Church taking an active part (7). The presence of these people is not merely passive, but active.

These people are important since they are themselves baptized and as such part of the baptized community. They not only role model but they exemplify what baptism means, insofar as each of them reflects *the* baptized one, Jesus. We see once more the progress: Jesus as *the baptized,* the Christian community as the basic sacrament of Jesus, and the actual baptism of a catechumen. In other words, the ritual of baptism means little unless it is seen in the context of the baptized and baptizing community. This community, however, means little, unless it reflects ("sacramentalizes") Jesus, *the* baptized.

5. *Baptism, confirmation, eucharist:* The RCIA clearly presents the sacrament of initiation as baptism, confirmation, and eucharist. The ritual calls for the actual baptism (220–222); then the explanatory rites, that is, the post-baptismal anointing (224), the clothing with the white garment (225), and the presentation of the lighted candle (226). This is immediately followed by the celebration of confirmation (227–231). After confirmation, there are the general intercessions, the offertory procession, the offertory itself and then the celebration of the eucharist.

The introductory material boldly calls this: "The Sacraments of Initiation." Even though the plural form is used (sacraments), the union of these three are called the "final stage" (27). With due acknowledgement to the ancient practice (this will be dealt with in the next chapter), an adult is to receive confirmation immediately after baptism (34). The basis for this is also presented: the unity of the paschal mystery, that is, the unity between the mission of Jesus and the sending of the Spirit, the unity of Father, Son and Spirit coming on those who are baptized.

These reasons are not unimportant, since they indicate to us that one really does not understand confirmation, except in its relationship with baptism. A non-baptismal theology of confirmation is basically erroneous. Baptism relates to confirmation and confirmation relates, in its turn, to baptism. To theologize on one without the other is to separate the unity of the paschal mystery. Secondly, one sees that Jesus, the center of the paschal mystery, focuses both baptism and confirmation and their interrelationship. The two sacraments, theologically, are at heart christological.

The eucharist is treated in n. 36. After baptism-confirmation, the neophytes have "the full right" to take part in the eucharist. The celebration of the eucharist is "the culminating point of their initiation" (36). The neophytes have received the dignity of the royal priesthood and thereby share in offering intercessions, bringing the gifts, taking part in the eucharistic prayer itself, reciting the Lord's Prayer, and receiving the consecrated bread and wine. Phrases such as "full right" and "culminating point of initiation" cannot be overlooked. These help us understand both baptism and eucharist. A non-baptismal theology of eucharist is not acceptable in the Christian faith; baptism has always been the "first" of the sacramental rites; on the other hand, a non-eucharistic theology of baptism is also inadmissible, since baptism, theologically, can only be fully appreciated in its relationship to the eucharist. Since the Church surrounds this initiation, the baptized and baptizing community should also share in the eucharist. This is expressly stated in n. 234. The Church as the basic sacrament of baptism can only be understood as such if the Church members partake in the baptismal eucharist.

This interconnection of baptism/confirmation/eucharist, however, poses an ecumenical problem today. In the divided Christian community, a stage has indeed been reached in which various Churches recognize the baptism of other Christian Churches. The Roman Catholic Church is one of these. In the *Rite of Receiving Baptized Christians into the Full Communion of the Catholic Church* we read that "the sacrament of baptism may not be repeated and conditional baptism is not permitted unless there is a prudent doubt about the fact or validity of the baptism already received" (7). It is up to the local ordinary to determine in individual cases what rites are to be included or excluded in conditional cases. Evidently, the Church tells us today that we are to accept the baptism of other Christian communities, unless there would be some serious doubt.

A baptized non-Catholic who becomes a Catholic may also be confirmed by the priest performing the ceremony, if confirmation has not been received (8). Again we see the connection of baptism and confirmation. Likewise, the reception can and is encouraged to take place in the context of the eucharist, and the larger community is urged to share in the eucharistic celebration (11).

However, if one does not wish to join the Catholic Church, but is baptized, may he or she receive the eucharist in a Catholic Church? There are restrictions to this, but the answer, in principle, is yes. The conditions will be discussed later when we treat of the eucharist, but, given some rather clear directives from the Vatican, we can say that in principle there is intercommunion in the Catholic Church. Nonetheless, a difficulty does arise from a theological standpoint. If baptism is thus recognized, why are non-Catholic Christians barred from Holy Communion in the Catholic Church ordinarily? Is there a theological reason for such an interdict? If baptism gives the neophyte "the full right" to receive communion (36) and the eucharist is seen as the "culminating point" of baptismal initiation, then on what theological basis can denial of eucharist to anyone whose baptism is recognized be made? One hears today of *full communion* or something similar, a sort of middle step between baptism/confirmation on the one hand and eucharist on the other. Historically, one looks in vain for such an intermediate step; canonically, one might be able to justify it, but canon law cannot be in opposition to solid theology. The dilemma remains: How can a Church accept the baptism of another Christian Church but deny eucharistic fellowship? Much more needs to be done on this matter.

6. *Original sin:* It is noteworthy that in the *Rite of Baptism for Children,* the term original sin occurs only once, namely, in the prayer of exorcism and anointing before baptism: "We pray for these children, set them free from original sin" (49). Original sin, naturally, does not play a role in the baptism of adults; this is in keeping with the theological opinion on limbo which we mentioned earlier. Adults do not have the option of limbo, and thus original sin is no longer operative in an adult. It has been taken away. For children, however, baptismal theology prior to the new rite was somewhat dominated by the original sin concept. The fact that it is mentioned only once is indicative of the Church's official stance: namely, a distancing from the emphasis on the original sin approach. Even postponement of baptism after birth (nos. 8–14) is seen as legitimate. "As soon as possible" is now understood as a few weeks, or a longer interval if pastoral reasons so determine. The faith-stage of the parents must also be kept in mind, since baptism without a continuous growth in the faith is fruitless.

7. *The Holy Spirit:* It would be unnecessary to cite all the references to the Holy Spirit in the RCIA and the Rite of Baptism for Children. It is abundantly clear that the presence of the Spirit is connected to baptism. This is, unfortunately, important to stress today, since a small minority of the charismatic movement has at times played off Christian baptism and the baptism of the Holy Spirit. At times, this small group seems to imply that the Holy Spirit is not really present or given except in the baptism of the Holy Spirit. This is clearly a heretical

view. That only a small section of the charismatic movement stresses this is to the credit of the majority of the charismatic movement which remains within the teaching of the Church.

Positively, one must understand the Spirit dimension of baptism. In the baptism of Jesus the Spirit is in the forefront; in the baptized and baptizing community of the local Christian Church, the Spirit is strongly present and operative. In the initiation process of baptism-confirmation-eucharist, the Spirit again is central. A theology of baptism, of confirmation, or of eucharist in which the Spirit of the Lord is not focal is unworthy of the very name of theology.

Such are some of the major issues involved in the new ritual of baptism. The emphasis has been on the RCIA, but the same issues are clear in the baptismal rite for children. There are, of course, liturgical considerations to the new rituals which cannot be addressed here. Rather, we have focused on the main theological issues, and, as mentioned previously, these are presented to us as official teaching of the Church. Clearly, one might envision a later revision of this ritual for baptism, but for the moment this is what the Catholic Church endorses.

Discussion Questions

1. Read through the actual Ritual of Christian Initiation of Adults and point out the occasions in the prayers in which Jesus is central.
2. What is the role of the Church in the four parts of the RCIA?
   a. Period of inquiry
   b. Period of catechumenate
   c. Period of purification and enlightenment
   d. Period of post-baptismal celebration
3. How do you explain the relationship of baptism, confirmation and eucharist?
4. How do you see baptism in an ecumenical way, especially as regards the Anglicans and the Lutherans?

The Sacrament
of
Confirmation

Confirmation
A Selected Bibliography

Only volumes in English are presented here; in the footnotes references are made to materials in other languages.

Many volumes, listed in the selected bibliography on baptism, refer to confirmation as well; these volumes are not repeated here.

Austin, Gerard	*Anointing with the Spirit: The Rite of Confirmation,* New York: Pueblo Publishing Co., 1985.
Dix, Gregory	*The Theology of Confirmation in Relation to Baptism,* London: Dacre Press, 1946.
Dunn, James D. G.	*Baptism in the Holy Spirit,* London, SCM Press, 1970.
Holmes, Urban T.	*Confirmation: The Celebration of Maturity in Christ,* New York: Seabury Press, 1975.
Lampe, G. W. H.	*The Seal of the Spirit,* London: SPCK, 1967.
Montague, George T.	*The Spirit and His Gifts: The Biblical Background of Spirit Baptism, Tongue-Speaking and Prophecy,* New York: Paulist Press, 1974.
Thornton, L. S.	*Confirmation: Its Place in the Baptismal Ministry,* London: Dacre Press, 1954.

6

Confirmation and the
Teaching of the Church

The solemn statements by the magisterium of the Church on the sacrament of confirmation have been quite limited. It is primarily the Council of Trent which has addressed itself to some of the issues involved in this sacrament.

1. CONFIRMATION IS A SACRAMENT

At the time of the Council of Trent, the ritual of confirmation was in the West almost totally separated from the sacrament of baptism. The scholastic theologians had considered the rite of confirmation on its own, and this approach was the prevailing view of the theologians and the bishops at the Tridentine council. The same scholastic theologians had various opinions as to the time at which Jesus "instituted" the sacrament, but the sense of all was clearly that confirmation was indeed a sacrament, and this is what was declared solemnly by the Church.

Allied to this positive statement that confirmation is a sacrament is the negative side: namely, one cannot say that confirmation is an "empty ceremony" or simply "a sort of instruction after the age of reason." Nor does confirmation insult the Holy Spirit. All such negative commentaries on confirmation are against the solemn teaching of the Church.

2. THE BISHOP IS THE ORDINARY MINISTER OF CONFIRMATION

In the Eastern Churches, the presbyter, not the episkopos, is the ordinary minister of confirmation, but at the Council of Trent, the bishops of the West wanted to maintain that in the Latin Church it was the episkopos or bishop who enjoyed the ordinary administration of the sacrament. The term "ordinary" has, in the recent renewal of the sacrament of confirmation after the Second Vatican Council, been changed to "original." In paragraph 7 of the *Praenotanda* we read: "The original minister of confirmation is the bishop." But then in the very next sentence, the text continues: "Ordinarily the sacrament is administered by the bishop . . ." The same ritual makes it a standard procedure for priests to confirm those just baptized who are adults or who are children but old enough for catechesis (ibid.).

As we shall see later on, the early Church's liturgies were dominated at first by the episkopos, and only from about 400 A.D. onward did the presbyters begin to take on more and more liturgical functions. In the East this included confirmation, while in the West this was generally reserved for the episkopos.

3. THE SACRAMENT OF CONFIRMATION CONFERS A CHARACTER

The Council of Trent, as we noted above in the discussion on baptism, defined that three sacraments, baptism, confirmation and orders, confer a character. It was noted above that the Council of Trent simply defined *that* there was a character, not *what* the character, theologically, was. The reason for this definition was the non-repeatability of these sacraments. As long as confirmation is seen as integral to baptism, the reason for the non-repetition of confirmation remains clear. The more that confirmation is separated from baptism, liturgically and theologically, the less reason there is to make confirmation a non-repeatable sacrament. In other words, the character of confirmation is intrinsically connected to the character of baptism, and cannot be understood except in this interrelationship. As we shall see, confirmation in the West did become separate from baptism and began to take on various meanings of its own. This process has made the sacrament of confirmation suspect, not only by the Protestants but also in an increasing way by Roman Catholics.

During this present period of renewal of the sacraments, a better understanding of the character of confirmation can only be achieved by theologically and liturgically relating confirmation to baptism, a step which the new ritual on these sacraments has clearly made.

A NOTE ON THE ISSUE OF CHRISM

In the East and the West, over the centuries, a question on the issue of chrism and/or the laying on of hands has been argued, with the West leaning toward the laying on of hands and the East leaning toward the chrismation. In Sola's presentation of the sacrament of confirmation, found in one of the better manuals of theology in use prior to and even during Vatican II, he mentions this issue, and then as the *valor dogmaticus* (dogmatic value) uses such terms as *certissimum* (most certain), *sententia communis* (the ordinary opinion of theologians), *certa et communis opinio* (a certain and common opinion). Nowhere does he refer to a solemn statement on the matter of chrism by the Church.[1] His analysis is typical of the manuals of theology and not simply an isolated voice. It would therefore be unscientific to state that the Church has made a solemn declaration on the issue of chrism or chrismation.

The following are the exact words of the canons of the Council of Trent on the matter of the sacrament of confirmation.

Canons on Confirmation

708
(871)

1. If anyone says that the confirmation of baptized persons is a useless ceremony and not rather a true and proper sacrament; or that at one time it meant nothing other than a certain catechesis by which those nearing adolescence gave an account of their faith before the Church: let him be anathema.

709
(872)

2. If anyone says that those who attribute some power to the holy chrism of confirmation are offending the Holy Spirit: let him be anathema.

710
(873)

3. If anyone says that the ordinary minister of holy confirmation is not the bishop, but any simple priest: let him be anathema.[2]

These solemnly promulgated words on confirmation clearly do not present us with a "theology of confirmation."[3] They deal, rather, with some individual points which the bishops at the Council of Trent felt were necessary to safeguard the correct doctrine on confirmation. As such they warrant great seriousness. Isolated from their historical context or considered apart from a larger theological context, these positions are not understandable. The difficulty arises as one begins to formulate a "theology of confirmation." If this theologizing occurs in a context which is not baptismal, that is, the relationship between confirmation and baptism is not kept in its centralizing role, the more tenuous is the "theology of confirmation." On the other hand, if the theologizing on confirmation is bound tightly to baptism, confirmation does become clearer. In this latter case, confirmation and eucharist can be reassociated, but only due to the basis of the baptismal link.

We will see in the next chapter the gradual disassociation process between baptism and confirmation, and we will see how this led to "theologies of confirmation" which are quite untenable. Historically, there is a clear baptism-confirmation-eucharist linkage, and it is precisely this reassociation which will provide a solid base for an understanding and a meaningful practice of confirmation.

Discussion Questions

1. What is the official teaching of the Catholic Church on the sacrament of confirmation?
2. What does the word "chrism" mean?
3. What does "Eastern Church" mean?

7

Confirmation and Its Historical and Theological Considerations

Since the eleventh century in the Western Church, theologians have worked long and hard to provide a clear theological understanding of the separated-from-baptism sacramental celebration of confirmation. The more differentiated and carefully organized attempts at this by the major theologians of the thirteenth century—Thomas, Bonaventure, etc.—appeared to bring the issues to some sort of stabilized base, but the critique at the time of the reformation, in the sixteenth century, raised many of the questions once again. This is not to say that the issue of confirmation itself was a major source of discord in the sixteenth century, but it is to say that some of the difficult questions relating to confirmation were once more noted and the traditional answers once more interrogated. Counter-reformation theology, as is well known, tended in many ways to be a siege-theology, defending positions rather than breaking into new frontiers. It was not until the contemporary biblical renewal and above all the studies on the history of the various sacraments that many of the questions related to the sacrament of confirmation were once again scrutinized. William Bausch entitles his chapter on this sacrament: "Confirmation: In Search of a Theology."[1] This is a somewhat dramatic, perhaps over-emphasized statement, but it has its kernel of truth, insofar as it reflects the present disquiet among Catholic theologians on the entire issue of confirmation. At the moment, no clear solution to all the problems regarding this sacrament seems to be evident, and the following pages must be seen as yet another attempt to further the theological enterprise on this topic of the sacrament of confirmation.

1. CONTEMPORARY PROBLEMS REGARDING CONFIRMATION

The first thing I would wish to do is to list in a rather undetailed way the major problem areas which have been raised today as regards confirmation. I will make no pretense at solving them, but it would, I believe, help to gather these difficulties together.

1. Probably the most worrisome difficulty relating to the sacrament of confirmation is its relationship to the sacrament of baptism. Historical research clearly indicates that the mother lode of the sacrament of confirmation is in the baptismal event, but the theological interpretations of confirmation have ranged from a view, on the one hand, that confirmation is simply a reaffirmation of baptism, to a view, on the other hand, that it is a totally separate sacramental rite in which a baptized Christian, out of a mature faith, is designated to a new ministry, e.g., to the lay apostolate, to be a soldier of Christ, etc. A theology of confirmation, today, must face quite forthrightly this issue of the relationship between baptism and confirmation.

2. A second problem as regards the sacrament of confirmation lies in the contemporary understanding of those texts in the Acts of the Apostles which apparently separate baptism in water in the name of Jesus and the reception of the Holy Spirit by the laying on of hands. In traditional Catholic theology, these were presented as the classical texts which gave scriptural evidence of a second sacrament after baptism, namely, Acts 8:16–20; 19:1–7. To these two passages, some authors also added the section in the Letter to the Hebrews, 6:1–6. Contemporary exegesis raises questions whether these passages truly indicate a post-baptismal second rite.

3. A third problem lies in the way in which one researches the history of the sacrament of confirmation. By this I mean, if one asks such a question as: "Does the New Testament or the early Church give evidence of the sacrament of confirmation?" the very formulation could be misleading, since there is an enormous danger of projecting a question, meaningful since the eleventh century, back into an earlier milieu, in which the very question, so expressed, is meaningless. In the eleventh century, the celebration of a separate rite called confirmation

had become general throughout the West. Prior to the eleventh century one discovers localized celebrations, and the farther back one goes from the eleventh century, the fewer localized situations are evident. A certain historical sensitivity is necessary.

4. The question has been raised today regarding the usual temporal flow of the sacraments, that is, the times that an ordinary Catholic receives the sacraments: first baptism, then first penance, then first eucharist, then confirmation. Is this sequence to be justified theologically, perhaps even made normative? Were the sequence to be altered, not just in exceptional cases, but as the general pattern for all Catholics, would such alteration affect the way one theologizes about confirmation? For instance, if the pattern in the Latin Church were to both baptize and confirm in infancy as a general rule, would theologians still speak about confirmation as a sacrament of mature faith, a sacrament for the lay apostolate, a sacrament in which one becomes a soldier of Christ? In other words, does the age of the recipient of confirmation tend to influence the way one theologizes about this sacrament?

5. There is as well the age-old question regarding the place of the laying on of hands, on the one hand, and the anointing with oil, on the other. The precise designation of either of these rites or both as constitutive parts of the confirmation liturgy has been argued back and forth for centuries, and is still of importance in the dialogue between the Western and Eastern Churches.

6. In this dialogue with the Eastern Churches, the Western Church has often addressed the issues with its own set of questions together with its own christological and ecclesiological context, and thereby skews the discussion. L. Ligier addresses this issue very strongly:

> Finally, ecumenism demands that one interpret the liturgical practice of a given church within the functioning of its own theology, not that of ours. Yet studies dedicated by us, Latins, to the eastern liturgy of confirmation generally make an abstraction of the teaching of these communities as regards the sacramental epiclesis. None of these works, save perhaps when there is a treatment of the Chaldean-Nestorian rite, take into account the great prayers made over the confirmandi or over the chrism. All of them proceed as they do for our own Roman liturgy. The viciousness of this method is clear and serious. In our case, the Greeks, the Syrians of Antioch, and

the Armenians do not reduce the essential rite of confirmation to the anointing with chrism and the brief formula alone.[2]

Ligier is pointing out that a person simply cannot compare a Western and Eastern "form" and a Western and Eastern "matter," since the very matter-form approach to sacraments is not the Eastern approach at all, and since it is not, a Westerner can easily miss the Eastern theology of sacraments.

7. There is as well the pastoral-theological question regarding the age at which a Christian might, even should, receive the sacrament of confirmation. This question has been especially rampant in current literature on the subject of confirmation, and has tended, in many instances, to over-shadow many other related questions.

8. A totally new question for contemporary Catholic theology as regards confirmation is this: What is the relationship between the humanness of Jesus as primordial sacrament and the sacrament of confirmation? Only because Jesus in his humanness is a sacrament is confirmation a sacrament. Secondly, what is the relationship between the Church as a ground sacrament and the sacrament of confirmation? In a derived and secondary way, only because the Church is a sacrament is there a sacrament of confirmation. The contemporary expanded understanding of sacrament and the understanding of Jesus' humanness as the primordial sacrament have raised these questions, which were clearly not part of the traditional approach to confirmation.

9. Confirmation, which theologically has never been described as "necessary for salvation," together with anointing of the sick and to some degree the sacraments of marriage and orders raises the issue today of a ranking of sacraments. Could not baptism and eucharist be considered *the* sacraments (as rites) of the Christian community, while the other five would be considered in a secondary way? Just as the scriptures are proto-canonical and deutero-canonical, could there not be a differentiation in the Catholic understanding of sacraments? This is, at least, a question which has been raised today.[3]

10. The ecumenical movement has raised the question regarding the Roman Catholic understanding of the sacrament of confirmation, and the similar rite, though not called a sacrament, in the major, and even at times the minor, Churches since the reformation.

11. The charismatic movement has raised the question as regards the Holy Spirit and all sacraments, but, in a special way, baptism and

consequently confirmation. Is there a baptism of the Spirit alongside water-baptism? With the Spirit at work in all of the sacraments and outside of the sacraments as well, what is the relationship between the sacrament of confirmation and the Holy Spirit?

These questions represent a formidable array of issues relating to the sacrament of confirmation, and no doubt other issues could also be added, but in my view the above areas seem to be the most prominent problematical areas today on the question of confirmation. It would take more than a chapter in a book of this size to unpack all these areas, and I am making no pretense to do so. But with these issues in mind, I would like to present briefly the emergence of a separated (from baptism) sacrament of confirmation (and the wording here is important). Secondly, I wish to approach confirmation from the standpoint of the humanness of Jesus as the primordial sacrament. The historical data is important so that we can focus more clearly on precisely what confirmation as a sacrament is and what it is not. Only then can we take up the issue of its sacramentality.

2. THE HISTORY OF THE EMERGENCE OF A
SEPARATED SACRAMENT OF CONFIRMATION

"Sometime in the eleventh century we find in the west (and only here!) a separated celebration of confirmation as the general practice. The development towards this new practice had, of course, causes and departure points which reach indeed further back."[4] This statement of Sigisbert Regli fairly well summarizes the conclusions of contemporary biblical, historical and systematic theologians, and the dating provides us, for our needs, with a *terminus ad quem*. An implication of this historical datum is that one will not find in the New Testament any description of a separated sacrament of confirmation. So, too, the farther one goes back in Church history beyond the eleventh century, there will be less and less evidence for a separate sacrament. It should be noted that Regli indicates a generalized practice in the eleventh century, which means that prior to that time, one will find here and there localized celebrations of confirmation, and the process of moving from a localized to a generalized situation becomes more intense the closer one approaches the eleventh century.

The New Testament data, particularly the passages in Acts and in Hebrews mentioned above, have in the past been seen by some scholars as an indication of a separate sacrament of confirmation. For instance, B. Neunheuser states:

> Our previous investigations . . . have yielded the certain fact that the Church was familiar as early as the age of the apostles with a second sacramental act subsequent to baptism and supplementing it.[5]

Neunheuser goes on to say that even though there is no mention at all of a laying on of hands after baptism in the Pauline corpus, "we must assume that the initiation rite of the primitive Church embraced both the water-bath and the laying on of hands."[6] A. Benning, in his own writing as late as 1972, concurs in this.[7] Still, it is an assumption, and Regli rightfully notes that one must rather assume with much stronger probability that there was no laying on of hands after the water-bath in the Pauline communities.[8]

A laying on of hands is, indeed, evident in the Old Testament period, and it was also a Jewish practice at the time of Jesus. For their part the gospels inform us that Jesus himself laid hands on people. For instance, the laying of Jesus' hands on someone was meant to be a blessing (Mk 10:16), or it was intended to be part of an act of healing (Lk 13:13; Mk 8:23, etc.). We find a laying on of hands in the apostolic Church; it was used for healing the sick (Acts 9:12; 28:8), or it was used as a conferral of some ministry (Acts 6:6; 13:3; 1 Tm 4:14; 2 Tm 1:6ff.). It might be noted that only in the third century do we have solid evidence of a laying on of hands for the reconciliation of a penitent. None of these instances, however, can be seen as an inchoative rite of confirmation. In other words, nowhere in the gospels nor in the Pauline corpus do we have any texts which might directly be the rootage of a laying on of hands for the conferral of the Holy Spirit, such as the later developed sacrament of confirmation intends.

By and large it is in the Acts of the Apostles that scholars have generally attempted to find the direct roots for the separate sacrament of confirmation, and particularly in those passages, almost the classical passages, one might say, mentioned above. The literature on these "classical texts" is, to say the least, abundant.[9] The traditional Roman Catholic exegesis of these passages, together with their context, moved along an axis of baptism-confirmation.

I will use the term "confirmation" during this discussion on the New Testament period and the first centuries of the Church, even though I am aware that this usage is anachronistic, since "confirmatio" as a technical term—and it is decidedly a Western term—did not appear until around the fifth century, as we see in the acts of the Council of Riez (439) and the Council of Orange (441). Naturally, as a technical term it did not appear out of nowhere and does have rootage in such New Testament ideas as strengthening (2 Cor 1:21). Still, I will use this anachronistic term since it is the general manner of speaking among most scholars.

There has been a decided move away from the baptism-confirmation axis, as the organizational framework for such exegesis, to a different axis, namely, baptismal initiation on the one hand, and on the other some sort of ecclesiological dimension—briefly, if you will, a baptism-Church axis. Such authors as J. Munck,[10] E. Kasemann,[11] J. Dunn,[12] E. Haenchen,[13] G. W. H. Lampe,[14] J. Fitzmyer,[15] G. Montague,[16] and L. S. Thornton,[17] to mention only a few, seem to be in this exegetical framework, each, however, with his own particular nuance. In the Acts of the Apostles the baptism under question seems to lack something, and rather than seeing this lack as a second rite, namely, confirmation, these authors tend to see the lack of the baptism in its non-relationship to the wider apostolic Church. This, they claim, seems to be the intention of Luke in the separation of water-baptism and the lay ing on of hands.

Nonetheless, rootage for the eventual appearance of a separated sacrament of confirmation does lie in the New Testament. First of all there is the frequent and important proclamation of the outpouring of the Holy Spirit. This is clear from the presence of this Spirit in Jesus himself, his humanness, and also in what he said and did. It is clear from the presence of the Spirit in the early community, as we see in some of the apparition narratives after the resurrection, in the dramatic episode of Pentecost, and in the many references to the Spirit in the Pauline corpus, the Acts of the Apostles, the pastoral letters, the Johannine letters and the Book of Revelation. In all of these the Holy Spirit is certainly not limited to specific, so-called sacramental actions, but the presence of the Spirit is attested to as a major phenomenon of the new age, which Jesus inaugurated.

Second, any early indications of confirmation are totally dependent and completely controlled by baptism. Throughout the entire New

Testament, baptism is presented as the occasion for the reception of the Holy Spirit. This baptism-confirmation relationship is so emphasized that every theological explanation, expressed in later centuries, will have to wrestle with it.

Third, certain other images and actions, mentioned in the New Testament, can also be seen as the rootage of the eventual separated sacrament, namely, both the metaphor and the actual practice of anointing; the metaphor and the actual practice of signing *(sphragis);* the practice of the laying on of hands.

All of these factors, in one way or another, are the *dramatis personae,* which historically appear and at times disappear only to reappear in the century-long development of a separate celebration of confirmation.

When we go beyond the New Testament data to the extant writings of the early Church, we note that the data for the last half of the first century and the entire second century are negative on this matter of a second rite after the water-bath. The *Didache,*[18] the *Letter of Barnabas,*[19] the *Apology* of Justin,[20] and the author of the Shepherd[21] make no mention of any rite other than the water baptism. In other words, from 100 to 200 A.D. we have no witness to any additional ceremony (the laying on of hands in the Acts of the Apostles notwithstanding) as regards the rite of Christian initiation. Only as we move into the third century do we begin to notice, not separate rites, but a multiplying of ceremonies within the *one* rite, which is, in its entirety, called "baptism." Actually, the data reveal to us that the total rite of *initiation* was "baptism-first eucharist." The new ceremonies which appear are, as to be expected, the laying on of hands, the anointing, and the signing *(sphragis).* There is no unified and generalized development of these additional ceremonies, and in fact local churches tended to be quite varied in the use or non-use of these ceremonies.

Toward the end of the second century we have the description of Clement of Alexandria as regards baptism.[22] Again, there is no mention of any additional ceremonies other than the baptism in water and first eucharist as the rite of initiation into the Christian community. However, shortly after, around 215, we have the detailed description of Hippolytus in his *The Apostolic Tradition.*[23] Scholars have continually noted that Hippolytus is anything but an innovator; he is, indeed, a traditionalist, and therefore his description of the rite of initiation certainly goes back further than 215, but how far back we cannot tell. For Hippolytus the rite of initiation includes: a water baptism with a profession of faith, an anointing by the presbyters, and the following prayer by the episcopos:

> O Lord God, who didst count these worthy of deserving the for-
> giveness of sins by the laver of regeneration, make them worthy to
> be filled with Thy Holy Spirit and send upon them Thy grace, that
> they may serve Thee according to Thy will; to Thee is the glory, to
> the Father and to the Son with the Holy Ghost in the holy Church,
> both now and ever and world without end. Amen.[24]

The episcopos says this while extending his hands over the newly baptized, which is not really a laying on of hands in the usual sense of the
term. He then anoints each of the newly-baptized singly, saying, ''I
anoint thee with holy oil in God the Father Almighty and Christ Jesus
and the Holy Ghost.'' The seal *(sphragis)* is then given on the forehead.
This is followed by the kiss of peace and finally the first eucharist. The
entire rite, other than the eucharist, is called baptism, and even the
added ceremonies are far more Christo-centric than Spirit-centric.
Clearly, there is no ''second sacrament.''

In Alexandria, about the same time as Hippolytus, Origen in his
Commentary on the Romans, quite in contrast to his predecessor Clement, makes mention of the water bath and the anointing.[25] Likewise,
around the same time, Tertullian, who gives witness to the Christian
community in North Africa, speaks of the water bath and the laying on
of hands in his *De Baptismo,*[26] but likewise mentions in *De Carne
Resurrectionis*[27] an additional ceremony, the scaling. In Tertullian we
see, as we do with all other early writers on this subject, that the emphasis is on the total rite, and what is effected is due to the total rite.
There is never a question of a second sacrament, to which in a particular
way the bestowal of the Holy Spirit is ascribed.

An interesting turn of events occurred around the middle of the
third century, which had to do with the baptism performed in heretical
communities. In the West a sharp division of thought took place on this
matter. For Cyprian, in North Africa, such baptisms were null and void,
and those who had been baptized in such heretical communities had to
be rebaptized when they joined the Orthodox church. Stephen, the
bishop of Rome, for his part, held that the baptism in these heretical
communities was valid and need not be repeated; those who had been

so baptized, on the other hand, received the Holy Spirit at the time of their profession into the true Church. There is no mention by any of the writers on this subject of the rebaptism of heretics that there is a "second sacrament" which would give the Holy Spirit.[28]

In Cyril of Jerusalem,[29] writing about the middle of the fourth century, we find a pre-baptismal anointing, which eventually one finds as a characteristic of the Syriac Church. The evidence of a variety of ceremonies for the *one* rite of initiation mounts as we go into the fourth, fifth and sixth centuries. At the time of Ambrose,[30] the ceremony in Milan included the washing of the feet, but not an anointing. There seems to be in the Milanese Church no laying on of hands, and Ambrose makes only a brief reference to a sealing. This kind of ritual seems to have been customary throughout the northern part of Italy.

Three factors begin to emerge in the fourth, fifth and sixth centuries, and each of these factors naturally did not occur in a brief moment of time, but took decades to evolve. These three factors are: (1) the deurbanization of Christian communities, (2) the growing predominance of the practice of infant baptism, and (3) the question of reordination of heretics. All three of these contributed to a separation of the rite of initiation, and, in the last instance, to an eventual difference of rite between the Western and Eastern Churches.

First of all, let us consider briefly the deurbanization of Christian communities. The Christian community began as an urban phenomenon, and during the centuries of persecution remained so by and large. Only with the cessation of the persecutions, the imperial justification of the Christian community, which began with Constantine, and the subsequent growth of catechumens did various Christian communities have to face the problem of what should be done pastorally for those Christians who lived in rural areas, particularly the more remote ones. At first such Christians had to travel to the major cities for any liturgical celebrations, but with the growth of Christians in these remoter areas, the so-called chore-episcopoi were established as the liturgical leaders of these small groups of isolated Christians. At times, simply a presbyteros was given charge of them. Still, for the major feasts and celebrations these Christians had to travel into the central urban community. Gradually, however, more and more of the liturgical actions were remanded to these chore-episcopoi and rural presbyteroi, including the actual baptism. Still, in order to provide some symbolization and liturgical celebration that such people were baptized into the wider community, e.g., the Christian community at Rome, at Milan, etc., in the West the post-baptismal laying on of hands (anointing) was reserved to the episcopos, who would "visit" the rural churches to fulfill this rite. As time progressed longer intervals between the baptismal rite by the presbyteros and the episcopal rite began to occur. With a more lengthy interval in the rite of initiation, and with an ever more liturgical celebration of this episcopal action, one is not far from a real separation, or, as N. Mitchell calls it, a disintegration of the one rite.[31] This separated practice gave rise to theological speculation on the meaning and distinction of the two rites. Rabanus Maurus, who died in 835, "argues that the episcopal imposition of hands and chrismation *confer* the Spirit. This sort of language forces him to explain the difference between the two post-baptismal acts. His explanation sounds ominously familiar: the first anointing done after baptism, done by the presbyter, effects the descent of the Spirit and the consecration of the Christian; the second anointing, the episcopal chrismation and laying on of hands, brings the grace of the Spirit into the baptized 'with all the fullness of sanctity, knowledge and power'."[32] The Western separation led eventually, then, to a theological justification of two distinct rites.

Still, the growing predominance of infant baptism over adult baptism, which triumphed almost completely in the fifth and sixth centuries, occasioned a further separation between the baptism in infancy and the episcopal laying on of hands and anointing at a much later age. This later age for reception of episcopal anointing, and therefore more maturity on the part of the person to be so anointed, was picked up in the theological justifications of these two rites, so that confirmation came gradually to be explained in terms of a mature profession of faith, an anointing to be a "soldier of Christ," and so on. We have here a clear example of a theologizing in terms of praxis, and I cannot say that this has been felicitous.

The third factor, the reordination of heretics, occasioned a change in the East. Ligier has argued that whereas, thanks to Tertullian, the West early on had developed a fairly technical vocabulary for ordination: ordo, ordinatio, etc., the East retained the more biblical terms connected with the laying on of hands: *cheirotonein, cheirotethein; cheirotenia, cheirothesia.*[33] Many of the early Eastern councils had to deal so strongly with this matter of reordination that gradually the laying on of hands was restricted almost entirely to ordination, while chrismation took over the place of such laying on of hands in the baptismal rite (if indeed there was a laying on of hands generally in the Eastern Churches). The result, as Ligier schematizes it, is as follows:[34]

ORDINATION	CONFIRMATION	PENANCE	ANOINTING
Imposition of hands without chrismation	No imposition of hands, chrismation	Neither an imposition of hands nor chrismation	Imposition of hands and chrismation

Because of this change in the Eastern Church, a division took place that would last for centuries: the Western Church celebrating confirmation with the laying on of hands, and the Eastern Church with the anointing with chrism. So it was that two different ways of Christian initiation developed.

Recently there has been some discussion on the matter of the early chrismation in the Roman baptismal ritual, particularly that based on Hippolytus' *Apostolic Constitution,* in which there is first of all a presbyteral anointing and then a second "post-baptismal" (a phrase which in itself is debatable) episcopal anointing. Kavanagh likens this latter chrismation to a "missa," i.e., "an archaic and independent rite."[35] Thomas Marsh, for his part, takes exception to this approach and stresses rather the Lukan approach to baptism, in contrast to the Pauline/Johannine approach. For Marsh, Luke tends to separate the gift of the Spirit from the water baptism. Marsh writes:

> The presentation of christian initiation throughout the Acts of the Apostles shows that this view is the correct one. Throughout this document baptism and forgiveness of sins are consistently related together, whereas the gift of the Spirit is just as consistently presented as distinct and separate from baptism. Indeed, in those key passages where Luke describes the *full* process of christian initiation, Acts 8:12–17; 19:1–7, the gift of the Spirit is an effect of a post-baptismal rite, imposition of hands. We are therefore justified in viewing the gift of the Spirit referred to in this text as an event envisaged as occurring after baptism.[36]

F. Quinn offers his own insights but does not advance much beyond Marsh, whom he seems to favor.[37] If I might offer a disagreeing note to this discussion (by no means limited to Kavanagh, Marsh and

Quinn), it would be the following. The very discussion would be un-thinkable had not a separation *de facto* taken place between baptism and confirmation. Had no separation taken place, then even the read-ing of Luke would be handled quite differently. The entire discussion is based, not so much on the textual evidence, as on the fact that a separation of confirmation from baptism did take place at a later date. Hippolytus, Tertullian, Ambrose and the other Fathers who wrote on baptism at this early stage would be completely bewildered by a dis-cussion on "two rites." In the baptismal rituals developed from the second century onward, there was a multiplicity of symbols: anoint-ing, water-bath, candle, clothing, etc. This multi-symbolic act was called baptism.

It is quite another thing to speak of multi-ritual, not multi-sym-bolic, actions. Once the process of separation began to occur, then, and only then, did the issue of multi-ritualism appear. This eventually led to the complete separation and therefore to the *de facto* dual ritual. The emphasis on this second "post-baptismal" chrismation by the episko-pos is the center of focus and not, for instance, the *photismos* or en-lightening aspect, which later did include symbols, i.e., the candle with all of its connection to the paschal candle and the ritualization which goes with the lighting of the fire and the lighting of the paschal candle. The reason why one is selected over the other lies more with the later development of confirmation as a separate ritual than with the material inherent in either the Acts of the Apostles or the early baptismal litur-gies.

Theologians will continue to discuss this, of course, but care must be taken not to read early material anachronistically.

The above admittedly general overview of the emergence of a sep-arate sacrament of confirmation in the Christian Church indicates, just as the New Testament data had done, that there was and is a strong interconnection between baptism on the one hand and confirmation on the other. It also indicates that there was and is a variety of practice in the historical development of this sacrament. The theologians of the eleventh, twelfth and thirteenth centuries did not, of course, have an awareness, as we do today, of the details of the history of confirmation. In the West, these theologians inherited this practice of a separate cel-ebration of confirmation, administered after a lengthy interval from an actual baptism. These theologians of the scholastic period took this practice for granted, and theologized on it.

The twelfth century theologians did little more than set the stage for the more thorough theologizing of the thirteenth century theologians, such as Alexander of Hales, Albert the Great, Thomas Aquinas, Bonaventure and Scotus. None of these twelfth and thirteenth century theologians raised the question whether confirmation was truly a sacrament; that was taken for granted. Concerning its institution by Christ, they struggled in a variety of ways to resolve the problem; none of the solutions were conclusive. It was accepted, as well, that a bishop was the ordinary minister of the sacrament, but being aware of the Eastern tradition as well as some statements from the Fathers of the Church, they left a door open so that a priest might, at times, confer the sacrament of confirmation. The "matter" of the sacrament was the anointing with oil, and generally a laying on of hands was either not mentioned or mentioned only in a secondary way. The "form" of the sacrament was accepted as: "I sign thee with the sign of the cross and confirm thee with the chrism of salvation." This indicative formula appears for the first time in the *Ordines Romani* of the tenth century, but by the twelfth and thirteenth centuries theologians considered it "of the essence" of the sacrament.

By far the most extensive area of their theological consideration revolved around the precise effect of confirmation, so that it could clearly be seen as a sacrament of its own right, distinct from baptism. Neunheuser summarizes the main thrust of their deliberations as follows:

> The task of confirmation is "con-firmatio," the strengthening of the baptized Christian, that he may "like a front line fighter (pugil) confess the name of Christ boldly and publicly" (Bonaventure, *Breviloquium,* p. 6, c.8). St. Thomas interprets the confirmation character similarly: "that a man may proclaim spiritual things by his bold confession" (Sent. IV,d.7 q.2 a.1 sol.). In the *Summa theol.* (III, q.72 a.5) he speaks of receiving the "power to carry out what belongs to the spiritual struggle against the enemies of faith." Thus the grace of confirmation does not serve the forgiveness of sins, like the grace of baptism, but "the increase and defence of righteousness" (loc. cit. q.72 a.7 d.1).[38]

Confirmation, then, in contrast to baptism, which is more personally oriented, has a social dimension, empowering a Christian to profess the faith boldly and publicly, particularly when faced by adversaries of the faith. This approach has remained within the Western Church down to the present century, and indeed the entire theologizing by these twelfth and especially thirteenth century theologians came to be seen as the "classical" theological interpretation of the sacrament of confirmation.

At the time of the reformation, the question whether or not confirmation was a sacrament was raised, which was far more foundational than such questions as regards the matter, the form, the minister, the effects, etc. The Achilles heel, of course, was the silence of the New Testament. The Council of Trent did not spend considerable time on this sacrament, since there were far more weighty issues to deal with, but the council did establish three binding canons on the sacrament of confirmation.

In the theology of the post-reformation period, the efforts of the Catholic theologians, such as Bellarmine, Suarez, etc., centered around a more solid scriptural analysis of the roots of confirmation, using, of course, the methods of interpretation of scripture characteristic of the seventeenth and eighteenth centuries. As mentioned at the beginning of this chapter, from the twelfth to the twentieth century, the Roman Catholic approach to this sacrament of confirmation remained consistent in this theological framework. D. Winzen in his commentary on the writings of St. Thomas, which appeared in 1935, offers a typical expression of this kind of theologizing:

> Confirmation is the sacrament of the messianic fullness of the Spirit. Therefore it elevates Christians to the highest ranks of the spiritual life, it ordains them to priests, prophets and genuine rulers in the kingdom of the Spirit. And because the Spirit of the Lord is destined to fill the whole world, confirmation makes Christians confessors and apostles of Christ's kingdom in the face of the world.[39]

Not without reason does Ligier take exception to this kind of hyperbolic language. "The confirmed Christian is neither a super-human nor a super-baptized."[40]

The historical overview raises question after question as regards the sacrament of confirmation. Periodically, during the Christian centuries, there have been "renewals" of sacramental action, and such renewals indicate that not all is well in certain sacramental actions, that murky elements are at play and need to be removed. The renewal of the sacrament of confirmation, stemming from the Second Vatican Council, attempts to come to grips with some of these murky areas. Whether this renewal truly effects a clearer understanding of the sacrament of confirmation remains to be seen, but it is a step forward.

3. CONFIRMATION AND ITS RELATION TO THE PRIMORDIAL SACRAMENT OF THE HUMANNESS OF JESUS

Throughout the centuries confirmation has been related to the Holy Spirit; indeed the Holy Spirit has been seen as the centering point of this sacrament. When we consider the relationship between the humanness of Jesus and the Holy Spirit, we notice a certain reticence in the synoptics on this matter, a much more expressed consideration in the gospel of John, and an even stronger emphasis in the Pauline corpus, and, as regards the Church, and therefore Jesus as well, in the Acts of the Apostles.

The Holy Spirit is constitutively present to Jesus at his conception, as Luke expressly narrates (Lk 1:35), and at the presentation of Jesus in the temple Simeon is described as a man in whom the Holy Spirit resided (Lk 2:25) and who was led that day into the temple by this same Spirit (Lk 2:27). Zechariah as well was filled with the Holy Spirit at the circumcision of his son John (Lk 1:67), and in his canticle he saw his son as the prophet of the Most High, going before the Lord to prepare his way (Lk 1:76). Likewise the baptism of Jesus in all of the gospels is seen as a moment of special presence of the Spirit over Jesus. Jesus, after reading the passage from Isaiah (Is 61:1-2; 58:6) in which the Spirit of the Lord is mentioned as being "upon me," says to those gathered in the synagogue: "Today this passage has been fulfilled among you" (Lk 4:18ff.). Jesus' ministry is a ministry in which the power of the Holy Spirit will be evident in Israel, and he will baptize in water and the Holy Spirit (Lk 3:16; Jn 3:5).

According to Jeremias, one of the themes in the preaching of Jesus was "the return of the quenched Spirit," which of course meant that the end-time had arrived.[41] Such a message was jolting to many of the Jews of his time, and Jesus is shown as working "mighty deeds" and "signs" in the power of the Spirit (Mt 12:28). God has sent his Spirit on him, who was his beloved and in whom his soul took delight (Mt 12:18). This presence of the Spirit, which ushers in the end-time, meant that true worship would be neither in Jerusalem nor on Mount Garizim, but people would worship the Father "in the Spirit and in truth" (Jn 4:21). In the discourse after the final supper, Jesus promises to send the Paraclete, the Spirit of truth and comfort (Jn 14:16–17; 16:5ff.). After the resurrection, he sends the Spirit upon his disciples (Jn 20:22).

Even though the Spirit may not be specifically mentioned, the gospel accounting of the life of Jesus cannot be understood except that the presence of the Spirit be seen as operative in Jesus. We could without hesitation say that the Holy Spirit:

1. is described as present to the very being and meaning of who Jesus is;
2. is associated with the baptism and so the beginning of his public ministry;
3. is part of the message of Jesus' own preaching;
4. is at work in the deeds that Jesus did;
5. is promised in a special way after Jesus' death and resurrection;
6. is bestowed on Jesus' disciples in the apparition to them.

All of this indicates that were one to eliminate the Holy Spirit from the very being of Jesus, from his work and his preaching, from his entire earthly life, death and risen life, Jesus would be meaningless. The relationship of the Spirit to Jesus, the presence of the Spirit in the humanness of Jesus, is constitutive for all that Jesus is, and this presence of the Spirit in the Lord is the basis for the entire Spirit christology of the early centuries. No created being, in the entire history of the universe, has been so profoundly and intimately related to the Holy Spirit than this humanness of Jesus. He is *the* one in whom the Spirit resides. Just as we noted in the chapter on baptism that Jesus is *the* baptized, so too we can say, even though the use of the term as far as the time of Jesus is concerned is anachronistic, that Jesus is *the* confirmed. Whatever confirmation as a sacrament intends to proclaim, it is to be found in Jesus, *the locus classicus* of what the sacrament of confirmation is all about. It was also noted above that Jesus is to be seen as the primordial sacrament in such a way that the individual sacraments are constituted as sacraments because of their relationship to this primordial sacrament. This indicates to us that theologically we must trace all sacramentality back to Jesus, and by presenting in a theological way Jesus as *the* confirmed we are doing just that. Remove this presence of the

Spirit within the humanness of Jesus, and the presence of the Spirit in the Church is meaningless; the presence of the Spirit in the individual sacrament of confirmation is equally meaningless. When we say, however, that Jesus was filled with the Holy Spirit, we are saying that he was filled in such a way with this Spirit that no other even comes close, no matter how strongly and deeply the Spirit is in him or her.

This Spirit in the Lord is there as a Spirit of holiness, making Jesus' humanness holy and, as the Greek Fathers loved to say, holy-making. This Spirit is in the Lord as a Spirit of love, enabling the human will and mind of the Lord to love God intensely and to love all men and women just as the Father himself loves them. This Spirit is in Jesus as the Spirit of life, so that Jesus can say: "I am the life." Not only is life, that is, the divine life itself, present in this humanness of Jesus, but the humanness of Jesus, again to quote the Greek Fathers, is life-giving. The Spirit is in Jesus as the Spirit of power, so that Jesus is greater than Moses, than Abraham, than Satan. This power not only enables Jesus to be a man of power, but this power in Jesus is also an enabling power, so that those who are related to Jesus are likewise empowered to fulfill the will of the Father. The Spirit is in Jesus as the Spirit of truth, so that Jesus can say: "I am the truth." This notion of truth, as well as that of power and strength, is particularly emphasized in the Johannine discourses after the supper. It is this Spirit of power, even over Satan, that makes the Spirit a forgiving Spirit. Theologically speaking, then, one could say: If you wish to know ultimately what baptism is all about, look to Jesus, *the* baptized; if you wish to know ultimately what confirmation is all about, look to Jesus, *the* confirmed. It seems to me that the entire discussion on the sacrament of confirmation would be strongly enhanced if there were more emphasis on this Christo-centric approach.

Still, one should not quickly go from the Spirit in Jesus to the Spirit in the sacrament of confirmation. The next step, methodologically, would be to discuss the Spirit in the Church and in the kingdom. The Acts of the Apostles presents in almost a panoramic way the outpouring of the Spirit. The Pentecost event, naturally, stands out as a remarkable event, and even if one were not as skeptical of the historical accuracy of the account as Haenchen is in his commentary, still Haenchen's insight that Luke wanted to express as dramatically as he could the presence of the Spirit remains valid.[42] The speaking in tongues, the large numbers who were baptized and all the other details are really secondary to the main thrust of the account: the unbelievable presence of the Spirit in this end-time.

Hans Küng rightfully describes the Church as the Church of the Spirit, and he even notes that the Church is the creation of the Spirit. He goes on to say that one must realize that we are not talking about "the Spirit *of* the Church" as though the Church possessed the Spirit, but rather the "Church *of* the Spirit."[43] The Acts of the Apostles indicates the freedom of the Spirit, present to those such as Cornelius and his family who are not yet baptized.

Contemporary theology has elaborated on that statement from Vatican II: "This Church, constituted and organized as a society in the present world, subsists in the Catholic Church, which is governed by the successor of Peter and by the bishops in communion with him."[44] An important distinction is being made here, namely, that the Church is not limited to the Roman Catholic Church; ecclesial communities outside the Roman Catholic Church are also to be considered in any theological consideration of "Church." Moreover, the Church and the kingdom of God are not co-extensive, since the kingdom of God is wider than the Church. Thus, we have the Spirit active in the Roman Catholic Church, in that wider understanding of Church, and in the kingdom of God no matter where and when this kingdom appears. The Spirit is freely and abundantly active in all the confluences of human life.

Without, then, saying that the Roman Catholic Church is the only locus of the Spirit's presence and activity, we still want to say, in faith, of course, that the Spirit is present and active in the Roman Catholic Church. This particular people of God is then a "confirmed" people, confirmed by the presence of the Spirit. It is Heidegger who uses the term "letting Being come to presence in being." As the people of God, we become what we are when we let the Spirit come to presence in our lives, our actions, our relationships. Only when and to the extent that we let the Spirit come to presence in what we are and do, have we the right to be called "Church." To the extent that we do not let the Spirit come to presence in our lives and actions, we are "unchurched."

Nonetheless, the reason for the presence of the Spirit in the Church must be sought at a deeper level. This Church is not simply a Church, but it is the Church of Christ, the *Christian* Church, the body of Christ, the people of God in Jesus. It is the presence of Jesus in his Church which is the reason for the presence of the Spirit, and it is this Jesus in whom the Spirit resides par excellence who is present to his Church. In other words, the presence of the Spirit is in the Church because the Spirit is present in Christ who is really present in and to the Church. We spoke above of the real presence of Jesus in the Church and that this understanding of real presence must go far beyond a "real presence" in the eucharist. The Church is a confirmed Church because of the presence of *the* confirmed one really and truly within it. In this way one can speak, I believe, meaningfully of the confirmed Church, just as one can speak of the baptized Church. In both instances it is not simply a sacramental rite which brings about this presence; it is, rather, the presence of the Lord and his Spirit, which ultimately gives meaning to the Church of the baptized and the Church of the confirmed.

This presence of the Spirit is found throughout the people of God, as the Vatican II Constitution on the Church reminds us:

> It is not only through the sacraments and the ministrations of the Church that the Holy Spirit makes holy the people, leads them and enriches them with his virtues. Allotting his gifts according as he wills (cf. 1 Cor 12:11), he also distributes special graces among the faithful of every rank. By these gifts he makes them fit and ready to undertake various tasks and offices for the renewal and building up of the Church, as it is written, "The manifestation of the Spirit is given to everyone for profit" (1 Cor 12:7). Whether these charisms be very remarkable or more simple and widely diffused, they are to be received with thanksgiving and consolation since they are fitting and useful for the needs of the Church.[45]

The vision here is of the Spirit acting in thousands of different ways, some remarkable and dramatic, others more humdrum and pedestrian. It does not matter; it is one and the same Spirit at work. The Church, then, is filled with the Spirit, and it is this presence of the Spirit, within and without the sacramental system, in marvelous ways and in quiet ways which must be gratefully acknowledged by the Christian community.

Only on the basis of this almost omni-presence of the Spirit in the Church should we begin to speak about the sacrament called confirmation. If the above is valid at all, and I surely think that it is, then we must be very careful when we speak about the sacrament of confirmation as the sacrament of the Holy Spirit. The phrase is surely not wrong, but it needs to be understood within certain parameters. We cannot speak, for instance, in terms which would indicate that *only* in the sacrament of confirmation is the Spirit given, is the Spirit poured out, or that the"fullness of the Spirit" is given *only* in confirmation. If we look back over the long history of the Christian Church, we note, as so many others have done before us, that in each century men and women have so lived their lives that they stand out as people of great holiness, and from early times on such people have been called "saints." What generations have been saying in all of this is that the presence of the Spirit was in these people in a very full and enriching way. There is no comparison, for instance, between some person who has just been confirmed and a Francis of Assisi. The presence of the Spirit in Francis was and remains a remarkable event for the Christian community. However, Francis did not receive such a fullness of the Spirit through confirmation; rather, it was through the lengthy conversion experience which one can trace from the time of his praying before the crucifix at San Damiano down to the overwhelming experience at Mount Alverna. In other words, the "fullness of the Spirit" in someone—and Francis is simply one example among thousands—has never been noticeable simply with the administration of the sacrament of confirmation. The very idea of "fullness," historically, arose as a theological interpretation of the relationship between baptism on the one hand and the then separated sacrament of confirmation. The idea was that confirmation was to "fill up" something that was only begun at baptism. Perhaps, a different approach to the sacrament of confirmation might accord more with the facts of Christian living and still stay within the tradition of the sacrament.

I would like to say that we should, on the basis of all that we noted about Jesus and the Church, see the sacrament of confirmation, first of all, as a moment of prayer, and the very confirming itself as a prayer. Confirmation has always been within a prayer liturgy, and so the aspect of prayer is not something superimposed; it is the context of the celebration of this sacrament from earliest times on. Prayer, at its center, is a reaction to something that God is primordially doing, and prayer is a reaction of wonder and awe.

God has acted, and the Church is responding to this action of God in a moment of prayer, which includes both word and sacrament. Once again the Church is celebrating what God has done and is continuing to do, only in this ritual of confirmation the Church is celebrating the presence of the Spirit in a particular and therefore special individual. The dynamic, which Rahner stressed, of the interplay in the sacraments between individual and community is at work here. If the presence of the Spirit is operative wherever there is Church, then in this one person, who is in the Church, we celebrate the presence of the Spirit to him or to her. Viewed in this way, the question of the age for confirmation is relativized. Whether this celebration is done as in the Eastern Churches generally in conjunction with baptism or whether it is done at some later age is, theologically considered, of minor importance, since in both cases the Spirit is present in an infant and the Spirit is present in someone more mature.

It seems to me that the current discussions on confirmation have gravitated around the question of age, and in many ways the "age of the one to be confirmed" has tended to control the theological thinking on the matter of confirmation. I would suggest that the controlling issue not be age, but the presence of the Spirit. Pastorally, it may be at times better that confirmation be administered in infancy; pastorally, given a whole other set of traditions and circumstances, it might be better celebrated at an age of some maturity, but deep down it does not really make any difference theologically. The theological axis is: the presence of the Spirit in the humanness of Jesus, the presence of the Spirit of Christ in the community called Church, and the presence of that same Spirit in a particular member of that community. The same rationale for the presence of the Spirit in an individual which was applied to the Church also holds for the presence of the Spirit in an individual, namely, the real presence of the Lord, *the* confirmed one, to and in the individual.

The Spirit, of course, is with the person at baptism, so that we are not at all talking about something that is completely distinguished from baptism. The mother lode of confirmation remains in and with the baptismal liturgy, so that what one says about baptism, with the exception of entry into the Church, one says about confirmation. The sacrament of confirmation simply takes one aspect of salvation, which we especially celebrate in baptism, and revels in it. Regli comments on this:

> "To receive the Holy Spirit" means, according to its inner reality, not a pinpointed, fixed, individual event, but a living personal relationship which is realized and developed throughout the entire course of our life. The Spirit of God draws us into a living and personal relationship. This relationship has its growth, its high points

of more intensive encounter and profundity, its lifelong history and development. Baptism is a definite and important milestone for this living in the Holy Spirit. Nonetheless, the entire Christian and ecclesial life is a developing and deepening of this Spirit-relationship. And as a central highpoint of this sealing and anchoring our life in the Spirit of God we celebrate the sacrament of confirmation. The celebration of confirmation is a one-time event, which takes place at a definite moment. The inner action of confirmation, the gift of the Holy Spirit, is, however, not a one-time, momentary event, which in this moment (of confirmation) and only in this moment occurs.[46]

Regli is clearly stating in his own way the phrase I have used again and again: we are celebrating what God has been doing and is continuing to do. What we celebrated at the baptism of an individual continues on a day-to-day basis; confirmation celebrates one aspect of that baptismal event, which has gone on continually since baptism: the gift of the Spirit to an individual.

Once again, the primordiality of Jesus as the fundamental sacrament helps us to recenter our discussion on confirmation, a recentering which from an ecumenical standpoint seems to be very helpful, since it takes our focus away from a ritual instituted by Christ with a clear promise of grace, and refocuses our attention on the very reason why confirmation might even be called a sacrament at all, namely, the presence of the Lord himself, as *the* confirmed, in the prayerful celebration called confirmation. Assuredly, not all the questions, either for Roman Catholics or for Protestant communities, have been answered here; rather, and this is all I had hoped to accomplish, an orientation is newly established which hopefully will provide for all a real breakthrough in an otherwise rather confused situation.

The Anglican tradition has always maintained confirmation, and its rootage in baptism has been emphasized. The present *Book of Common Prayer* sees confirmation as a mature profession of Christian faith, on the one hand, and as public affirmation of faith within the larger diocesan structure.

In the course of their Christian development, those baptized at an early age are expected, when they are ready and have been duly prepared, to make a mature public affirmation of their faith and

commitment to the responsibilities of their Baptism and to receive
the laying on of hands by the bishop.

Those baptized as adults, unless baptized with laying on of hands
by a bishop, are also expected to make a public affirmation of their
faith and commitment to the responsibilities of their Baptism in the
presence of a bishop and to receive the laying on of hands.[47]

Hatchett notes the same emphases: "Confirmation can now be re-
established as a time for a mature public affirmation of faith and commitment."[48] The author notes that this is "based on the Renaissance-
Reformation rationale for the rite of 'confirmation.' " Nonetheless,
with the understanding of Christ as the primordial sacrament, the various traditions in the Western Christian community can, perhaps, move
away from the "age" aspect of confirmation, and move into a deeper
meaning of this rite.

The Lutheran renewal of worship lays stress, equally, on the in-
tegration of baptism and confirmation. "Nothing can be added to Baptism, except a life of growth and maturation in the faith."[49] The
Lutheran synods, in their study on confirmation, took into account the
various meanings of confirmation in its history within the Western
Church. On the basis of such studies, the Joint Commission in 1970
stated:

> Confirmation is a pastoral and educational ministry which helps the
> baptized child through Word and Sacrament to identify more deeply
> with the Christian community and participate more fully in its mis-
> sion.[50]

The authors go on to note that confirmation marks a continuing obli-
gation of the Church to each member, a dynamic which often is not
mentioned in sacramental theology. Generally, the dynamic is from the
individual to the Church; here, the stress is on the Church to the individual.

Because confirmation in the past was done at a mature age, and
was followed often by first eucharist, there had been a tendency in some
Lutheran communities to overstress confirmation and understress baptism. This is now rectified in the new *Lutheran Book of Worship*. Confirmation's connection with baptism is brought into high relief, since
the rite is entitled "Affirmation of Baptism."[51]

Even with the Anglican, Lutheran and Roman Catholic renewals of this sacrament of confirmation, there is still much to be done, since the history of this rite has fluctuated over the centuries with a variety of meanings. Today we are not yet totally in a position of agreement, not because of doctrinal differences on the matter, but because of the various historical forms which this sacrament has taken within the Christian community. It would be advantageous, so it seems, to come together on this matter of confirmation around the primordial sacramentality of Jesus, and see where the various Western traditions might move. Even though the rituals of the Anglican, Lutheran and Roman Catholic communities do show remarkable unity, still the underlying theological stance for such ritualization needs much more solid ecumenical attention.

4. SUMMARY ON CONFIRMATION

1. The separate ritual of confirmation is attested to generally in the West from the eleventh century onward. Prior to this the evidence becomes less and less generalized.

2. The early baptismal rituals include at times a post-water-bath laying on of hands and somewhat later a post-water-bath anointing with oil.

3. The Roman document, *The Apostolic Tradition*, of Hippolytus includes a second post-water-bath anointing: the first is done by a presbyter, the second is done by the episkopos. This has raised some questions by scholars.

4. Other baptismal rituals do not have a dual-anointing after the water-bath. However, the Roman practice eventually carried great influence, because of Hippolytus' writing, in the West, but not in the East.

5. Nowhere in the early Church documents do we find mention of "two sacraments." The entire service was called "baptism," and was followed by the eucharist. The baptism-(confirmation)-eucharist sequence was the rite of Christian initiation.

6. As a technical term, confirmation *(confirmatio)* is first found in the fifth century and seems to be of Gallic origin, not Roman. It indicated the intervention of the episkopos in the baptismal service, especially if he had not been present at the actual water-bath service.

7. The term *confirmatio* tended to have the same meaning as other terms found in the liturgical literature about the same time (fifth century), namely, *perfectio* or *consummatio,* all of which meant the completion of the baptismal rite itself.

8. Outside of southeast Gaul, the word confirmation is not used of this post-water-bath ritual, but of eucharistic communion following baptism. The reception of the consecrated bread and wine confirms (perfects, consummates) the reception of the consecrated bread. One finds this in Alcuin.

9. The first time that we find the term *confirmatio* in an actual ritual occurs in the tenth century. A German manuscript *(Ordo Romanus L)* has the phrase: "I confirm you in the name of the Father, Son and Holy Spirit."

10. The first time the word confirmation appears in an officially approved Roman ritual is in the Castellani Pontifical of 1520.

11. When the episkopos in the early Church could not attend the baptismal ritual, the West reserved the laying on of hands/anointing to him. In this way, in the West, a separated rite of a post-baptismal anointing/laying on of hands developed, which in time was liturgized and also given several theological interpretations which were separate from both the liturgy and theology of baptism and eucharist.

12. An impetus for this was given by a (pseudo) homily of Faustus of Riez, which was incorporated into the canonical writings of the eleventh century and even ascribed (erroneously) to two previous popes.

13. On the basis of a separated ritual, both liturgically and theologically, the great medieval theologians, Thomas Aquinas, Bonaventure, etc., also interpreted the sacrament of confirmation as a separate ritual. Through their influence, the sacrament of confirmation continued to be theologized as a sacrament of maturity.

14. The Protestant Churches, though not calling confirmation a sacrament, have kept the ritual of confirmation and have associated it with a mature profession of baptismal faith. This, too, lacks precedent in the early Church.

15. Today, with a sense of the history of this ritual, both Roman Catholic and Protestant theologians are attempting to reintegrate confirmation into the baptismal context from which it was separated.

Discussion Questions

1. What are the major problems regarding the sacrament of confirmation in the Catholic Church today? Why are they problems? Can anything be done to alleviate them?

2. What are the regulations for the sacrament of confirmation in your diocese? What are the governing ideas behind these regulations?

3. Explain how baptism and confirmation began to be separated from each other.

4. What is the difficulty in calling the sacrament of confirmation a sacrament for the "soldiers of Christ"? A sacrament of "mature Christians"?

5. How is Jesus the primordial sacrament of confirmation?

6. How is the Church the basic sacrament of confirmation?

The Sacrament
of
The Eucharist

The Eucharist
A Selected Bibliography

Bouyer, L.

Eucharist, trans. C.U. Quinn, Notre Dame: Univ. of Notre Dame Press, 1968.

Daly, Robert, S.J.

Christian Sacrifice: The Judaeo-Christian Background before Origen, Washington, D.C.: The Catholic University of America Press, 1978

―――

The Origins of the Christian Doctrine of Sacrifice, Philadelphia: Fortress Press, 1978.

Delorme, J., et al.

The Eucharist in the New Testament: A Symposium, Baltimore: Helicon Press, 1964.

Duffy, R., O.F.M.

Real Presence, San Francisco: Harper & Row, 1982.

Emminghaus, Johannes H.

The Eucharist, trans. Matthew J. O'Connell, Collegeville, Minn.: The Liturgical Press, 1978.

Guzie, Tad

Jesus and the Eucharist, New York: Paulist Press, 1974.

Jasper, R.C.D. and
Cumming, G.J.   *Prayers of the Eucharist: Early and Reformed,* London: Collins, 1975.

Jeremias, Joachim   *The Eucharistic Words of Jesus,* London: SCM Press, 1966.

Jungmann, Josef   *The Early Liturgy* trans. Francis Brunner, Notre Dame: University of Notre Dame Press, 1959.

———   *Missarum Solemnia,* 2 vols. New York: Benziger, 1955.

Keifer, Ralph A.   *Blessed and Broken,* Wilmington, Del.: Michael Glazier, 1982.

Kilmartin, E.J.   *The Eucharist in the Primitive Church,* Englewood Cliffs: Prentice-Hall, 1965.

Lash, Nicholas   *His Presence in the World,* London: Sheed & Ward, 1968.

Martelet, G.   *The Risen Christ and the Eucharistic World,* London: Collins, 1976.

Martimort, A.G., ed.   *The Eucharist,* edited by A Flannery and V. Ryan, New York: Herder and Herder, 1973.

Mitchell, Nathan, O.S.B.   *Cult and Controversy: The Worship of the Eucharist outside Mass,* New York: Pueblo Publishing Co. 1982.

NCCB   *Eucharistic Celebrations,* study text no. 5, Washington, D.C.: USCC, 1978.

Paul VI   *Mysterium Fidei,* Huntington, Ind.: Our Sunday Visitor, 1965.

Powers, Joseph, S.J.   *Eucharistic Theology,* New York: Herder and Herder, 1967.

Ramsey, I.T. et al.   *Thinking about the Eucharist,* London: SCM, 1972.

Rordorf, Willy, et al.   *The Eucharist of the Early Christians,* trans. Matthew J. O'Connell, New York: Pueblo Publishing Co., 1978.

Schillebeeckx, E., O.P.   *The Eucharist,* trans. N.D. Smith, New York: Sheed & Ward, 1968.

Seasoltz, Kevin, O.S.B.   *Living Bread, Saving Cup: Readings on the Eucharist,* Collegeville, Minn.: The Liturgical Press, 1982.

Sheerin, Daniel J.   *The Eucharist,* Wilmington, Del.: Michael Glazier, 1986.

Swidler, Leonard, ed.   *The Eucharist in Ecumenical Dialogue,* New York: Paulist Press, 1976.

Wainwright, Geoffrey   *Eucharist and Eschatology,* New York: Oxford University Press, 1981.

8

Eucharist and the
Teaching of the Church

Once more it is the Council of Trent which has most solemnly spoken on the sacrament of the eucharist. The council divided its deliberations into the section on the *Most Holy Sacrament of the Eucharist,* secondly on the *Most Holy Sacrifice of the Mass,* and lastly on some issues dealing with communion under both forms and the communion of little children. Let us follow this division, even though the sacrament/sacrifice division has its theological difficulties, which we will note later on at greater length.

1. THE HOLY EUCHARIST IS A SACRAMENT

For the theologians and the bishops at the Council of Trent, the understanding of the eucharist as a sacrament was presupposed. This had been and remains the constant teaching of the Christian community. When we spoke of the term "sacrament" in the section on baptism above, we noted that the term itself is not to be found in the New Testament as applying either to baptism or eucharist. The early technical terms were "mystery" for the Greek-speaking world and subsequently "sacrament" for the Latin-speaking world. These same ideas apply here, in the case of the eucharist.

Likewise, the Protestant groups which employ the term "ordinance" do so to avoid the seven-sacrament approach. In the *Lima Document* we find the term "sacrament" used with no hesitation. One could easily say, then, that the entire Christian community, Roman Catholic, Orthodox, and Protestant, accepts the truth of the eucharist as a sacrament. To deny this would be clearly against all that Christian tradition stands for and therefore heretical.

The major leaders at the time of the Reformation, Martin Luther and Jean Calvin, did not dispute the issue of the eucharist as a sacrament. In fact they strongly upheld the sacramentality of the eucharist. There were indeed issues on the eucharist which were part of the controversy, but this issue on sacramentality was not one of them.

For the theologians and the bishops at the Council of Trent, the last supper was a very normative event, both in the life of Jesus and in the life of the Church. At the last supper Jesus gave bread and wine to his disciples but in reality was giving his own presence to them. One might state the position of the Church in an even more specific way by saying:

2. THE HOLY EUCHARIST IS A SACRAMENT OF THE REAL PRESENCE OF JESUS

It is the mystery of the real presence of Jesus in the eucharist which is at the heart of the Church's teaching on the eucharist and is the basis for all theology on the eucharist. The *fact* of the real presence—a "fact" which we have access to only in faith—is the central eucharistic teaching in the Church. Denial of the real presence would clearly be heretical.

3. THE PRESENCE OF JESUS IS TRUE, REAL AND SUBSTANTIAL

Each of these terms was chosen with great care: *true,* to avoid any semblance of a merely symbolical presence; *real,* to avoid any notion of merely imagined presence, a merely remembered presence; *substantial,* to avoid any teaching that would diminish the full presence of Jesus, both in his humanness and in his divinity, in the eucharist.

Not until the ninth century is there really any argument about the real presence of Jesus in the eucharist. In 831 Paschasius Radbertus wrote *De corpore et sanguine Domini;* this was followed by several other treatises on the eucharist. Ratramn of Corbie wrote an opposing treatise in 850. A controversy ensued on the question of the real presence. Gottschalk and Rhabanus Maur entered into the controversy. In the beginning of the eleventh century Berengarius continued the dispute, opposed by Lanfranc, Alger of Liege and Guitmund of Aversa.

It was during this time that the word "substantial" began to appear in eucharistic writings and, with Roland, the term "transubstantiation." It is also against all of these disputes that the theologians of the twelfth and thirteenth centuries developed their approach to the real presence in the eucharist, including the works of Thomas, Bonaventure, and Scotus.

The Council of Trent relied on scholastic theology, but in no way wanted to "define" Aristotelian philosophy nor to settle the issues which separated the Dominican and the Franciscan schools of theology. Actually, the intent of the council bishops was pastoral: to speak out on errors and to provide the pastoral ministry of the Church with some solid guidelines for the eucharistic teaching, preaching and liturgical celebration.

As we will see later, the council did not settle the issue of "how" Jesus is truly and really present in the eucharist, but it maintained with the entire tradition of the Christian world the "that" of Jesus' presence in the eucharist.

4. THE BREAD AND WINE IN THE EUCHARIST IS NOT MERELY BREAD AND WINE BUT "CHANGED" INTO THE BODY AND BLOOD OF JESUS

Theologians make a distinction of what some term the "fact of transubstantiation," on the one hand, and the "term transubstantiation" on the other. The "fact" of change is solemnly declared by the Church; one is not handling ordinary bread and wine. The "name" transubstantiation is not part of the defined teaching. All the major manuals of theology, in use prior to Vatican II, make this kind of distinction, thereby providing us with a solid understanding of the solemn teaching of the Church on this matter.

*** *** ***

One can see that there is a certain circumspect approach by the Church in the discussion on the real presence of Jesus as regards the "how" of this presence. There is no such circumspect position as to the belief of Christians in the real presence of Jesus in the eucharist.

We turn now to the issue of the *Most Holy Sacrifice of the Mass.*

5. THE MASS IS A TRUE SACRIFICE

As we shall see in detail later, the issue was not that the Mass was a "sacrifice of praise." Rather, it was seen by the bishops and the theologians at the Council of Trent as a "propitiatory sacrifice." The crux of the issue is the relationship between the sacrifice of Jesus, which alone and totally is propitiatory, and the Mass, which the council wanted to define as related to this once and for all propitiatory sacrifice of Jesus. This issue was the central issue in the deliberations on the Mass at the Council of Trent. The terms "bloody" and "unbloody" came to be the conciliar terminology to express such an interrelationship. What is at stake in this teaching of the Church is that there is a true interrelationship between the once-and-for-all sacrifice of Jesus and the Mass. To deny this would be outside Christian belief. This will be explained in detail in a further chapter.

Sacrifice was a major issue between the Roman theology and the reformation theology in the sixteenth century. The issue has divided Protestant and Catholic ever since, at least down to our present time. Documents of our present age, e.g., the Lima Document and the statements from the Lutheran/Roman Catholic dialogues, take up the issue of sacrifice and the eucharist. In doing this, the authors face up to the many issues involved and have developed solid areas of agreement.

6. IN THIS SACRIFICE OF THE MASS, JESUS IS PRIEST AND VICTIM

The eucharist is essentially christological, and the presence of Jesus controls all theological thinking on the matter, including all one wants to say about "sacrifice." This is the import of the Church's statement: Jesus alone is the one who offers and Jesus alone is the one who is offered. All others, i.e., the human priest, the use of bread and wine, the eucharistic prayer, are parts of the sacrament of this single sacrifice. It is this christological centering which has made some dialogue on the matter of the "sacrifice of the Mass" possible today within the ecumenical movement.

7. THE EUCHARIST IS A SOURCE OF GRACE

Since in the eucharist we acclaim the real presence of Jesus, who is grace, the essential relationship of the eucharist to grace is a clear and unquestionable teaching of the Church. When one enters into the question of "how" precisely the sacrament of the eucharist "gives" grace, one enters into the area of theological opinion and these opinions are in no way the solemn teaching of the Church. The relationship, and an essential one at that, between eucharist and grace must, however, be seen as clear Church teaching.

In a later chapter we will discuss in detail the issue of the Mass as a sacrifice. The above points are the clear and defined statements of the Church. As one sees, there is a certain brevity on the matter. When one moves into the explanation of these points, differences of opinion begin to show themselves. Nonetheless, one must recall that behind all the arguments between the Roman Catholic theologians and bishops on the one side, and the reformation theologians on the other side, the issue of the Mass as a sacrifice was actually and only the most illustrative of the instances in which there was a question of grace and good works. Behind all the argumentation, the good works issue was dominant. One cannot, accordingly, hope to settle the difficulties in the area of the "Mass as a sacrifice" unless one first clarifies the issue of "grace and good works."

8. THE PASTORAL CANONS

There were two situations which the bishops at the Council of Trent pastorally wanted to clarify on the matter of the eucharist:

a. If a Christian receives only the consecrated bread, does he or she truly receive the eucharist? The Tridentine answer was emphatically "yes." At the time of the reformation, there was a strong move to provide the lay people with both the consecrated bread and the consecrated cup. So intense was the feeling on this that some denied a sacramental reception of the eucharist if only one form were used. The bishops at Trent did not want to start up anew the custom of communion under both forms, and in many ways this issue became a dividing point between Catholic and Protestant.

b. As we noted in our discussion of baptism, communicating infants was the custom in the East and had been the custom in the West until the early middle ages. There was a movement afoot at the time of the reformation to reinstate this custom. It fits in clearly with the baptism-eucharist connection. However, the bishops at the Council of Trent did not wish to reestablish this custom, and they said clearly that communicating little children was not necessary for their salvation.

Several points need to be stated on both of these pastoral concerns. First of all, the Council statement cannot be understood as if reception of only the bread was preferable, either liturgically or theologically. From the standpoint of Vatican II and all the liturgical renewal which we have been a part of, reception under both forms is indeed liturgically and theologically preferable.

Secondly, the Council of Trent cannot be interpreted as if it meant that communicating children was theologically unacceptable. Given the history of this practice both in the East and the West, we can easily see that there are excellent theological and liturgical reasons for doing so. Rather, the council was stating that *at the time of the Council of Trent* in the Roman Catholic Church, neither reception of holy communion under both species nor communicating infants was to be part of the prevailing pastoral practice.

The above statements present the official and solemn Roman Catholic teaching on the eucharist. Denial of any of these points would be heretical. In the case of the canons on eucharistic reception under only one form and the reception or non-reception of eucharist by infants, a heretical stance would only arise were one to *deny* that the Church itself had power to make such pastoral prescriptions. If such a denial were made, then the focus is no longer specifically on the eucharist, but rather on the Church, and more specifically on Church hierarchy, and the heresy would be ecclesiological and not eucharistic.

Let us look now at the canons developed by the Council of Trent. The statements are not verbatim from the Protestant reformers, but rather they are statements reshaped and refocused so that the main point of the Church's teaching might be expressed more clearly. The bishops at the Council of Trent, however, did not start with a Catholic "formulation of eucharistic doctrine"; rather, they started with selected statements which in one way or another were considered the teaching of the Protestant Reformers and which were out of step with the Roman Catholic position. Because of this, the canons tend to jump from one idea to another in, at times, a rather disjointed way. One must read these canons but then restate them in a clearer way as was done above. This is the method one finds in the manuals of theology in which the various authors developed theses—not the verbatim words—expressive of solemn Church teaching on the eucharist.

Canons on the Most Holy Sacrament of the Eucharist

728
(883)

1. If anyone denies that the body and blood, together with the soul and divinity, of our Lord Jesus Christ and, therefore, the whole Christ is truly, really, and substantially contained in the sacrament of the most holy Eucharist, but says that Christ is present in the Sacrament only as in a sign or figure, or by his power: let him be anathema (*see* 719, 721).

729
(884)

2. If anyone says that the substance of bread and wine remains in the holy sacrament of the Eucharist together with the body and blood of our Lord Jesus Christ, and denies that wonderful and extraordinary change of the whole substance of the bread into Christ's body and the whole substance of the wine into his blood while only the species of bread and wine remain, a change which the Catholic Church has most fittingly called transubstantiation: let him be anathema (*see* 722).

730
(885)

3. If anyone denies that in the venerable sacrament of the Eucharist the whole Christ is contained under each species and under each and every portion of either species when it is divided up: let him be anathema (*see* 721).

4. If anyone says that after the consecration the body and blood of our Lord Jesus Christ are not present in the marvelous sacrament of the Eucharist, but are present only in the use of the sacrament while it is being received, and not before or after, and that the true body of the Lord does not remain in the consecrated hosts or particles that are kept or are left over after Communion: let him be anathema (*see* 721).

731
(886)

5. If anyone says that the principal effect of the most holy Eucharist is the forgiveness of sins, or that other effects do not come from the Eucharist: let him be anathema (*see* 720).

732
(887)

6. If anyone says that Christ, the only-begotten Son of God, is not to be adored in the holy sacrament of the Eucharist with the worship of latria, in-

cluding the external worship, and that the Sacrament, therefore, is not to be honored with extraordinary festive celebrations nor solemnly carried from place to place in processions according to the praiseworthy universal rite and custom of the holy Church; or that the Sacrament is not to be publicly exposed for the people's adoration, and that those who adore it are idolators: let him be anathema (*see* 723). 733 (888)

7. If anyone says that it is not permissible to keep the sacred Eucharist in a holy place, but that it must necessarily be distributed immediately after the consecration to those who are present; or that it is not permissible to carry the Eucharist respectfully to the sick: let him be anathema (*see* 724). 734 (889)

8. If anyone says that Christ present in the Eucharist is only spiritually eaten and not sacramentally and really as well: let him be anathema (*see* 726). 735 (890)

9. If anyone denies that each and everyone of Christ's faithful of both sexes, is bound, when he reaches the age of reason, to receive Communion at least every year during the Paschal season according to the command of holy Mother Church: let him be anathema (*see DB* 437). 736 (891)

737 (892) 10. If anyone says that it is not permissible for a priest celebrating Mass to give Communion to himself: let him be anathema (*see* 726).

738 (893) 11. If anyone says that faith alone is a sufficient preparation for receiving the sacrament of the most holy Eucharist: let him be anathema. And, lest this great sacrament be received unworthily and thus be received unto death and condemnation, this holy council has determined and decreed that those who have mortal sin on their conscience, no matter how contrite they may think they are, must necessarily make a sacramental confession before receiving, provided that they have access to a confessor. If anyone presumes to teach, or preach, or stubbornly maintain, or defend in public disputation the op-

posite of this, he is excommunicated by his action (*see* 725).

Canons on the Most Holy Sacrifice of the Mass

1. If anyone says that in the Mass a true and proper sacrifice is not offered to God or that the sacrificial offering consists merely in the fact that Christ is given to us to eat: let him be anathema (*see* 747).   756 (948)

2. If anyone says that by the words, "Do this in remembrance of me" (*Luke 22:19; I Cor. 11:24*), Christ did not make the apostles priests, or that he did not decree that they and other priests should offer his body and blood: let him be anathema (*see* 747).   757 (949)

3. If anyone says that the Sacrifice of the Mass is merely an offering of praise and of thanksgiving, or that it is a simple memorial of the sacrifice offered on the cross, and not propitiatory, or that it benefits only those who communicate; and that it should not be offered for the living and the dead, for sins, punishments, satisfaction, and other necessities: let him be anathema (*see* 749).   758 (950)

4. If anyone says that the Sacrifice of the Mass constitutes a blasphemy to the sacred sacrifice that Christ offered on the cross, or that the Mass detracts from that sacrifice: let him be anathema (*see* 749).   759 (951)

5. If anyone says that it is a deception to celebrate Masses in honor of the saints and to ask their intercession with God, according to the mind of the Church: let him be anathema (*see* 750).   760 (952)

6. If anyone says that there are errors in the Canon of the Mass and that it should therefore be done away with: let him be anathema (*see* 751).   761 (953)

762 (954)   7. If anyone says that the ceremonies, vestments, and external signs which the Catholic Church uses in the celebration of its Masses are the source of godlessness rather than helps to piety: let him be anathema (*see* 752).

763 8. If anyone says that Masses in which the priest
(955) alone communicates sacramentally, are illicit and
     should be done away with: let him be anathema (*see*
     754).

764 9. If anyone says that the rite of the Roman
(956) Church prescribing that a part of the Canon and the
     words of consecration be recited in a low tone of
     voice, should be condemned; or that Mass should
     be celebrated only in the vernacular; or that water
     should not be mixed with the wine offered in the
     chalice since that would be contrary to Christ's de-
     cree: let him be anathema (*see* 752, 754 *f.*).

*Canons on Communion under Both Species and on
Communion of Little Children*

742 1. If anyone says that each and every one of
(934) Christ's faithful ought to receive both species of the
     most holy sacrament of the Eucharist, because of a
     command from God or because it is necessary for
     salvation: let him be anathema (*see* 739).

743 2. If anyone says that the holy Catholic Church
(935) was not led by good reasons to have the laity and
     the clerics who are not celebrating Mass commu-
     nicate under the species of bread alone, or that the
     Church erred in so doing: let him be anathema (*see*
     678).

744 3. If anyone denies that the whole and entire
(936) Christ, the source and author of all graces, is re-
     ceived under the species of bread alone, alleging,
     as some falsely do, that such a reception is not in
     accord with Christ's institution of the sacrament
     under both species: let him be anathema (*see* 739,
     740).

745 4. If anyone says that Eucharistic Communion is
(937) necessary for little children before they reach the
     age of reason: let him be anathema (*see* 741). 1

One might also find solemn statements on specific issues
from other Church sources. On the question of the real presence of Jesus
in the eucharist and that the bread and wine are truly changed, one could

cite the brief statement from the IV Council of the Lateran, held in 1215. (Cf. Denzinger, 802.) The ideas presented there in very summary form are more clearly enunciated by the Council of Trent.

As regards the reception of the eucharist under only one form the thirteenth session of the Council of Constance, held in 1415, upholds the right of the Church hierarchy to prescribe such a practice because of "pericula et scandala" (dangers and scandals). (Cf. Denzinger, 1200.) Again the Council of Trent presents the same teaching in a fuller way.

One might ask about the *Decree for the Armenians,* promulgated in the *Bulla Unionis,* "Exsultate Deo," on November 22, 1439. Eugene IV was the pope at that time, and he had worked hard for reunion with the Greek and also the Armenian Churches. A counter-council was being held at Basel at the same time that the papal council was being held, first at Ferrara and then at Florence. Eugene IV, in the section on the sacraments, presented the Armenians with the basic teaching of St. Thomas Aquinas as found in his *De articulis fidei et Ecclesiae sacramentis.* Since the *Decree,* because of this, presents many theological opinions, rather than assured statements, it is more than difficult to use the *Decree* as a solemn teaching of the Church on the sacraments. For this reason I have not included the *Decree for the Armenians* as a source for the solemn teaching of the Church on the sacraments. The *Decree for the Armenians* surely indicates a general teaching of the Roman Church at the time of the Basel-Ferrara-Florence councils. Nonetheless, since the *Decree for the Armenians* is based in almost a literal way on one of Thomas Aquinas' small works, other theological positions, such as the Scotistic position, which were quite acceptable to the Latin Church, are not presented. In other words, the *Decree* takes into account only certain areas of theological opinion, and this makes the *Decree* at times quite difficult to read. In the *Decree* where does one draw the line between "official and solemn teaching" on the one hand, and the Thomistic "interpretation" on the other? The two are not equated by any means. At the Council of Trent, we know, almost half of the conciliar theologians were Scotistic, and a large part of the bishops were also Scotistic. This indicates the strength of the Scotistic position shortly after the *Decree* was issued, and would argue to the strength of the Scotistic position at the time of the *Decree* as well.

As a result, we are cautioned in making a *carte blanche* use of this *Decree,* nor did the Council of Trent subscribe in any official way to all that we find in this Thomistic *Decree*. For these reasons one must use the *Decree for the Armenians* in a most circumspect way.

Discussion Questions

1. What is the Catholic Church's teaching on "real presence" of Jesus in the eucharist?

2. Theologians speak of the "fact" of the real presence and the "how" of the real presence. What does this distinction mean?

3. What is the basis for saying that the Mass is a "sacrifice"?

4. Who is the real priest at the Mass? What does this mean?

5. If one receives only the consecrated bread, does one receive the eucharist? If one receives both the consecrated bread and the consecrated wine, does one receive anything more?

6. Is it acceptable, theologically, to give communion to infants? Why?

9

The Eucharist in
the New Testament

The influence of the mural depicting the last supper by Leonardo da Vinci has been enormous not only on Western art, but also on the religious piety of people at large. Almost all portrayals of the last supper since da Vinci's time have emulated his work in one way or another. Holy cards given to school children, illustrations in missals and other prayer books, church windows, replicas of the last supper to be hung in home dining rooms—all these have perpetuated the image of the last supper for countless numbers of Christians, Catholic and Protestant. Remarkably, the old adage that one picture is worth a thousand words finds strong verification in the matter of the last supper. The da Vinci image and its imitations with all their realism often control the way Christians tend to understand that final meal. Although contemporary theology, from an historico-critical method, has written much about the last supper, the theological and historical ideas they present do not have the force of the da Vinci image.

It would be totally out of place to attempt here a history of the eucharist, which in our day and age has been done on many occasions and by eminent scholars.[1] In spite of this abundance of critical historical theology, however, many questions, regarding the last supper and early Christian eucharist have not been resolved. There is a solid core of critical historical material, but there are also large areas in which not a little speculation is needed to fill in the gaps. In the following pages, an effort will be made to indicate those areas that are fairly solid as regards New

Testament interpretation, and those areas that remain theological or even historical opinion.

At the end of the eighteenth century with S. Reimarus and throughout the nineteenth century, especially with F.C. Bauer, not only has the literal interpretation of both the Old and the New Testament been questioned, but above all new interpretations have been developed. These are referred to often as "criticisms." There is tradition-criticism, editorial-criticism, etc. A literal interpretation of the last supper, for instance, has much in common with da Vinci's approach. What we really have, however, in the New Testament data are accounts which have been affected by traditions, editorializings, liturgical overlay, etc. All of this makes it very difficult to state what actually happened. When the gospels were being written, sometime after 70 A.D., the then local way of celebrating the eucharist played no small role in the manner in which each of the evangelists recorded that final meal. Theological and liturgical considerations, far more than simply historical considerations, shaped the actual wording and even sequencing of events.

1. NEW TESTAMENT TEXTS

All scholars, treating of the eucharist, begin with the textual data. A synoptic presentation of the words of institution helps us see both the similarities and the differences.

1 Cor 11:23–26: "For this is what I received from the Lord, and in turn passed on to you: that on the same night that he was betrayed, the Lord Jesus took some bread, and thanked God for it and broke it, and he said 'This is my body, which is for you; do this as a memorial of me.' In the same way he took the cup after supper and said, 'This cup is the new covenant in my blood. Whenever you drink it, do this as a memorial of me.' Until the Lord comes, therefore, every time you eat this bread and drink this cup, you are proclaiming his death, and so anyone who eats the bread or drinks the cup of the Lord unworthily will be behaving unworthily toward the body and blood of the Lord."

Lk 22:14–20: "When the hour came he took his place at table, and the apostles with him. And he said to them, 'I have longed to eat this passover with you before I suffer; because I tell you, I shall not eat it again until it is fulfilled in the kingdom of God.' Then taking a cup, he gave thanks and said, 'Take this and share it among you because from now on, I tell you, I shall not drink wine until the kingdom of God comes.' Then he took some bread and when he had given thanks, broke it and gave it to them, saying, 'This is my body which will be given for you: do this as a memorial of me.' He did the same with the cup after supper, and said, 'This cup is the new covenant in my blood which will be poured out for you.' ''

Mk 14:22–25: ''And as they were eating he took some bread, and when he had said the blessing he broke it and gave it to them. 'Take it,' he said, 'this is my body.' Then he took a cup, and when he had returned thanks, he gave it to them, and all drank from it, and he said to them, 'This is my blood, the blood of the covenant, which is to be poured out for many. I tell you solemnly, I shall not drink any more wine until the day I drink the new wine in the kingdom of God.' ''

Mt 26:26–29: ''Now as they were eating, Jesus took some bread, and when he had said the blessing he broke it and gave it to the disciples. 'Take it and eat,' he said, 'this is my body.' Then he took a cup, and when he had returned thanks he gave it to them. 'Drink all of you from this,' he said, 'for this is my blood, the blood of the covenant, which is to be poured out for many for the forgiveness of sins. From now on, I tell you, I shall not drink wine until the day I drink the new wine with you in the kingdom of my Father.' ''

The sixth chapter of John's gospel is also a very eucharistic passage even though in the Johannine account there are no words of institution or interpretation in connection with the last supper. Scholars have variously understood this Johannine omission. The discourse in the synagogue at Capernaum centers around Jesus himself as the bread of life; indeed, the key concept is ''life''—a word that dominates the first eleven chapters of the fourth gospel. The comparison and contrast with Moses is pronounced. Union with Jesus and union with the Father are at the heart of this message, and the eating of the flesh and the drinking of his blood is the way to this life with God. This chapter, with all its eucharistic overtones, is important for still another reason: the author indicates here the Galilean crisis, that time in the life of Jesus when ''many of his disciples left him and stopped going with him.'' For Jon Sobrino, and other contemporary writers on christology, this Galilean crisis represents a major turning point in the life of Jesus and his own vision and interpretation of his life and death. Jesus, as bread of life, provides a stumbling block to many of his disciples.[2]

These accounts of the last supper are, with the exception of 1 Corinthians, connected to the arrest, suffering and death of Jesus, the "passion accounts." Jeremias, in his studies, sees that at first there was a brief account of the arrest, suffering and death.[3] A *short account* developed around this earliest kerygma, as more details were added. Third, a *long account* was drawn together. This *long account* is basically the material which all four evangelists have regarding the arrest, suffering and death of Jesus. Finally, each evangelist added his own specific material, and we have the accounts as contained in the written gospels today.

A similar process went on as regards the last supper material, which he outlines as follows:

1. The earliest part of the accounts of the Last Supper are the words of interpretation (Mark 14.22–24 par.), whose antiquity approaches that of the early kerygma (I Cor. 15.3b–5).
2. The announcement of the betrayal (Mark 14.17–21 par.) is an original part of the *long account;* it is common to all four gospels and in the synoptics is firmly embedded in its context.
3. Everything else is part early special tradition (so the avowal of abstinence, Luke 22.15–18; Mark 14.25; Matt. 26.29 and the feet washing, John 13.1–20), part composition (so the Lukan table conversation, Luke 22.24–38) and part expansion (so the account of the preparation for the passover meal, Mark 14.12–16 par., which has its analogy in Jesus' miraculous foreknowledge, Mark 11.1–6).[4]

Jeremias notes that the "words of interpretation" are the oldest and therefore closest to the time of Jesus. Other details are added at later dates and are due to liturgical and theological factors, not necessarily historical.

The words of interpretation, as the Protestants often call them, or the words of institution, as the Catholics often call them, line up in two somewhat different traditions. On the one hand, Paul and Luke are similar; on the other hand, Mark and Matthew are similar. Even though Paul's actual writing is chronologically first, there are good reasons to think that the Mark-Matthew presentation reflects the older tradition and is therefore closer to the actual words of Jesus himself. This question will probably be argued for decades to come, but it is important to note that there is a divergence even in the accounts we have in the gospels and Paul. A literal approach, therefore, can raise only additional difficulties and in no way resolve these diverging texts.

There is, as well, a history between the Lord's supper just before he died and the appearances or accounts of early Christian eucharists. Fitzmyer notes that the synoptics seek to root the Christian eucharists in the words and deeds of Jesus at that meal. Paul mentions the eucharist prior to his reference to the Lord's supper. The steps between the Lord's supper and the Christian eucharist will remain speculative at best, but one cannot simply go from the first accounts of Christian eucharist (nor from the accounts of the Lord's supper itself) to the actual supper that Jesus had with his disciples before he died.[5]

Let us move now to some background material for the Lord's supper and for the subsequent Christian eucharists.

Nowhere in the New Testament is this supper called the "last supper." Paul refers to it as the "Lord's supper" (1 Cor 11:20). Frequently, one begins with this supper as a "starting point" for discussion on the eucharist. Perhaps, one might do well to go beyond the supper to the many meals of fellowship which Jesus shared with his disciples, both men and women. This will help situate the last supper in a more realistic way.

2. JEWISH MEALS AT THE TIME OF JESUS

Howard Z. Cleveland notes that "Meals in the bible periods varied greatly in time of eating, diet, and table customs. Generally two meals were served daily, although three were not uncommon."[6] The first meal seems to have been shared somewhat later in the day than our current "breakfast." This is understandable for an agrarian population, in which numerous chores need to be done shortly after daybreak. Once the chores are out of the way, then there is leisure for a meal. The evening meal came at the end of the day, and since candlelight was fairly expensive, the poorer people would eat at dusk so that the clean-up would be done before nightfall. The daylight, in so many ways, governed the activities of the poorer classes.

Meals were taken around a fire, at least by the poorer classes. The richer Jewish people did have dining rooms and servants. This would mean again that the poorer people squatted around the fire, while richer people would sit or recline. Knives, forks and spoons were not used in eating by the lower classes; rather, a meat in a gravy dish would be placed on bread and scooped into the mouth.

However poor it might have been, there was a fellowship connected with such meals. Jeremias highlights the factor of reconciliation which was part of the Jewish meals:

> To understand what Jesus was doing in eating with ''sinners'', it is important to realize that in the east, even today, to invite a man to a meal was an honour. It was an offer of peace, trust, brotherhood and forgiveness; in short, sharing a table meant sharing a life.[7]

Jeremias refers to 2 Kings 25:27–30 and to sections of Josephus to exemplify this. He continues

> In Judaism in particular, table-fellowship means fellowship before God, for the eating of a piece of broken bread by everyone who shares in the meal brings out the fact that they all have a share in the blessings which the master of the house had spoken over the unbroken bread.[8]

Fellowship and forgiveness, a sharing in one's life and in one's blessings, were all part of the ordinary meal at the time of Jesus. In other words, there are themes which one finds in the last supper and in the eucharist which are already rooted in the ordinary meals of Jesus and his disciples. The fellowship which he enjoyed and in so many ways brought about in the ordinary meals during his own lifetime are carried over into that final meal and into the eucharistic meals.

This fellowship is not simply the sharing of bread and wine and food, but it is also the sharing of one's real presence to others. In so many ways these fellowship, ordinary meals of Jesus with his disciples anticipate and flow into the eucharistic meals of the post-resurrection area.

Some meals were, of course, more festive than others: meals for a marriage, meals at the time of circumcision. Other meals were more sober: meals at the passing of a loved one in the family. There were meals celebrated in a quite religious way. Not simply the sabbath nor the paschal meal, but other festive holydays were celebrated with a meal.

There were prayers to be said, which at least the more pious Jews practiced, and these prayer-blessings seem to have been developed into special patterns. L. Bouyer, particularly, focuses on these various blessings as background for the Christian eucharist.[9] Important as the blessings are, and important as the various feastdays were, it was the basic fellowship meal of daily life that is the substrate of Christian eucharist. Therefore some acquaintance with ordinary meal customs among Jewish people, particularly poor people, at the time of Jesus helps one immensely to understand the dynamics which eventually enter into the Christian eucharist.

3. THE LAST SUPPER AS A PASSOVER MEAL

Probably, it will never be fully determined whether the last supper was a passover meal or not. The gospels indicate that it was, at least in some degree, while John's gospel narrates that it was celebrated the day before passover. Clearly, the evangelists, and St. Paul as well, align the last supper to the paschal event, just as they align the arrest, trial and death of Jesus to the paschal event. One can at least say that the passover motif is one of the major ways we find in the New Testament to interpret the last supper. This, in turn, helps us to interpret, to some degree, the meaning of the Christian eucharist.

Jeremias has lined up the dominant indications to interpret the last supper as a passover meal in an historical way. These indications are as follows:[10]

1. *The last supper took place in Jerusalem.* All the synoptics mention this. After the meal Jesus went to Gethsemani, a place within the established city-limits during the passover. Although Bethany might be the more logical place for Jesus to go, it was outside these passover city-limits. Accordingly, the mention of Jerusalem fits in well with passover customs.

2. *A room was made available to him.* The inhabitants of Jerusalem, due to the large number of pilgrims, had to open up their homes, if rooms were available, for strangers to celebrate the passover. Nor could they collect a fee for this.

3. *The last supper was celebrated at night.* As noted above, the ordinary time for the evening meal among the Jews at the time of Jesus was just prior to sunset. The passover, however, was celebrated after sundown.

4. *Jesus celebrated the last supper with the twelve*. For a passover meal at least ten persons were required, and a year-old lamb was to be consumed. Jeremias notes, however, that the presence of women at the last supper cannot be excluded.

5. *At the last supper they reclined*. Generally, Jewish people squatted around the fire, but at the passover they reclined. This was done in imitation of the Egyptians; for in Egypt the wealthy Egyptians reclined at table. The passover celebrates the freedom from slavery and the entry into the land flowing with milk and honey, that is, into a rich land. At passover, the Jewish people "played rich."

6. *A state of levitical purity was required*. A washing was mandated, and this gives strong explanation for the washing of the feet, a ritualized washing, which we find in the gospel of John.

7. *Bread is broken during the meal*. Both Mark and Matthew indicate that the bread was broken during the meal. As we saw above, the breaking of the bread and the "blessing" began the meal. Since there was to be an interpretation given to this breaking of the bread at the passover, it was not the beginning ritual.

8. *Wine was served with the meal*. Special celebrations included the drinking of wine with meals, and the passover required it. Again, there is the aspect of "playing rich." Ordinarily, less affluent people drank water with their meals.

9. *Red wine was used*. Jewish people had, at the time of Jesus, red, white and a black wine. It is not certain that red wine was the more common, but it is certain that red wine was required for a passover meal.

10. *A purchase was made*. In emergencies purchases that were required were allowed, even purchasing at night. This is a very strange detail, but possibly in accord with passover regulations.

11. *Something was given to the poor*. It was the custom to assist the poor on the passover evening. It seems that the temple gates were

opened at midnight on passover night so that the poor could begin to gather and be aided.

12. *The last supper ends with a hymn*. This seems to be the passover *hallel*.

13. *After the supper Jesus did not go to Bethany*. During the high feast, the usual limits of Jerusalem were insufficient to provide for the number of pilgrims. However, the regulation was that all pilgrims had to remain inside the "city of Jerusalem." To accommodate the large number of pilgrims, an extended "city limits" was established. Gethsemani fell within this, but Bethany did not.

14. *Jesus interprets the bread and wine*. At passover there was indeed a "word of interpretation" for some of the foods which were eaten. Only at passover was this done. At the last supper, Jesus "reinterprets" the meal—clearly, a passover detail.

Such are the major indications that the last supper was a passover meal. Jeremias may or may not be correct and some of the details he mentions may not have the strong backing he assumes. At any rate, a case is made for the last supper as a passover meal, and yet there are still inconclusive aspects. Probably, the exact historical situation may never be clarified.

For a theology of the eucharist, the determination of the passover character of the last supper may not be central. The crucifixion of Jesus was one of the most embarrassing aspects of the early Jesus movement. How could the Messiah, the Son of God, the Savior of all, be crucified. The New Testament authors go to great lengths to "interpret" Jesus' death, and one of the interpretations is the new paschal event. As Paul mentions in 1 Corinthians 5:7: "Christ our passover has been sacrificed." The entire turn of events, from the supper to the pouring out of the Spirit at Pentecost, is considered "paschal" or passover. This new paschal event far surpasses the old paschal event, and in this sense the very term "paschal" is reinterpreted.

The early Christian community however did not select the yearly passover as the basis for the eucharist. Rather, the meal-fellowship was seen as the basis for the eucharist. Eucharist was not confined to an annual event; it was celebrated more often, eventually weekly, and eventually daily.

Even more than this question of the rootage, the eucharist cannot be understood apart from an understanding of the resurrection. Let us consider this aspect of eucharistic theology more at length.

4. THE RESURRECTION AND THE EUCHARIST

Easter faith involves the acceptance of Jesus as *Kyrios,* which has profound and extensive ramifications for the entire Christian belief structure. Only after the resurrection event did the disciples accept Jesus as *Kyrios,* Lord and God.[11] It is with this faith that they understood the eucharist, and so accordingly we can speak meaningfully of the eucharist only after the resurrection event. The eucharist is much more an Easter event than it is a last supper event. Without any doubt there is a definite relationship between a post-resurrectional celebration of the eucharist and the meal fellowship of Jesus with his disciples prior to his death. Nonetheless, the heart of the meaning of the eucharist, and the very depth of what the eucharistic presence of Jesus is all about, so focuses the eucharist on the risen body of Jesus that the eucharist cannot simply be attributed to a pre-resurrection event. Assuredly, this demands that we once again rethink the relationship of eucharist as a post-resurrectional Christian event with the pre-resurrection last supper event. To state that the last supper was the first eucharist and that the post-resurrectional eucharistic celebrations essentially repeat the last supper does an injustice to all that resurrection theology has developed over the Christian centuries. Such a way of thinking is clearly scholastic, namely, to develop an "essence" of eucharist and then apply it univocally to (a) last supper and (b) any and all post-resurrectional eucharists. This approach dehistoricizes the resurrection, which later in this scheme would play only a secondary and tangential role, and because of this dehistoricizing would actually dehistoricize the eucharist itself, since it removes it from its historical roots in the Easter faith of the early Christian community.

Betz, who has done so much research into the early material on the Christian eucharist, sums up the data of the New Testament material on the eucharist in this way: "The NT institutional narratives were not first formulated by their witnesses, but a part *(ein Stück)* of the gospel prior to the gospels—and indeed the oldest part—stem from the community worship, and on the basis of their linguistic coloration reach back into the Palestinian community. They portray the last supper of Jesus, not in an historical way with all its significant details, but simply in the light and the perspective of what was of value for the liturgical celebration of the community.''[12] This community is post-resurrectional in belief, as is also the liturgical expression of this belief. This does not mean that the liturgy as such dominates the New Testament presentation of the eucharist, although the liturgical construct of the passages is more than evident, but that the belief of the Christian community in the presence of the risen Lord (and therefore the belief in the resurrection itself and the acceptance of Jesus as Lord and his presence which goes far beyond the eucharist) is absolutely central to the very meaning of the eucharist itself. This is the reason why one should clearly emphasize that the eucharist, both in its reality and in its theological interpretation, is a post-resurrection event; that the "institution" of the eucharist is likewise post-resurrectional and depends very much on the action of the Spirit of Jesus which was "sent" as an integral part of the post Easter event of "instituting the Church." Indeed, the very meaning of the eucharist (its "essence" if you will) is not to be found in the last supper nor in the death of Jesus, in spite of all the references to the blood "being poured out" and the body "which will be given up for you" which are in the New Testament texts themselves, but, like every other faith item in our Christian context, in and through the resurrection of Jesus itself. The eucharist is the celebration by the Christian community of the real presence of the risen Lord in their communal meal. In this sense, the eucharist as a meal, i.e., people-eating-together, is a sacrament or sign *of* the presence of the risen Lord *to* the community of believers.

5. THE EUCHARIST AND ST. PAUL

The importance of the resurrection on eucharistic theology is a necessary preface to the eucharist and St. Paul. Paul's entire eucharistic approach is focused in the christological mysteries, and although he speaks of the eucharist only in 1 Corinthians, what he says there can only be understood against his understanding of the mystery of Christ. In 1976/1977 Jerome Murphy-O'Connor, O.P. summarized the eucharistic teaching of Paul in a series of articles published in *Worship*.[13] Murphy-O'Connor first contextualizes the eucharistic thought in Paul's approach to the Christian community. He states:

> The Christian community is an organic unity in which the members are vitally related to each other through participation in a common life. By love they are bound together in a mode of existence which is the antithesis of the individualistic mode of existence that constitutes the "world."[14]

The community is the basis for eucharist. What Murphy-O'Connor is indicating here is that the Church is the basic sacrament. Prior to and constitutive of the eucharistic sacrament is the sacrament of the Church. The eucharist is not constitutive of the Church; the Church is constitutive of the eucharist. Murphy-O'Connor continues:

> This community is Christ in that it prolongs incarnationally the power of love that was the essence of his mission. It represents the saving force of Christ because in the world it demonstrates the reality of an alternative mode of existence in which humanity is not dominated by the egocentricity that provokes possessiveness, jealousy and strife. To enter this community is to abandon the individualism of self-affirmation. In a group which possesses "the mind of Christ" (1 Cor 2:16) the individual is distinguished only by different Spirit-given gifts of service.[15]

The basis of the community, called Church, however, is Jesus, the primordial sacrament, in today's language. The sacrament of Jesus constitutes the sacrament of the Church which constitutes the sacrament of the eucharist—this is the progression of the mystery of Christ.

Only on this basis does Murphy-O'Connor move to the eucharist in St. Paul. What dominates Paul's thought is the realism. Such realism is not poetry, not a flight into mysticism, but a real Jesus, a real community of faith, a real body and blood of Jesus in the eucharist—in other words, a *real presence*.

> Not by the Eucharist in itself, because Paul would energetically repudiate any mechanical approach to the sacrament. The person of Christ is really present under the sacramental species, only when the words of institution are spoken by "Christ," an authentic com-

munity animated by the creative saving love which alone enables
humanity to "live." The power of Christ is released and becomes
effective only when the participants demonstrate a lived realization
of the demand implicit in the organic unity of which they are members.[16]

It is not simply a Jesus in the eucharist which rivets the theology
of Paul, but the Jesus who lived and who died and who rose from the
dead and is sitting now at the right hand of the Father, making intercession for us, which dominates his thought. Too often, one can begin talking about the eucharist, and get focused on bread and wine, on
transubstantiation, on how the eucharist re-presents the sacrifice of the
cross, and forget about the Lord and all that salvation history and eschatology involve. Paul never abandons that vision; nor does he so focus on the eucharist that he forgets the community-base, which is only
a community filled with Jesus if it is a community filled with the Holy
Spirit.

In the section from 1 Corinthians we see that there is a meal connected with the eucharist, although some who are more affluent eat and
drink well, while others who are needy remain hungry. The connection
of eucharist to a meal, however, indicates that the table-fellowship is
still a major feature of the eucharist at this early stage.

It is evident that the eucharist is seen as a great moment of reconciliation. First of all, there are the words of the Lord, which Paul
recounts, but are clearly seen to be interpreted: "This is my body,
which is for you." "This cup is the new covenant in my blood." The
"for you" and the "new covenant in my blood" are all indications of
forgiveness, of salvation, of reconciliation, of justification—a multiplicity of terms, but all with the same meaning: in Jesus, both in his
own life, death and resurrection, and in this same Jesus present in the
eucharist, there is reconciliation. Indeed, the eucharist, next to Jesus
and the Church, is *the* sacrament of reconciliation, not the sacrament
of penance, not even the sacrament of baptism. The eucharist, because
of the centrality of Jesus, must be seen as the sacrament of reconciliation.

On the basis of Paul and the gospels, the early Church continued
to celebrate the eucharist without controversy. The only question which
plagued the early Church was that of rebaptism and reordination (and
therefore the legitimacy of the eucharist in a heretical group), but there

were no specifically eucharistic controversies. Transubstantiation is not a part of this early eucharistic doctrine, either in the East or in the West, and attempts to see "transubstantiation" in the New Testament data is clearly "eisegesis" or a reading into the text. Similarly, the question which developed at the time of the reformation—Is the Mass a sacrifice?—cannot be read into these texts, either, with all the theological niceties of the sixteenth century. Sacrificial language is clearly in evidence (e.g., the "pouring out of the blood," etc.), but the questions of the reformation period are too theologically specified to be transferred in an unqualified way to the New Testament materials. The fact that these issues of transubstantiation and sacrifice came only to the fore in the middle ages and the sixteenth century indicates that they were not the focused issues prior to those times.

6. SUMMARY OF NEW TESTAMENT TEACHING ON THE EUCHARIST

This summary is not a comprehensive summary of everything that the New Testament teaches on the eucharist, but it summarizes the main issues which were treated in this chapter. Naturally, there are many more New Testament items which deal with the eucharist.

1. The synoptics and St. Paul present us with the words of institution for the eucharist; there seems to be two different approaches: (a) that of St. Paul and Luke, (b) that of Mark and Matthew.

2. Although Paul is the earliest *written* form which we know of, the tradition expressed in Mark-Matthew might be the older and therefore the closest to the very words of Jesus.

3. John's gospel, which does not give any words of institution, presents a profound eucharistic teaching in chapter 6.

4. The accounts of the last supper are not separate accounts in any of the gospels or in St. Paul. They are imbedded in the salvation history of Jesus; particularly, they are associated with the arrest, death and resurrection of Jesus. In other words, the eucharistic accounts can only be understood in their christological framework, and not in isolation.

5. The eucharist can be only understood against the background of the many meals of fellowship which Jesus enjoyed with his disciples, both men and women. The last supper alone is insufficient to explain the eucharist.

6. Scholars argue on whether or not the last supper was a passover meal. The argument may never be settled. There are, however, many details, described by the evangelists, which point to a passover meal.

7. An understanding of the meaning of the resurrection is necessary for an understanding of the eucharist, since the eucharist is basically a post-resurrection, Christian celebration of the new paschal mystery, i.e., the life, death and resurrection of Jesus.

8. St. Paul, who writes about the eucharist only in a very occasional manner, emphasizes the christological background of the eucharist, and the ecclesiological or community background in Christ. Without Jesus and the believing community the eucharist, for St. Paul, makes no sense.

9. The New Testament gives evidence of the early eucharist within the context of a meal, and particularly a Jewish meal. It is celebrated in a home situation, not in a church-building.

10. The New Testament also gives evidence of a liturgical and theological interpretation of the eucharist, connecting the eucharist with the life, death and resurrection of Jesus, and therefore with a sacrifice motif, not because the eucharistic meal is in itself a sacrifice, but because of the intrinsic relationship with Jesus.

11. St. Paul particularly presents us with a strong statement of belief in the real presence of Jesus in the eucharist, but there is absolutely no trace of any doctrine such as transubstantiation.

Theologians and biblical scholars will continue to go over the New Testament material again and again. New insights will be developed, as new understandings of the biblical material continue to unfold. The above touches only in a cursory way on some of the major issues involved. Let us go now to the early Church. One issue, however, will not be treated: namely, the issue of the eucharistic minister. This is a complicated matter and will deserve a treatment all its own. Naturally, the eucharist and the ministry are intertwined, but the question of eucharistic ministry in the New Testament and the early Church is too extensive for this present volume.

Discussion Questions

1. What are the differences you see in the four accounts of the institution of the eucharist? What are the similarities?

2. Compare the accounts of the institution of the eucharist in the synoptics and Paul, on the one hand, with the sixth chapter of St. John, on the other. Are there any similarities in the theology of the eucharist?

3. Compare the style of eating among the Jewish people at the time of Jesus with the style of eating you are used to today. What are the similarities and what are the differences?

4. What does the theology of the resurrection bring to an understanding of the eucharist?

5. What does St. Paul say about the community in 1 Corinthians 11:17-34? Read the text carefully for all its details.

10

Eucharist in
the Early Church

A history of the entire development of the eucharist, even in the period of the early Church, goes far beyond the needs of this volume. Instead, I would like to present a few early passages which indicate the gradual liturgizing of the eucharist, as also some changes which occurred due to pastoral needs.

At first the data that we have remains rather close to the data for baptism, namely, the *Didache*, the writings of Justin and those of Hippolytus. However, Ignatius of Antioch, Clement of Rome, Irenaeus of Lyons, Clement of Alexandria—all have important reflections on the eucharist. We cannot enter into the thought of each of these here; rather, we will look at a few representative, and perhaps key authors of this period, pointing out some important details for an understanding of eucharistic development.

1. THE DIDACHE

In this ancient document of the early Christian community, the eucharist is mentioned in chapters nine, ten and fourteen. Quasten notes that chapters nine and ten contain the oldest eucharistic prayers yet recorded. For Catholics,[1] Quasten's view has been rather common. On the other hand, P. Drews and M. Goguel saw the two chapters (9 and 10) as referring to an ordinary meal; only chapter 14 referred to the eucharist.[2] Lietzmann, in his work, *Messe und Herrenmahl,* distinguished between an early eucharist in which the redemptive death of Jesus was celebrated, and therefore a sacrifice, and another eucharist in which this is all absent. In the *Didache* Lietzmann sees the commemorative eucharist in chapter 14, the non-commemorative one in chapters 9 and 10.[3]

More recently Willy Rordorf attempts to show that the early chapters are simply ''prayers spoken at table before the eucharist proper'' while chapter 14 presents us with a brief description of a true early eucharist.[4] No doubt, the discussion will continue on this matter, but what Rordorf, following Audet, clearly indicates is that a stage of eucharistic celebration was reached in the early Church, when the presence of the non-baptized was problematical. It was a major pastoral problem. To separate the non-baptized from the eucharist proper, a meal was held first, and then after the absenting of the non-baptized, the baptized Christians celebrated the eucharist. There is little doubt that this pastoral problem, the presence of the non-baptized, contributed to the separation of the meal proper from the eucharist. It may not have been the only pastoral problem. The growing numbers of Christians tended to make a meal somewhat problematic. Only larger homes could be used for such celebrations, which meant that only the homes of rich Christians became available. We have the Church of St. Clement in Rome, built over the wealthy home of Flavius Clemens, as a possible indication of this other factor. If Rordorf and Audet are correct, then the *Didache* presents us with an early example of a meal, at which baptized and non-baptized were present, followed by a eucharist, at which only the baptized were present. *That* such a situation developed is fairly well established; *that* the *Didache* reflects this may remain a subject of controversy.

Let us consider, however, the blessing prayers of Chapters 9 and 10 in the *Didache:*[5]

> 9. Regarding the eucharist, give thanks *[eucharistize]* thus: First, concerning the cup:
>> We give thanks to you, our Father,
>> for the holy vine of David your servant,
>> which you have made known to us through Jesus your Servant.
>> To you be glory unto the ages!
>
> Concerning the broken bread:
> We give thanks to you, our Father,
> for the life and knowledge
> which you have made known to us through Jesus your Servant.
> To you be glory unto the ages!

As this broken bread was scattered over the hills,
and then, when gathered, became one,
so may your church be gathered
from the ends of the earth into your Kingdom.
For yours is the glory and the power,
through Jesus Christ, unto the ages!

Let no one eat and drink of your eucharist but those baptized in the name of the Lord; to this, too, the saying of the Lord is applicable: "Do not give what is holy to dogs (Mt 7.6)."

10. After you have been satisfied, give thanks *[eucharistize]*thus:

We give you thanks, O holy Father, for your holy name
which you have enshrined in our hearts,
and for the knowledge and faith and immortality
which you have made known to us through Jesus your
Servant.
To you be glory unto the ages!
You, Master Almighty,
have created all things for the sake of your Name,
and have given food and drink to the sons of men for
enjoyment, that they may give thanks to you.
But to us you have granted spiritual food and drink
for eternal life through Jesus your Servant.
For all this we give thanks to you, for you are mighty.
To you be glory unto the ages! Amen.

Be mindful, O Lord, of your church, to deliver it from all
evil, and to perfect it in your love;
and gather it, the sanctified, from the four winds
into your Kingdom which you have prepared for it.
For yours is the power and the glory unto the ages!

May grace come and this world pass away!
Hosanna to the God of David!

The injunction at the end of chapter 9 against the unbaptized sharing in the eucharist raises the issue that perhaps these are indeed eucharistic prayers and not simply meal prayers, even in preparation for the eucharist. Likewise, the injunction at the end of chapter 10 that prophets be allowed to "eucharist" as often as they wish fits in well with the eucharistic minister question of the early Church. Moreover, the text itself of both chapters easily adapts itself to eucharistic theology and not merely to blessing prayers at a meal.

In chapter 14 we have reference to the ordinary Christian eucharist:[6]

On every Lord's Day, after you have assembled, break the bread and give thanks, first confessing your sins, that your sacrifice may be pure. Let no one who has a quarrel with his neighbor gather with you before they are reconciled, lest your sacrifice be profaned (*cf* Mt 5.23ff). For this is what the Lord said: "In every place and time a pure sacrifice is offered to me, for I am a great king, says the Lord, and my name is wonderful among the gentiles" (*cf* Ml 1.11,14).

The phrase "On the Lord's own day . . ." is important. Already at this early time (around the turn of the first to the second century) Christians celebrated eucharist on the day after the sabbath. This was the Lord's day, i.e., the day the Lord rose from the tomb. The connection with Easter is once more established as regards the eucharist. This "Lord's day" can also be found in Revelation 1:10 and also in St. Ignatius of Antioch's letter to the Magnesians (9:1); these are all written about the same time and give separate witnesses to the Christian disuse of the sabbath and their use of the day after in honor of the risen Jesus. The split between the synagogue and the Christian community has, at this time, widened considerably.

The final sentence is taken from the prophet Malachi (1:11), although differently from the Rahlfs' edition of the *Septuagint,* but indicates that early Christians connected the suffering and death of Jesus and therefore the eucharist with an understanding of "sacrifice." This prophetic understanding of sacrifice is reflected in the two preceding sentences as well.

2. ST. JUSTIN

In the *First Apology* of St. Justin (around 150) we have a description of early Christian eucharist for two different occasions: first for those who have just been baptized; then for the regular Sunday eucharist. In neither of these descriptions do we find a meal-setting. Rather, we see a liturgized setting, at which only bread and wine are used. Let us consider first of all the description of the eucharist which occurs immediately after the baptismal liturgy.[7]

65. But we, after thus washing the one who has believed and joined us, bring him to the place where are assembled those called the

brothers, to offer prayers in common for ourselves, for the newly-illumined person, and for all other persons wherever they may be, in order that, since we have found the truth, we may be found worthy also through good works to be reckoned good and devout and observers of what has been commanded, and thus attain to eternal salvation. At the conclusion of the prayers we greet one another with a kiss (1 Pt 5.14). Then bread and a cup containing wine and water are presented to the one presiding over the brothers. He takes them and offers praise and glory to the Father of All, through the name of the Son and of the Holy Spirit, and he makes a lengthy thanksgiving to God because He has counted us worthy of such favors. At the end of these prayers and thanksgiving, all express their assent by saying *Amen*. This Hebrew word, *Amen*, means "So be it." And when he who presides has given thanks, and all the people have acclaimed their assent, those whom we call deacons summon each one present to partake of the bread and wine and water over which the thanksgiving was said, and they carry it also to those who are absent.

66. We call this food the "Eucharist." No one is allowed to partake of it except him who believes that our teachings are true and has been cleansed in the bath for the forgiveness of his sins and for his regeneration, and who lives as Christ commanded. Not as common bread or as common drink do we receive these, but just as through the word of God, Jesus Christ, our Saviour, became incarnate and took on flesh and blood for our salvation, so, we have been taught, the food over which thanks has been given by the prayer of His word, and which nourishes our flesh and blood by assimilation, is both the flesh and blood of that incarnate Jesus. The apostles, in their memoirs which are called gospels, have handed down that they were commanded to this: Jesus took bread, and, after giving thanks, said "Do this in remembrance of me; this is my body." In like manner, He also took the cup, gave thanks, and said "This is my blood." And to them alone did He communicate this. The evil demons, in imitation of this, have ordered the same thing to be performed in the Mithraic mysteries. For, as you know or may easily learn, bread and a cup of water, along with some incantations, are used in their mystic initiation rites.

67. Henceforward, we constantly remind one another of these things. We who have possessions come to the aid of the poor, and we are always together. For all the favors we enjoy we bless the creator of All, through His Son, Jesus Christ, and through the Holy Spirit. On the day which is called the day of the Sun we have a

common assembly of all who live in the cities or in the country, and the memoirs of the apostles or the writings of the prophets are read, as much as there is time for. Then, when the reader has finished, the one presiding provides, in a discourse, admonition and exhortation to imitate these excellent things. Then we all stand up together and say prayers, and, as we said before, after we finish the prayer, bread and wine are presented. He who presides likewise offers up prayers and thanksgiving, to the best of his ability, and the people express their assent by saying *Amen,* and there is the distribution and participation by each one in those things over which thanksgiving has been said, and these are sent, through the deacons, to those not present. The wealthy, if they wish, contribute whatever they desire, and the collection is placed in the custody of the president, and he helps the orphans and widows, those who are needy because of sickness or any other reason, and the captives and the strangers in our midst; in short, he takes care of all those in need. The day of the Sun, indeed, is the day on which we all hold our common assembly, because it is the first day. On it God, transforming darkness and matter, created the world; and our Saviour Jesus Christ arose from the dead on the same day. For they crucified Him on the day before that of Saturn, and on the day after that of Saturn, the day of the Sun, He appeared to His apostles and disciples and taught them the things which we have passed on to you also for your consideration.

Justin is describing, perhaps, a eucharist which immediately follows baptism, not two different eucharists. M. Jourjon highlights some of the main points of this eucharistic presentation of Justin: (a) once more we see the Christian day of assembly, "on the day named after the sun"; (b) a clear distinction is made between presider and people; (c) "deacons" help to minister; (d) similar to the *Didache,* the eucharistic prayer in Justin is a prayer of praise for blessings received. Neither the *Didache* nor the presentation of Justin includes the words of institution.[8]

There is no connection with a meal. Perhaps by 150 A.D. the meal part of the eucharist had been rather commonly eliminated. We do see a ritualization process: there is a reading or several readings from the prophets or from the apostles; there is a homily or address. Bread, wine and water are brought up in a sort of procession. The eucharistic prayer is proclaimed by the presider, and the people, at the end, all say "Amen." Communion follows and deacons take some of the eucharist to those who were absent. In a very simplified way, we have the outline of the Christian eucharist which will be celebrated for centuries.

Jourjon indicates, along with many others, that this "presider" cannot at this early date be identified with "priest." But, as mentioned earlier, the issue of the minister of the eucharist is one which goes beyond this current study.[9]

In the second century there are other authors who treat of the eucharist. Ignatius of Antioch has many eucharistic passages. Clement of Rome, likewise, alludes to the eucharist. The works of Rordorf, Sheerin, Jasper and Cuming, Thurian and Wainwright, as well as the older works of Martimort, Bouyer, Jungmann, Quasten, and many others gather together this early material.

3. THIRD CENTURY SOURCES AND BEYOND

Hippolytus of Rome, once again, provides us with the first complete anaphora or eucharistic prayer which is extant. It was not a set prayer, which one had to follow. Rather, it was a model which the presider could use as a guide. Only at a later date, and outside of Rome, did the prayer become literally mandated. This prayer had enormous influence on the celebration of the eucharist in its own time, and was the basis for contemporary efforts to renew the eucharist in the Roman Catholic (Eucharistic Prayer II) and in the Anglican (Eucharistic Prayer B). This is no doubt one of the most important eucharistic prayers which the Christian community possesses, and ranks alongside the eucharistic prayer of St. Basil as far as influence is concerned.

> Let all offer the kiss of peace to him who has been made a bishop, saluting him because he has been made worthy. Let the deacons present the oblation to him, and, after placing his hands upon it, along with the entire presbytery, let him say, giving thanks:
>
> The Lord be with you.
> And let all say: And with your spirit (2 Tm 4.22).
> [Let us lift] up our hearts.
> We have them [lifted] to the Lord.
> Let us give thanks to the Lord.
> It is fitting and right (2 Th 1.3).

And then let him continue as follows:

We give thanks to you, O God, through your beloved servant Jesus Christ, whom you have sent to us in the last times (Ga 4.4) as Saviour and Redeemer and Angel of your Will (Is 9.5). He is your inseparable Word, through whom you have created all things (Jn 1.3), and in Him you were well-pleased (Mt 3.17). You sent Him from heaven into the womb of the Virgin, and He, dwelling in the womb, was made flesh, and was manifested as your Son, born of the Holy Spirit and the Virgin.

When He had fulfilled your will, and obtained (Ac 20.28) a holy people (1 P 2.9) for you, He stretched forth His hands when He suffered, that He might free from suffering those who believed in you.

When He was handed over to His voluntary suffering, that He might destroy death, and burst the bonds of the devil, and tread upon the nether world, and illumine the just, and fix the limit, and reveal the Resurrection, taking bread, He gave thanks to you, and said: Take, eat, this is my body, which will be broken for you.

Similarly also the cup, saying: This is my blood which is shed for you. When you do this, you are making a remembrance of me.

Wherefore remembering His death and Resurrection, we offer to you the bread and the cup, giving thanks to you because you have accounted us worthy to stand in your presence and serve you. And we ask that you send your Holy Spirit upon the oblation of holy church, and that gathering it together into one, you grant to all who partake of the holy things a fullness of the Holy Spirit for the strengthening of faith in truth, that we may praise you and glorify you through your Servant Jesus Christ, through whom be glory and honor to you, to the Father and to the Son with the Holy Spirit in your holy church, both now, and unto the ages of ages. Amen.

The view of salvation history is of special notice here, since it speaks of the Logos with the Father, with creation, in the incarnation, in the death and in the resurrection. The epiclesis will take on even more importance, in the Eastern church, particularly, as the years go on. A memorial and a presentation (an offering) are important: memores offerimus.

In the third century we have the Alexandrian theology of Clement and Origen and then Eusebius of Caesarea, Athanasius, Serapion of Thmuis, Didymus, Cyril, and to these should be joined the Cappadocians, Basil, Gregory of Nazianz and Gregory of Nyssa. In the eucharist, the Logos is present because of the incarnation. In this sense we can speak of these authors as incarnational in their approach to the eucharist. We are divinized in the eucharist not by sharing in the body of a man, but by sharing the body of the Logos. This reality of the Logos finds a sacramental presence in the entire gamut of incarnational thinking, so that one might speak of a relativizing of the eucharist in reference to the entire incarnational reality of the Logos made flesh. One might also sense a sort of spiritualizing of the eucharist, with the emphasis not only on the more subjective approach to eucharistic efficacy which we find in Origen, but also with respect to the clear and overwhelming activity of the Spirit. Indeed, the insight on Spirit and salvation in Cyril of Alexandria stands as a highpoint in the patristic theology of the eucharist. Because of the Logos and because of the Spirit we are not dealing with mere symbolization but with a reality.

The theologians at Antioch, at least prior to the council of Ephesus, stressed the humanity of Jesus in a much more forthright way. For them the anamnesis is not only of the death of Jesus, but also of his birth, his life, his death, his resurrection and his sending of the Spirit. John Chrysostom presents us with a classical text:

Do we not offer every day? Indeed, we do offer daily, but while we celebrate the memory of his death, this is a one-time occurrence, not a multiple one. How is it once and not many? Because it was only offered on one occasion, just as the offering which was brought into the Holy of Holies. This latter was a type of the other and in a similar way our own offering is a type of his. For we always offer the same [Christ] not today this lamb and tomorrow that lamb but always one and the same. Therefore, there is only one unique offering. Are there then many Christs, since he is offered in many places? By no means! Rather, everywhere there is the one Christ, completely here and completely there, one unique body. Just as the offering which is made in many places is one body and not many bodies, so is there only one unique offering (thysia). Our high priest is he who has offered the victim which cleanses us. That offering which we now present is the one which was once offered, which is inexhaustible. What now takes place occurs as a remembrance of what once took place. For he said: Do this in remembrance of me. Not any other high priest as the one of that time do we present on each occasion, or rather: We make a remembrance of that victim.[11]

Theodore of Mopsuestia stands in the same tradition and even goes further in relating distinct parts of the eucharist with distinct parts of the life, death and resurrection of Jesus. Both authors, indeed, place a strong emphasis on the Spirit. Since these authors make such express identification with the historical Jesus, we find a realism to the eucharist that is not part of the Alexandrian tradition. The Spirit brings about this change in the bread and wine, and the terms used to express this action of the Spirit are *metaballein* and *metapoiein*. These words are to be understood in a functional and dynamic way, but not in an ontological way. Above all there is no technically theological understanding of the ''how'' of the eucharistic presence of Jesus in this early period of the Church.

The Alexandrians, and the Cappadocians who shared their eucharistic views, have left us powerful insights into the presence of the Logos in the incarnation and the entire Christ-event. The Logos is present in an individual Christian, accomplishing his or her spiritualization. Such Christians are the true ''gnostics.'' For these theologians the confluence of Logos (Word) and Spirit is at the heart of their eucharistic spirituality.

For their part, the Antiochenes with their deep and comprehensive understanding of the reality of the humanness of Jesus and the ''re-presencing'' of this same humanness in the eucharist provide us with a rich approach to eucharistic theology. The christological insight regarding the full humanness of Jesus has remained a strong part of the christological tradition both of the East and the West due in large measure to the Antiochenes. At Chalcedon their position, in spite of the Alexandrian counter-measures, was solemnly declared. This emphasis on the humanness of Jesus, not on the Logos, provides us today with the key to the full sacramentality of the eucharist. We will resume this theme later on.

After Ephesus and after Chalcedon the Alexandrian theologians, and those affected by them, began to speak less strongly about a change in the elements of bread and wine. Eutherius of Tyana and Theodoret of Cyr evidence this change. Undoubtedly, christological factors are at work here: monophysitism is suspect and duophysitism (two natures) is acceptable. ''Bread and wine remain; what they are undergo no change of nature (*ousia* or *physis*) but rather a change of name which our faith affirms. The elements are called the body and blood of Jesus as, vice versa, Christ calls himself the bread of life and the true vine.

Still, the event is not simply a change of names and a mere semantic move. According to Eutherius, Theodoret and others, the elements, which remain in their nature, receive the grace of the Spirit, and consequently a supernatural growth, and are therefore called "the body and blood of Jesus."[12] The basis for this is christological: in the incarnation the nature of the humanness did not change (monophysitism) but remained; still, we can speak of this humanity as the humanity of the Lord (duophysitism). Pope Gelasisus, Ephraim of Antioch and in an implicit way Leontius of Jerusalem rejected any change in the elements.

The Latin tradition of the West is also rich and extensive on the matter of the eucharist. Tertullian is quite realistic in his approach to the eucharist, and the whole emphasis in the West is sharply focused on the elements. Tertullian identifies them clearly with the body and blood of Jesus. The Lord makes his body present *(repraesentat)* through the bread (cf. *Adv. Marc.* 1, 14; also *De cor.* mil. 3).

On his part Cyprian had to deal with those who employed water instead of wine at a eucharist, the Aquarians. This emphasis tended to focus even more concentratedly on the elements. Sacrifice too is an important part of Cyprian's approach to the eucharist, and the sacrifice of Jesus is present in the eucharist, but likewise the sacrifice of the Christian community. The realism of the West continues in Ambrose, while in Augustine we find an ambiguity in his teaching that has remained with us down to the present time. Is there a realism? Is there a spiritualism? Is there a symbolism? Harnack, Loofs, Seeberg, and Holl have stressed the spiritual side. Catholics have tended to emphasize the realistic aspects of this thought. More recently such scholars as Karl Adam and Josef Ratzinger have taken a middle position.

In all of this richness of the patristic period the presence of Jesus in the eucharist was really not an issue; it was rather presumed and in faith strongly believed. For Cyprian the community was not seen so much as the fruit of the eucharist, but rather the other way around; true ecclesial community needed to be first and only then communion in the eucharistic celebration. The practice of the "Fermentum," so common in the West, was an indication of this acceptance of another community. All of this indicates that Jesus is so central: the Logos of the Eastern Fathers, the historical Jesus of the Antiochenes, the reality of Jesus in the eucharist in the West.

During this entire time that goes from the apostolic age down to that of John Damascene eucharistic theology developed very strongly, and the liturgy of the eucharist likewise took on an enriching number of forms. During this period one really does not find any major controversy as regards the eucharist. The "Aquarians" in North Africa present a rather singular case; for Augustine and others, eucharists which are celebrated outside the recognized church community are heretical (just as baptisms and ordinations are). But these instances are not major eucharistic issues.

There is a richness clearly both in the faith and in the theology of the eucharist in these early times, but there is really no in-depth attempt to philosophically or even theologically "explain" how the presence of the Logos comes about in the eucharist. The entire approach that we associate with transubstantiation is clearly not evident in these early centuries. For centuries, both in East and West, belief in the real presence in no way involved belief in transubstantiation.

Liturgically, there is a wealth of material in these early centuries, and we can only touch on some very disparate items here. The move from home liturgies to "Church" liturgies tended to take away the closeness of the early communal celebrations and move the eucharist into a more formalized celebration. This included a formalized liturgizing of the eucharistic prayer. Secondly, the growth in numbers of the early Christian community precluded the use of many smaller homes, moving the eucharist into the larger homes and eventually into "church" buildings. Also with the presence of the non-baptized at early eucharistic liturgies, the separation of the eucharist from the meal became a pastoral necessity, since feeding large numbers becomes increasingly impossible, and the separation of the meal from the eucharistic part preserved the celebration of the eucharist for the baptized alone. The non-baptized could be dismissed prior to the eucharist part. The second century saw the rise of catechumenate, and the first part of the separate eucharistic celebration (separate from the meal) tended more and more to focus around the catechumens as the second part of the eucharist focused more on the real presence of Jesus in the community and in the eucharist, i.e., the stylized community meal. Even the historical process of clericalization, through which the actions of the priest (bishop) in the eucharistic part of the liturgy focused more and more on the elements, tended to emphasize the presence of Jesus in the eucharist. Indeed, the liturgical development as such, in this early Church period, is dominated by the presence of the Lord and how one liturgically and symbolically makes this presence ever more active within the gathered community.

In all of this, however, the reality of the presence of Jesus in the eucharist centralizes the faith of the early Christian communities. Certainly, this presence is not merely mental or logical; whether the term "real" might say too much, given its later development, is a factor that cannot be overlooked. Certainly, too, such theological constructs as transubstantiation, transfiguration, transfinalization, etc., would be totally out of place in this early milieu. The "how" of the presence of Jesus was not an issue on which theologians of those times spent any effort. The emphasis of the early church on the presence of Jesus in the eucharist, but also, and very much connected to this, his presence in the community, and because of the tremendous discussions on christology during those ages, the presence of Jesus in the flesh helps us today to reconsider the eucharist in the perspective of Jesus as *the* original and primordial sacrament.

However, consider for a moment the following statement: "Since the substantial bodily presence of Christ under the forms"—of bread and wine—"becomes the proper center of the eucharist *(das Proprium der Eucharistie)*, we are able, along with the tradition, to consider this as *'the'* real presence."[13] What makes the eucharist a sacrament, from the standpoint of Jesus as the primordial sacrament, is not something proper to the eucharist itself, namely the substantially, bodily presence of Jesus in the elements, but rather Jesus, in his humanness as the primordial sacrament, is the very reason that a eucharist can be called a sacrament at all. Even more than this, the Church as a basic sacrament is also a more profound reason why the eucharist can be called a sacrament than anything proper to the eucharist celebration itself. Truly the understanding of primordial sacramentality of Jesus as a sacrament and the basic character of the Church as a sacrament requires of us today to rethink the entire sacramentality of the eucharist on grounds wider than the eucharist itself. The early Church, far more than the medieval and even more so than the reformation and post-reformation Church, appreciated the christological and ecclesiological basis of the eucharist, and it is this appreciation, which we have emphasized in the preceding pages, which helps us to understand this new way of considering the eucharist. But before we press this point, let us consider two historical aspects of eucharistic thought which have overly dominated the theological scene: the eucharist as sacrifice and the matter of transubstantiation.

4. SUMMARY

1. In the New Testament and immediately following the New Testament period, we see that eucharistic meals were part of the Christian community celebration. The meal was an integral part of such celebrations.

2. The earliest accounts outside the New Testament relate baptism and the eucharist, e.g., in the *Didache* and in Justin. However, one cannot conclude that the eucharistic meal was celebrated only in conjunction with baptism. It appears that a weekly celebration (on the eighth day) begins to take place.

3. Gradually, the eucharistic part of these meals was separated from the meal itself. Eventually, the meal was dropped completely, and the eucharistic part became liturgized.

4. It would seem that the Jewish word service of the synagogue had some influence on the development of this early non-meal, eucharistic celebration of the Christian community. The extent of such Jewish influence, however, is still a matter of debate.

5. After the development of the catechumenate (c. 150 A.D.) began, the custom gradually arose to see the first part of the eucharistic liturgy, especially during the Lenten and Easter times, focused rather specifically on the catechumens. Much later, this first part of the Mass was called the "Mass of the Catechumens."

6. Belief in the real presence of Jesus was not contested during this early Church period. No heresies arose regarding the eucharist. Belief in the real presence did not involve any theory such as transubstantiation.

7. During the entire patristic period, sacrifical terminology is quite strong as far as interpreting the eucharist is concerned. The connection between the death of Jesus and the eucharist was a part of faith. Nonetheless, the question on sacrifice which the reformers of the sixteenth century posed was not addressed specifically by the early Church.

8. The eucharist, in the early Church, was christological and ecclesiological. A theology of the sacraments had not yet been developed, with the result that the eucharist was imbedded in christology generally.

The connection with the incarnation was especially strong in the Eastern Church.

9. The presence of Jesus in the eucharist, as also in the Church, was a presence of the risen Jesus. There was never a question of a re-performance of the Jesus who lived and died.

10. The community was integral to an understanding of the eucharist during the patristic period. Reception of the eucharist meant that one was a welcome member in the community. In both the East and the West the practice of the *fermentum* exemplified this community relationship.

11. The flow: Jesus-Church-eucharist, provides us today with a solid basis for the contemporary understanding of Jesus as the primordial sacrament, the Church as the basic sacrament and the eucharist as the sacrament of the presence of the risen Lord. Although the specific sacramental terminology was not used by the early Fathers of the Church, nonetheless, their stress on the interconnection of these three indicates to us, today, the validity of this new sacramental approach.

Discussion Questions

1. Read carefully the text from the *Didache*. What are the most important ideas on the eucharist that you find in this early document?
2. Read through the text from St. Justin. What are the most important ideas on the eucharist that you find in this early document?
3. Read through the text from Hippolytus on the eucharist. What are the most important ideas on the eucharist you find in this eucharistic prayer?
4. Why did the meal section of the early eucharist get separated from and eventually dropped from the Christian eucharist?

11

The Eucharistic Question of the Middle Ages and Beyond

Not until the early middle ages was there any controversy regarding the theology of the eucharist, but in the controversies of that time a manner of speaking about the real presence of Jesus in the eucharist was first formulated and then to some degree canonized. This manner of speaking has been called "transubstantiation." Eventually this manner of speaking began to divide the Roman Catholics from the remainder of the Christian world: Orthodox, Anglican, and Protestant. The issue of transubstantiation remains one of the dividing issues as far as the contemporary ecumenical movement is concerned, although much progress in this area has been made.

This chapter is divided as follows. First of all, I want to present a brief overview of the emergence of the term "transubstantiation" and its implications and use in official Roman Catholic documents. Second, I want to indicate what representative Roman Catholic theologians today are saying about the issue of transubstantiation. Third, I want to indicate some specific areas which have caused a change of thinking on the part of many Roman Catholic theologians as regards transubstantiation. Finally, I want to point out how the primordial sacramentality of the humanness of Jesus is the reason why the eucharist is a sacrament.

1. THE EMERGENCE OF THE TERM "TRANSUBSTANTIATION" AND ITS IMPLICATIONS AND USE IN OFFICIAL ROMAN CATHOLIC DOCUMENTS

Numerous and lengthy books have been written on the subject of transubstantiation,[1] and various theories have been proposed by eminent theologians. Indeed, it has been a theme in eucharistic theology for many centuries. In spite of this vast material, however, an explanation of what transubstantiation means is not easy to come by, and it is my hope in the following pages to indicate that transubstantiation is not a self-evident term within Catholic theology.

The idea of transubstantiation first began to appear in the writings of Guitmund of Aversa (d. c. 1095) and Lanfrank of Bec (1010–1089). Although Guitmund did not use the term transubstantiation specifically, his language indicates this kind of thinking; for instance, he writes: "Bread and wine . . . are substantially changed into . . . the flesh and blood of Jesus Christ." He is present "not only in the sign and power of the sacrament, but in the uniqueness of nature and truth of sub stance."[2] Guitmund and Lanfrank laid the foundation for the eventual transubstantiation discussion on the eucharist.

The first usage of the term "transubstantiation" itself can be found about a half century later in the writings of Magister Roland (c. 1150), Stephen of Tournai (c. 1160), and Peter Comestor (c. 1170). The idea of transubstantiation was picked up and developed by all the major scholastics: Alexander of Hales, Albert the Great, Thomas Aquinas, Bonaventure, Scotus. It was because of this use in theology that the Church in official statements began to use the term "transubstantiation."

The first occasion for such *official* usage is in the profession of faith required by Berengar of Tours:

> I, Berengar, believe with my heart and confess with my lips, that the bread and wine, which are placed on the altar, are through the mystery of the sacred prayer and the words of our Savior substantially changed (converti) into the true and proper and life-giving flesh and blood of our Lord Jesus Christ, and after the consecration they are the true body of Christ, which was born of the virgin, and which hung on the cross, an offering for the salvation of the world, and which is seated at the right hand of the Father, and [also] the true blood of Christ, which poured from his side, not only by way

of symbol and by the power of the sacrament, but in the characteristic of nature and the truth of substance.[3]

Berengar, basing himself on Augustine's understanding of sacrament,
had proposed a symbolic interpretation of the real presence of Christ in
the eucharist. The council demanded of him a more realistic interpretation, and, as one notes, utilized terminology similar to Guitmund of
Aversa. It must be remembered that at this early date no clear theory of
transubstantiation had been formulated within Christian theology,[4] and
that the point of the statement is the real presence of Jesus in the eucharist, a presence that is not merely symbolized.

Innocent III in 1202, writing to John of Belesmes, uses the term
transubstantiation for the first time in a papal document. "Others," he
writes, "hold that the water together with the wine is transubstantiated
into the blood [of Christ] . . ."[5] Under this same pope, in 1215, the
Fourth Council of the Lateran was held. Part of the agenda of this council was to condemn the teachings of the Albigenses and the Cathari. As
regards the eucharist, the council declared:

> The universal church of the faithful is truly one, outside of which
> no one at all is saved, and in which Jesus Christ himself is both
> priest and sacrifice, whose body and blood are truly contained in
> the sacrament of the altar under the species of bread and wine, once
> the bread by divine power has been transubstantiated into his body
> and the wine into his blood.[6]

In 1274 at the Second Council of Lyons, held under Pope Gregory
X, a profession of faith was drawn up for Michael Palaeologus, the emperor of the East. This was a reunion council and the West was spelling
out points of belief that the East need accept for any such reunion. As
regards the eucharist, the profession is worded as follows:

> The same Roman church consecrates the sacrament of the eucharist
> from unleavened bread, and she holds and teaches that in this sac-
> rament the bread is truly transubstantiated into his body and the
> wine into his blood.[7]

It is interesting to note that an understanding of the term transubstantiation is taken for granted, and that even the Greek form *metas-
tocheiosin* needs no clarification for the Greek church. Yet it is also

interesting to note that no definition of transubstantiation is given and that it is simply understood. By this time, of course, transubstantiation was a common word within scholastic theology. However, as we shall see later, the imprecision of the term as it appears in official Church statements does present some serious drawbacks.

At the Council of Constance in 1418, the errors of John Wycliffe were condemned. The very first error that the council listed was this: "The material substance of bread and likewise the material substance of wine remain in the sacrament of the altar."[8] In the official documents of the Council of Constance there is no mention of the word transubstantiation, but it is clear that the council fathers were working out of a eucharistic theology that was grounded in the theory of transubstantiation.

In 1438–1445 the Council of Florence drew up another statement to facilitate the reunion of the Latin and Greek Churches. On the matter of the eucharist the following was stated:

> In virtue of these words [the words of institution] the substance of bread is changed (convertuntur) into the body of Christ and the substance of wine into his blood: in such a way that the entire Christ is contained under the species of bread and the entire Christ under the species of wine.[9]

Again, the word transubstantiation does not appear, but the substantialist theology is clear. The same council, in the decree of reunion for the Jacobites, used a clearer expression: "After the aforementioned words of consecration of the body, spoken by a priest with the intention of consecrating, it [the bread] is immediately transubstantiated into the true body of Christ."[10]

The major document is, of course, the statement of the Council of Trent. Some preliminary observations need be made:

a. The Council of Trent again and again made it clear that the intention of the council fathers was not to settle any theological issues between the various theological schools within the Roman Catholic Church. This meant especially the differences between the Dominican and Franciscan theologians, but it also meant at least secondarily differences between Greek theologians, namely those who at that time belonged to an orthodox church which had united itself to the Roman church.

b. A very large proportion of the *periti* who were in attendance at the council were Scotistic or Franciscan in theological bent, and were alert to those sensitive areas where diverse opinion between themselves and the Dominicans lay. Wording of the documents had to be broad enough not to close the door on such diverse opinions.

c. Over and over again the council fathers made it clear that their condemnations were directed to the Protestant reformers, and so the most official statements, the canons, must be read as opposing statements of Luther, Calvin and Zwingli.[11]

Let us, then, first look at the document on the eucharist itself, and then consider what the Council of Trent intended to say.

In the Tridentine decree on the eucharist, we read first of all the brief statement of chapter four, entitled "On Transubstantiation." This is the background for the dogmatic canons on the eucharist. It reads as follows:

> Moreover, since Christ our savior said that what he offered under the species of bread was truly his body [cf. Mt. 26:26ff; Mk. 14:22ff; Lk. 22:19ff; I Cor. 11:24ff], for this reason it has always been held in the church of God and this holy synod now declares it once again: through the consecration of the bread and wine there occurs a change (conversio) of the entire substance of bread into the substance of the body of Christ our Lord, and of the entire substance of wine into the substance of his blood. This conversion (conversio) has been aptly and properly called by the holy Catholic church transubstantiation.[12]

The two canons which address themselves to our topic read as follows:

> If anyone says that in the sacrament of the most holy eucharist the body and blood together with the soul and divinity—and therefore the whole Christ—are not truly, really and substantially contained (contineri) but rather says that he is there only by way of a sign or figure or power, let him be anathema.[13]

> If anyone says that in the most sacred sacrament of the eucharist the substance of bread and wine remains along with the body and blood of our Lord Jesus Christ, and thereby denies that wonderful and singular conversion (conversio) of the entire substance of wine into his blood, while the species of bread and wine alone remain, a con-

version (conversio) indeed which the Catholic church has most suitably called transubstantiation, let him be anathema.[14]

Certainly, the main point in both the chapter and in the two canons is to restate as strongly as possible the real presence of Jesus in the eucharist. With regard to transubstantiation as a term, it should be noted that in all instances where it is mentioned, it is really in a secondary position, namely, in a relative clause. Karl Rahner's remark on the matter is, I think, important: "A genuine debate regarding transubstantiation did not take place at the council. The council considered this teaching as something already definitively established, beyond which one could no longer go."[15] At the most, regarding the use of this term, Bishop Fridericus Nausea mentioned that the word was not very ancient and that it was not used by the Fathers of the Church,[16] a point which was repeated by Peter de Augustinus.[17]

It is Schillebeeckx' view that the main aim of the fathers at Trent was to maintain the unique real presence of Jesus in the eucharist, and that through the use of transubstantiation language. He writes: "This means, in other words, that the Council of Trent was unable to express this unique presence in any other way but on the basis of a transubstantiation. Anyone denying this transubstantiation would at the same time be denying this particular presence, and this was what was at stake in the Catholic faith."[18] We will return to his interpretation later.

Subsequently, other official documents use the term transubstantiation, but always on the basis of the Tridentine statement—for instance, the papal bull *Inunctum nobis* of Pius IV in 1564; similarly the papal constitution *Nuper ad nos* of Benedict XIV in 1743; the condemnation by Pius VI in 1794 of the synod of Pistoia; the responses of the Roman Inquisition, July 7, 1875 and December 14, 1887; the encyclical of Pius XII, *Humani generis;* and finally the encyclical of Paul VI, *Mysterium Fidei,* in which the very infelicitous term "the mystery of transubstantiation" is used.[19] Such are the official statements of the Roman Catholic Church on this matter.

2. TRANSUBSTANTIATION AND CONTEMPORARY ROMAN CATHOLIC THEOLOGIANS

Naturally, when going into detail on the matter of transubstantiation, theologians over the last centuries have taken diverse routes, so that one must say that there are several theologies of transubstantiation, and not just one theology of it. In this chapter, it would take us too far afield to discuss all the opinions of these theologians, but the following areas have been the most controverted:

a. Since both the cessation of the bread/wine-substance and the presence of Christ in the eucharist are the focal points of this doctrine, theologians have been divided as to whether or not God's action is a *single* action (effecting the presence of Jesus in the eucharist) or a *two-fold* action (one action affecting the presence of Christ, another action affecting the cessation of the bread/wine-substance).

b. The second area of dispute concerns the *relationship* between the cessation of the bread/wine-substance on the one hand, and the coming to presence of Jesus in the eucharist, on the other. Some theologians argue for an intrinsic relationship, others for an extrinsic relationship.

Let us consider these two points in some detail, and particularly note the implications which each of them contains.

a. The two-action approach: For the theologians in this camp, properly speaking, transubstantiation is not simply one action of God, but in some way or another a twofold action, since the cessation of the bread/wine-substance is not the same formally as the coming to presence of Jesus in the eucharist. The point which is being made here is that an action of God which simply brings about the cessation of bread/ wine in no way, of itself, and therefore formally, demands that the presence of Christ's body and blood fill in the void. According to Doronzo[20] the following theologians have maintained this view: Scotus, Occham, Biel, and the nominalists and Scotists generally. Moreover, Vasquez, Suarez, Bellarmine, Lessius, Lugo, Pesch, Franzelin and De Augustinus have also defended this view in one way or another. However, when these authors further advance their argument and describe the kind of action which affects the bread/wine-substance, there is a diverse span of opinions: the action of God is described in one of the following ways:

1. an annihilation properly speaking;
2. an annihilation but in a non-proper sense of the term;
3. a productive action;
4. an adductive action.

Beyond this, these theologians disagree as to the *relationship* between the two actions: some say the relationship is merely an extrinsic one (Bellarmine, Lessius, among others), or that the two actions are physically related (for instance, Lugo).

    b. The single-action approach: In this view, God's action brings about the presence of Jesus in the eucharist and the entire substance of bread/wine is converted into the body of Jesus, not, however, in the understanding that one thing is changed into another, e.g., water into wine as at Cana, but in the sense that the wine/bread-substance *is* no more and instead there is now the real presence of the Lord. In such a view, there is a *necessary* relationship between the cessation of the bread/wine-substance and the coming to presence of the Lord in the eucharist.

    This single-action approach is the view of St. Thomas and, following him, almost all Thomistic theologians. In many ways this approach has dominated the manuals of theology and the various catechisms from the end of the nineteenth century and into the first half of the twentieth century. In spite of this popularity, it must be recalled that the single-action approach is, strictly speaking, a theological opinion, and at the Council of Trent, neither the opinion of the Thomists nor that of the Scotists was in any way officially approved. Both were left acceptable and valid ways of Catholic theologizing.

    Even when transubstantiation was being taught in all the seminaries and at the popular level through catechisms, there were some theologians at the end of the nineteenth century who cautiously began to move in a different direction. The number of these theologians, though small, still disturbed the theological equilibrium of that day.

    In 1912 a theologian who is quite traditional, Joseph Piccirelli, wrote a book, *On the Catholic Understanding of the Dogma of Transubstantiation,* and in this book he states:

> However, as regards the formal *terminus a quo,* or the total physical substance of bread and wine, it has indeed been defined that it must not remain, that it must cease: how, nonetheless, it must not remain, how it must cease, so that it can be called "changed" whether through resolution into some underlying matter, whether through annihilation properly so-called, whether through some improper form of annihilation, or through some sort of corruption or

through an intrinsic mutation without the destruction of the substantial reality—none of this was defined by the church.[21]

Again, this same author states what the dogma of the church, in his
view, is as regards the *terminus ad quem* of the change:

> In the profession of faith [at Trent] it is most certainly held that the
> bread and wine are changed into the body and blood of Christ, or
> into that very Christ who is seated at the right hand of the Father,
> and who therefore is at least substantially changed [sic], through the
> power of the conversion, and is placed and is under the species of
> bread and wine.[22]

Furthermore, Piccirelli goes on to say:

> Finally, it is most certain that from the rule of faith an action, truly
> "conversive," must be admitted.[23]

What disturbed Piccirelli the most is the idea, somewhat prevalent in
his lifetime, that transubstantiation is not necessarily connected to the
real presence of Christ in the eucharist. It was his intention to show as
forcefully as possible that there is a clear and necessary connection between these two items.

Let us turn to another theologian, De Aldama, whose writings on
this subject appeared in one of the best of the so-called manuals of theology. De Aldama summarizes his "doctrine of the Church" regarding
transubstantiation in this way:

> a) The body and blood of Christ are so present in the eucharist, that
> the substance of bread and wine does not remain there [i.e., in the
> eucharistic elements];

> b) The substance of bread and wine does not remain therefore be-
> cause it is changed into the body and blood of Christ;

> c) Consequently, the body and blood of Christ begins to be present
> in the eucharist in virtue of a true change, of which the extremes
> [the terms] are on the one hand the bread and wine, and on the other
> the body and blood of Christ:

d) This change (conversio) most suitably is called transubstantiation; undoubtedly because the entire substance of bread and wine becomes the entire substance of the body and blood of Christ;

e) This doctrine is gathered from the truth of the words of institution.[24]

De Aldama summarizes his position in this: the fact of transubstantiation, namely the cessation of the entire substance of bread and wine and its change *(conversio)* into the body and blood of Christ, is *de fide divina catholica definitum*. That the word transubstantiation is most apt and ought to be retained is *doctrina catholica*.[25]

It will be remembered that Schillebeeckx, in his book on the eucharist, as noted above, says that the canons on transubstantiation were drawn up by Trent merely to safeguard the real presence against symbolism and spiritualization.[26] Along this very same line is the thought of Karl Rahner who first of all states that he is not sure that all Catholic theologians will agree with him on what he has to say.[27] Then he makes the distinction between a logical explication and an ontic explication: for him, a logical explication is a statement which states in another way an earlier statement that needed to be clarified. An ontic explication is a statement which expresses some new content other than that expressed in the statement which needed clarification. Utilizing this distinction for the statement of Trent, Rahner clearly says that the Tridentine statement is a logical statement, expressing precisely that which Christ himself said: that which he gave to his disciples is his own flesh and blood and no longer bread and wine. In other words:

$$\text{The statement of Trent} = \frac{\text{This is my body;}}{\text{This is my blood.}}$$

According to Rahner, Trent's statement merely makes clearer and less able to be misunderstood Christ's own statement at the last supper. When one moves into the ''how'' of such a statement regarding Christ's body and blood on the one hand, and bread and wine on the other, one has moved into an ontic statement, utilizing new content beyond that in the original statement of Jesus.

It seems to me that all of these authors see quite clearly the implication that if a person were to define the meaning of transubstantiation in some detail, that very definition would involve a theory of conversion, or a theory of production, or a theory of annihilation, etc., all of which are merely theological positions and therefore can in no way be understood as the "dogmatic teaching of the Catholic Church." Nonetheless, to say simply that what Trent said is only a clearer expression of what Jesus said is totally unsatisfactory. Other content is being employed; otherwise, *substance, conversion* and other such terms would have no meaning. Such terms have meaning of their own, applicable to situations quite distinct from the eucharist. To say that the following statement from Trent is merely a logical statement, i.e., a clarification of Jesus' words *without* adding any new content, seems a denial that words have meaning. Trent's expression is as follows:

> The conversion of the entire substance of bread into his body and the entire substance of wine into his blood, while the species of bread and wine alone remain . . .[28]

Even were we to minimize the Aristotelian overtone of the statement (as Schillebeeckx does), even were we to disassociate ourselves from any philosophical bias, we would still need to discuss at least the common understanding of such words as "substance," "bread," "wine," "species." People use words which have a definite meaning, at least in a general, though not too technical, sense, and the fathers at Trent clearly and deliberately made use of some general theological terms which of themselves have content. Something "more" is being said than simply: This is my body; this is my blood.

Piccirelli's entire endeavor, as he inveighs against his so-called "modern theologians," is to underscore the necessity of an *intrinsic* relationship between the real presence of Jesus in the eucharist on the one hand, and the whole matter of transubstantiation on the other. He maintains that there is a *necessary* connection between the cessation of the substance of bread and wine and the presence of Jesus in the eucharist. The reason for this is clear: if there is no necessary connection between the two, then one can explain the real presence of Jesus in the eucharist *without* the theory of transubstantiation.

It seems to me that one of the major difficulties why certain Catholic theologians, and others as well, recoil at the entrance of transignification, transfinalization, etc., into eucharistic theology lies precisely in this theological view that there is a *necessary, intrinsic* relationship between cessation of the substance of bread and wine and the presence of Jesus in the eucharist. Because the two ideas are intrinsically connected, the rejection of one implies the rejection of the other. Out of such a stance a person cannot readily dialogue about transignification.

I would wish to argue that the definition of Trent does center on a reaffirmation of the real presence of Jesus in the eucharist. The positions of Schillebeeckx and Rahner are valid. But I would also wish to argue that Trent's presentation of the real presence is in and through transubstantiation-theology, which involves new content. This vehicle of presentation is not defined.[29] Just as the Tridentine document utilizes the vehicle of the Latin language to express its dogmatic decisions, but in no way makes the Latin language part of the dogmatic decision (Latin is not defined), so too the dogmatic definition focuses on the real presence, while the theological vehicle to express this is not made part of the definition. The bishops at Trent had to use some language if they were going to draw up a document. The fact that it was Latin is due only to historical processes. Other councils utilized Greek. So, too, council fathers, from Nicaea to Vatican II, have utilized a theological framework out of which their writings have meaning, but the framework used in the early councils, the framework used in the medieval councils, the framework used in Trent, in Vatican I and Vatican II are not part of dogmatic definitions.

C. Vollert, in his article on transubstantiation, makes the following remark: "Although the Church has defined the doctrine of transubstantiation, theologians disagree about its precise nature."[30] Vollert proceeds to describe the various theories, similar to the outline given above. But is it not logical to ask: If the "precise nature" remains unclear, what has really been defined when one says that the "doctrine of transubstantiation" has been defined? Something imprecise? Something unclear?

E. Gutwenger, in his turn, takes issue with Schillebeeckx' view that the Council of Trent wished to affirm nothing more than the real presence. He writes: "Hence, the Council went beyond the real presence to envisage the eucharistic change as such and affirm it directly."[31] Over the centuries, in Catholic theology, including our present century, there has been a continuous wrangling as regards this definition by Trent. All Catholic theologians certainly maintain that the council defined (again) the real presence of Jesus in the eucharist. This is not the issue. Disputed theological positions arise over the issue whether the Council of Trent defined anything more than this real presence, and the reason for the dispute is in the evaluation of the theological vehicle or framework (transubstantiation) out of which the council necessarily for its time had to speak.

This section began with the title "Transubstantiation and Theologians," and hopefully it is clear, even from this brief overview, that there are numerous theological opinions on the precise meaning of transubstantiation, and since these views can only be classified as theological opinions, none of them can be propounded as the teaching of the Catholic Church. This diversity of interpretation on the vehicle of expression has occasioned, to some degree, a newer approach to the sacrament of the eucharist which utilizes a *different* vehicle. The main issue, namely, the real presence of Jesus, is forthrightly maintained, even though a vehicle of expression quite different from that of substance-formulation is used. Let us turn now to this new approach.

3. SPECIFIC AREAS WHICH HAVE CAUSED A CHANGE OF THINKING

By now it is clear that in the period of scholasticism and most significantly in the writings of Thomas Aquinas, Bonaventure and John Duns Scotus, sacramental theology, including that of the eucharist, received a fairly systematic format, and terms such as matter, form, cause, effect, and transubstantiation received acceptability and eventually became quite standard in Roman Catholic thought. In the sixteenth century the Council of Trent overlaid this kind of thinking with a sort of official endorsement. In the centuries following this council, Catholic theology on the eucharist operated generally within this scholastic-Tridentine framework. Neunheuser, in his historical study on the eucharist within Roman Catholic thought from the middle ages to the present, *Eucharistie in Mittelalter und Neuzeit*,[32] surveys the situation from the end of the sixteenth century down to the beginning of the twentieth century in a *single* page. As pioneers of some change he cites the distinguished work of such theologians as L. Billot (d. 1931), M. de la Taille (d. 1933), Odo Casels (d. 1948) and A. Vonier (d. 1938). This indicates that for a good three hundred years no clearly significant change took place within Roman Catholicism regarding eucharistic theology. What work was done in those centuries, important as it might have been, operated totally within the scholastic-Tridentine framework. It must also be said that even the scholars Neunheuser cites did not really approach the eucharist from a position outside of that same framework.

Actually, it was a non-theological area that forced theologians other than those mentioned above to reconsider the Catholic teaching on the eucharist. This non-theological source was *science,* more particularly *physics.* Contemporary physics, with its molecular, atomic and sub-atomic structures, with Heisenberg's theory of quantum mechanics and Einstein's theory of relativity, raised some fundamental questions regarding the meaning of the term "substance." A few Catholic theologians, such as J. Ternus, A. Maltha and F. Unterkircher,[33] addressed themselves to this issue in the years just preceding the Second World War. Not much really developed from this initial consideration. After the Second World War the issue was raised again, particularly in the exchange of articles between F. Selvaggi and C. Colombo. The fundamental issue raised in all this discussion is certainly not trivial, and this issue has two aspects. First of all, there is the question whether or not the theologian is so autonomous in his work that he need not enter into dialogue with contemporary scientific modes of thought. The second question is equally important: Is or is not the presence of Christ in the eucharist related in some way to our physical reality, and if not, then are we free to describe this presence purely within metaphysical or symbolical terms?[34]

The positions which both Selvaggi and Colombo took on this matter might appear to us today as somewhat ridiculous, but they do highlight the division of thinking on the fundamental issues mentioned above. For his part, Selvaggi affirmed the necessity of theologians entering into straightforward dialogue with contemporary science and equally affirmed that the presence of Christ in the eucharist relates to the physical reality of our world in some way or another. However, when he went on further to specify the mode of eucharistic presence, based on these affirmations, he became ridiculous, since he argued that whereas the basic substance within bread or wine consists of thousands of molecular structures, there must correspondingly be the same number of transubstantiations.

Colombo, on his part, took an opposite stand and in his reply to Selvaggi stated that theologians are really dealing with a metaphysical reality quite beyond the parameters of contemporary physics. This position affirms both that the theologian does not have to engage in serious dialogue with contemporary physics, and that the eucharistic presence can be adequately described in purely metaphysical terms. Such a position tends equally to become one-sided and unrealistic.

Of itself, this Selvaggi-Colombo debate, joined into, of course, by other theologians of that day, led nowhere. Nonetheless, the issue that it raised influenced in no small degree a number of other theologians who eventually became associated with the term "transignification."[35]

A second major influence for a change of approach to eucharistic theology within Roman Catholicism is the philosophical movement called *phenomenology*. Phenomenology is more a method and a movement than a system of philosophy, and its primary concern is that of meaning, particularly meaning within a human context. More important than the question of what a thing is in itself, or substantially, is the question of what it means within its relationship to human existence and the way in which we from our human standpoint can unlock this meaning. The question of meaning was posed most strongly by Merleau-Ponty, and the question of interpretation or hermeneutics most pointedly by Ricoeur. This philosophical style, phenomenology, finds its echo in the efforts of some Catholic theologians in their discussions on the eucharist, particularly in their efforts to situate the eucharist not in a physical or ontological framework, but within the framework of human existence.

A third causative factor for a change in eucharistic thinking derives directly from *ecumenical dialogue*. Such dialogue has forced Catholic theologians to be more cautious in the use of terms such as transubstantiation, to be more open to the insights of other traditions, and to rethink the presuppositions out of which one theologizes.[36]

Other causative factors, such as the rise of historical consciousness, the development of theological pluralism, and the confrontation of the Church with the third world, could likewise be enumerated. In fact, all of the causative factors which gave rise to the change of theological thinking within the total gamut of Catholic theology and which was so dramatically highlighted by the Second Vatican Council could be enumerated, but the three instances above undoubtedly played the most significant role as regards Catholic eucharist theology specifically.

4. TRANSUBSTANTIATION AND JESUS AS THE PRIMORDIAL SACRAMENT

One might think that since the eucharist is the sacrament of the body and blood, soul and divinity of Jesus himself, the connection between the primordial sacramentality of the humanness of Jesus and the eucharist is self-evident. The sacrament of the eucharist is the sacrament of the real presence. However, there is indeed more to this relationship than simply the sacrament of the real presence. It is, rather, due to the fact that the humanness of Jesus itself, quite apart from the eucharist, is a sacrament, and at that the primordial sacrament, and it is due to the fact that the church is a basic sacrament that the eucharist itself can even be called a sacrament. It is this line of relationship that must be further unpacked.

The humanness of Jesus is the sacrament of the presence of God. This is the starting point. We do not directly enter into the presence of God, but we do so indirectly, that is, through the incarnate Word. The "inhumanization" of God makes God, sacramentally, present to the world. One could say that the Incarnate Word is essentially *the* real presence. The Christian proclamation in faith that Jesus is Kyrios, God, is a proclamation made in and through the primordial sacrament of Jesus's humanness. Any theological understanding of real presence must begin with this incarnational or christological focus. To speak of the real presence in exclusively eucharistic terms can only be misleading. The real presence of God in Jesus and the real presence of Jesus to his fellow men and women, both in and through his bodiliness while here on earth and in the bodiliness of his risen life, is indeed *the real presence*. All other presences of the Lord derive from this primordial source and find their meaning only through this primordial source.

Secondly, there is a presence, and a real presence, of Jesus in the Church. To deny this is to deny the very meaning of the Church. The Constitution on the Church of Vatican II was entitled "Lumen gentium" (Light of nations), yet the true light is not the Church but Jesus, and the Church is meant to reflect that light, just as the moon reflects its source of all light, the sun. Paul VI, basing his ideas on the Constitution on the Sacred Liturgy, also issued by Vatican II (n. 7), notes: "All of us realize that there is more than one way in which Christ is present in his Church.''[37] He then goes on to enumerate some of these various presences:

> Christ is present in His Church when it prays.
>
> He is present in the Church as it performs works of mercy.
>
> He is present in the Church in its pilgrimage of struggle to reach the harbor of eternal life.
>
> He is present in the Church as it preaches.
>
> He is present in the Church as it governs the people of God.
>
> He is present in His Church as it offers in His name the sacrifice of the Mass.
>
> He is present in the Church as it administers the sacraments.[38]

He then goes on to say: "But there is yet another manner in which Christ is present in His Church, a manner which surpasses all the others; it is His presence in the sacrament of the eucharist."[39] Of all the ways in which Christ is present in the Church the eucharist is indeed the most sublime, but this does not mean that the presence of Jesus in the eucharist surpasses his presence through the incarnation. On the basis of the primordial sacramentality of the humanness of Jesus, the most surpassing presence of Jesus is in and through this very humanness. The incarnational presence, in its own right, far surpasses the presence of the Lord in the sacrament of the eucharist. Secondly, the presence of Jesus to the Church is what entitles the Church itself to be a basic sacrament, and again it was Vatican II that called the Church a sacrament, and the major theologians of our time, in the Roman Catholic Church, highlight the basic or foundational sacramentality of the Church. It is only because the Church, constitutively, is a sacrament that one can speak meaningfully of baptism and eucharist as sacraments, and it is only because Jesus is present to his Church that the Church is a basic sacrament. In other words, the real presence of Jesus in and to the Church is the basis why we can speak of eucharist as sacrament at all. In this sense, the presence of Jesus to his Church is more surpassing than the eucharistic presence. This in no way demeans or disparages the eucharistic mystery; rather, from this new approach to sacramental theology, it provides an even deeper christological centering for eucharistic theology.

It would seem correct to say, on this matter, that if one moves in the direction of the primordial sacramentality of Jesus' humanness and the foundational sacramentality of the Church itself, then readjustments to eucharistic theology have to be made, and of primary importance in this situation is a rethinking of real presence. One cannot have it both ways: an understanding of Jesus as primordial sacrament with the Church as basic sacrament, on the one hand, and on the other, the scholastic understanding of the eucharist as sacrament. Certain ways of speaking about the real presence of Jesus in the eucharist will, of necessity, be modified and changed within this newer framework of sacramental theology.

An effect that this different field of discourse will have on the eucharistic discussions will be to turn the emphasis away from the transubstantiation, transignification, etc., emphasis (although this would not be omitted completely), and to refocus on the more fundamental relationship: the incarnate Lord, the Church, and then, and only then, the eucharist. This stress will indicate that christology fundamentally controls the shape of eucharistic theology, not vice versa. Too often has the understanding of transubstantiation, in Roman Catholic circles, controlled eucharistic theology; this new approach severs such a controlling factor and reestablishes the christological control. Moreover, this stress will emphasize the ecclesiological dimension of the eucharist to an even greater degree than in the scholastic approach, since the real presence of Jesus in the Christian community is seen as constitutive of the real presence of the Lord in the eucharist. The communal aspect of the eucharist is thus strengthened, and the contextualizing of the eucharist in the Christian community and not just in transubstantiated bread and wine is effected.

The most obvious question, of course, arises as regards the distinctiveness of the presence of the Lord in the eucharist. As argued above, Jesus is present, really present, in all the sacraments, not only in the eucharist, and it is the real presence of the Lord in the Church and in each of the sacraments which is the constitutive relationship between the primordial sacramentality of the humanness of Jesus and all other derivative sacraments. From this viewpoint, then, there is no difference between the real presence of Jesus in the Church and in each and all of the sacraments. Were one to counter that the teaching on transubstantiation has generally, if not always, pointed to a special eucharistic presence of the Lord, then one must indicate that, once again, it is transubstantiation that is attempting to control eucharistic theology, and the primordial sacramentality of Jesus' humanness is being left to one side. To say, however, that there is no essential difference between the presence of the Lord in the eucharist and in other sacraments, including the Church, does not in any sense defraud the eucharist of its importance and of its mystery. Indeed, the christological centering of the presence of the Lord in such a primordial way brings us even closer to the heart of all Christian mysteries, the incarnate Jesus himself. The eucharist is not the greatest of all Christian mysteries; it is the incarnation of the Logos which is the greatest of all Christian mysteries.[40]

A move to rethink eucharistic theology in this direction cannot help but have a very salutary ecumenical effect, for it displaces the focus of the argument away from the controverted (even in Roman Catholic circles) transubstantiation theme, and moves it to an area that is far more profound and, in a truer sense of the term, substantial. The eucharist should bring Christians together, and it clearly does this. There is something amiss when the theology about the eucharist drives Christians apart. The *reality* of the eucharist has been and always will be a magnetizing force of union among the Christian community; every *theology of this reality*, then, must reflect this same magnetizing force of unity, if it is to be reckoned a true eucharistic theology. If the larger Christian community has not been able to rally around a teaching, such as transubstantiation, if in our day and age new factors have arisen from physics, from phenomenology, from a contemporary worldview generally which raise serious questions regarding some aspects of some forms of eucharistic thought, then a rethinking is in order. Fortunately, it would seem, the direction of the primordial sacramentality of Jesus' humanness helps us to see the eucharist in ways which remove those obstacles, at least in many ways, for it centers our thinking differently, and our view is thereby somewhat altered. In all, however, the main aspect is retained: the presence of the Lord.

The Lutheran-Catholic dialogues on the eucharist and the various statements from the Anglican/Roman Catholic discussions have indicated a strong consensus on eucharistic theology. The liturgical renewals as found in the *Lutheran Book of Worship* and the *Book of Common Prayer,* and the approved eucharistic prayers of the Roman Catholic Church, were worked out in deliberate mutuality. The history of the eucharist in the Anglican and Lutheran traditions has been researched rather well in contemporary theology, and this historical material provides a genuine context for a more profound understanding of the eucharist within these traditions. The hesitation on the part of Roman Catholic theologians today to avoid a discussion on the ''how'' of the real presence arises in part from the cautions of the Anglican tradition in this matter. Likewise, the elaborate, and at times extreme, paraliturgical celebration involving the eucharist within the Roman Catholic community has been substantially modified, due to the theological and pastoral questioning of both the Anglican and Lutheran communities.[41]

This combined effort on the part of the mainstream churches of the West has enchanced the appreciation of the eucharist and has been one of the major sources of unity, not only marking a unity achieved, which has been considerable, but also acting as a means of unity, so that the oneness of the Lord is visible in the oneness of the eucharistic celebration.

4. SUMMARY ON TRANSUBSTANTIATION

Even though the issue of transubstantiation in Roman Catholic theology is so multi-dimensional, we could summarize the material, at least in a general way, in the following manner:

1. The primary objective of a theology of transubstantiation is to safeguard the real presence of Jesus in the eucharist. This is true from the time of Berengar down to the present. The real presence, not transubstantiation, is the key to the doctrine on the eucharist.

2. Only the Roman Catholic tradition has maintained in some way or another an understanding of transubstantiation. It is not part of the Eastern Churches' approach to the eucharist, nor is it part of the Anglican or Protestant approach to the eucharist. These Churches, however, maintain a belief in the real presence of Jesus in the eucharist without a doctrine of transubstantiation.

3. Until the eleventh century, it should be remembered, the Latin Church itself professed its belief in the real presence of Jesus in the eucharist, without a doctrine of transubstantiation. This indicates that for an entire millennium a doctrine of transubstantiation was not part of a theology of the eucharist in the Roman Church.

4. Official statements, both by individual popes and by councils,

have been very circumspect in this matter. The real presence of the body and blood of Jesus in the eucharist has been solemnly defined. That the word "transubstantiation" should be retained and is most apt is, theologically, only *doctrina catholica*.

5. The position of theologians that there is a *necessary* and *intrinsic* relationship between real presence and transubstantiation is not part of the solemnly defined Catholic faith, but only a theological opinion.

6. Both the ecumenical dialogues of our present times and the eucharistic theology of competent Roman Catholic theologians who suggest alternatives to transubstantiation (transignification, transfinalization, etc.) indicate that the *fact* (in faith) of real presence is the central issue, not the *how* of this real presence.

7. The contemporary theology of the Church as the basic sacrament (Vatican II documents) and of Jesus as the primordial sacrament indicates that the foundation for real presence is not the eucharist, but (a) the real presence of the Logos in the humanness of Jesus and (b) the real presence of Jesus in the Church. Only on the basis of these instances of real presence will the real presence of Jesus in the eucharist make theological sense.

This material on the issue of transubstantiation which arose in the middle ages has been a critical part of eucharistic discussion ever since. It is difficult to treat the Roman Catholic theology of the eucharist without dealing with the issue of transubstantiation. Of itself, the theory does not advance the issue of this volume: namely, the issue of baptism (confirmation) and eucharist as the sacrament of initiation. However, if one could realize that the focal point is the real presence and not the manner in which the real presence comes about and if one could transcend the details of the transubstantiation discussion by moving the entire discourse into the framework of Jesus as the primordial sacrament, then eucharist will be seen much more in its christological and ecclesiological framework and the connection with baptism can be made even more strongly.

However, before we take this further step, another issue arose in the course of history which has traumatized eucharistic discussion. This did not arise specifically in the middle ages, but rather at the time of the reformation and has remained critical down to our own times. Let us consider this issue: the eucharist as "sacrifice."

Discussion Questions

1. Try to write down in one or two sentences what transubstantiation means to you. Where does your answer fit into the theological discussion on transubstantiation?

2. What are the reasons for change in thinking about transubstantiation, and why are these reasons moving theologians to change their approach to transubstantiation?

3. What does "real presence" mean?

4. How is Jesus really present in the Church?

5. How is the incarnation the main source of real presence?

12

The Eucharistic Question of
the Reformation and Beyond

Today we live in an "ecumenical age." This means primarily a time when Western divisions in Christianity have begun to dialogue and seek ways of mutual reconciliation. It is, of course, also a time when the Eastern Church and the Western Church dialogue and seek ways of mutual reconciliation. The division of East and West was not occasioned by a division of the theology of eucharist. The divisions within the West were also not occasioned by a division on the theology of eucharist, but in the West the eucharist became one of the most focal areas for this division. In the West the eucharistic issue revolved around the understanding of sacrifice, with the Roman Church emphasizing the term and reality of the "sacrifice of the Mass." The Reformation Churches shied from such usage.[1]

To say that the theological position on the issue of the sacrifice of the Mass has been one of the major issues is to say the obvious, but it must be remembered that there is an even deeper issue. The Mass, as a sacrifice, is simply one instance of this deeper concern: namely, the concern for the relationship between grace on the one hand, and good works on the other.

From the standpoint of eucharistic theology, any omission of the "sacrifice" issue would be unacceptable. "Sacrifice" has caused some of the most heated and difficult discussion in the ecumenical bilaterals. Unless there comes a meeting of the minds on this issue of "sacrifice" and "eucharist," ecumenical dialogue on this sacrament will never be successful.

We will approach the issue from three aspects. First, we will consider the difficulties which the reformation theologians brought against the term ''sacrifice'' when applied to the eucharist. Second, we will consider the Roman Catholic response to these difficulties. Third, and finally, we will look at the theology of sacrifice and the theology of Jesus as the primordial sacrament as a possible reorientation of the issue.

1. DIFFICULTIES OF THE REFORMATION THEOLOGIANS

Initially, Luther did not have much difficulty with the term ''Mass,'' but as time went by, the term ''Mass'' came to be associated, for Luther, with the phrase: ''the sacrifice of the Mass.'' In Luther's view, this implied a denigration of the sacrifice of the cross. John Calvin, for his part, preferred to use the terms ''the sacred supper'' or the ''Lord's supper.'' The term ''Mass'' became then a ''Catholic'' name and was connected with ''Catholic'' theology on grace and good works.

Calvin's *Institutes of the Christian Religion* leaves the reader quite aware of the ''evil of the Mass.'' In book IV, chapter 18, we find the following sub-titles:[2]

> The Mass as blasphemy against Christ
> The Mass as suppression of Christ's Passion
> The Mass brings forgetfulness of Christ's death
> The Mass robs us of the benefit of Christ's death
> The Mass as nullification of the Lord's Supper
> Private Masses a repudiation of communion
> The Mass not scriptural and not primitive

When one reads carefully each of these sections, one sees that the issue is clearly christological and deals with the value of Jesus' sacrifice. Calvin saw in the theology of the Mass, as propounded by the ''Roman'' theologians of that time, a denigration of Christ.

Luther shared this view. In the *Smalcald articles* he wrote: ''Campeggio would suffer himself to be torn to pieces before he would give up the Mass. So, by God's help, I [Luther] would suffer myself to be burned to ashes before I would allow a celebrant of the Mass and what he does to be considered equal or superior to my Saviour, Jesus Christ.''[3]

The *Church Order of Kurpfalz,* written in 1563, includes the following statement:

> What is the difference between the Supper of the Lord and the papist Mass? The Supper testifies to us that we have full forgiveness of all our sins through the one sacrifice of Jesus Christ, inasmuch as he has offered it once and for all on the cross; and that we are one body with Christ through the Holy Spirit—with Christ who is with his true body in heaven at the right hand of the Father and who is to be adored. But the Mass teaches that the living and the dead do not have forgiveness of their sins through the suffering of Christ; and so Christ is daily offered up for such sins by the Mass-priests. . . . The Mass basically, then, is nothing else than a denial of the one sacrifice and suffering of Christ and a cursed idolization.[4]

In all of the above, and there are many more citations from the reformation theologians, the issue is christological: Was the "sacrifice" of Jesus completely adequate, or was an additional "sacrifice," namely, the sacrifice of the Mass, also required? It seemed to these reformation theologians that the Roman position was a "yes." Besides the sacrifice of Jesus, an additional sacrifice was necessary. It was this which they roundly condemned.

There was no problem with the eucharist as a "sacrifice of praise." Any prayer is a sacrifice of praise *(sacrificium laudis).* The issue focused on the propitiatory sacrifice of Jesus. In the propitiatory sacrifice, a sacrifice which took away sin and reconciled us anew with God, was the sacrifice of Jesus incomplete? Again, the reformation theologians believed that the Roman position was yes: Jesus' propitiatory sacrifice needed to be completed by the propitiatory sacrifice of the Mass. The *grace* of Jesus' sacrifice needed the *good work* of the Mass. This is the crux of the problem.

Looked at from still another angle, we could say it is the question of justification, the central issue, perhaps, both of the reformers and of the Council of Trent. In justification what is the role of God and God's grace, and what is the role of human activity? Again, an application of this twofold aspect is seen in the Mass. In the Mass do we celebrate God's gracious gift of justification, or do we also "do something" which brings about our justification?

Undoubtedly, there were teachers and preachers at the time of the reformation who spoke in a very unhealthy way about the "human" contribution to the propitiatory sacrifice of the Mass. In many instances, the preaching on indulgences gave a clear indication of this heretical view: the earning of indulgences on the part of the faithful brought about the salvation of those who had died, at least to some degree. Since the popes were often behind such indulgences, the impression could easily be given that the official Roman Catholic Church was teaching that the work of Jesus needed to be completed by human work. It was this christological problem which beset the reformers.

Actually, it would be difficult to verify that the official teaching of the Roman Church was precisely what the reformers stated, but the rather common preaching and teaching in this line, at times with ecclesiastical approbation, did present cause for concern. What is important here is to note that the issue of the "sacrifice of the Mass" is not so much eucharistic as it is christological, and the topics from Calvin, enumerated above, are almost all christological and not eucharistic.

2. THE COUNCIL OF TRENT

When the bishops at the Council of Trent took up the issue of justification, of grace and good works, and of the sacrifice of the Mass, not all at once but on different occasions, they realized the gravity of the topics. There were long discussions by the conciliar theologians; there were divisions of opinion between the Franciscan and Dominican schools; there were uncertainties and unclarities in many of the statements which were made both orally and in writing. The story of these deliberations is a long and involved one, which has been documented elsewhere.[5] In the end, after much heated debate, the following theological presentation was developed and solemnly defined.

A. JUSTIFICATION

In the issue of justification the Roman Church at Trent stated again that no one is saved by his or her own merits. Every human being is sinful and stands in need of God's grace. No good work can save him or her from sin and its effects.[6]

First justification comes from the sacrament of baptism, which is seen as a grace or gift of God. There is a preliminary "disposition" or "preparation" (these words were carefully selected since the Dominican and Franciscan schools were at odds on this matter and the council did not intend to favor either of them or condemn either of them). Still this preparatory disposition is also a grace or gift from God. The most important of these antecedent gifts is not one's personal disposition, but God's gracious will to send his own Son, Jesus, to save us from our sinful state. Again, no good work occasioned or caused this merciful will of God on our behalf. Those who respond to Jesus are "called." Moreover, this call is a gift or grace, not a human good work. The response to this call includes: aversion from sin and conversion to the Lord, a movement of one's heart which is due to grace, but is at the same time a human activity. There is no "quietism" here nor denial of human activity. Free will plays a role, but this free will must always be seen as a gift of God, not something "over and against" God.

After this preparatory disposition, there is the acceptance of Jesus through baptism or its *votum* and sin is totally removed. But the removal of sin is not the main part of justification; more important is the superabundance of God's grace which is poured into our hearts. Justification, then, is not simply a "return" to Adam's original state, but it is a sharing in the unexpected grace of the second Adam, Jesus.

In all of this God *alone* is the efficient cause and the glory of God and Christ is the final cause. The initiative is totally God's. The meritorious cause is Jesus, who by his holy passion on the cross merited our justification and made satisfaction for us to God the Father.

Neither Luther nor Calvin would have any problem with the above. It is all God's work, and the role of Jesus is clearly safeguarded. In the next step the instrumental cause is baptism, according to the Council of Trent, restating Roman Catholic faith. Again, neither Luther nor Calvin would have any problem with this, with the exception of a theology of sacraments which would see the sacraments themselves as "good works" making up what is lacking in the work of Christ. The council, however, does not say this. Luther and Calvin both clearly believed in the necessity of baptism; in this they were one with the mainstream of the Christian faith. Only a theology of sacraments which would see the sacramental activity as an instrument or a good work was at issue, and the council in no way says this.[7]

Next, the Council says that the only formal cause is the justice of God. The term "only" *(unica)* was used because of Seripando's "two justice" theory as also in part the Dominican approach of grace as the "formal" cause.

Faith itself is a gift of God, not a human work, and therefore faith is the very beginning of salvation, the foundation and root of all justification. "We may be said to be justified freely, in the sense that nothing that precedes justification, neither faith nor works, merits the grace of justification" (ch. 8).

On this decree, Harnack writes: "The decree on justification, though an artificial product, is in many respects an excellent piece of work; in fact one may doubt whether the Reformation would have developed if this decree had been issued by the Lateran Council, at the opening of the century, and had really passed into the Church's flesh and blood."[8] This is a strong statement, and indicates that the Council of Trent clearly did not place good works ahead of God's grace.

B. THE SACRIFICE OF THE MASS

A further stage in this grace-good work controversy occurred when the issue of the "sacrifice of the Mass" became the topic under discussion at the Council of Trent. From July 19, 1562 until September 5 of that same year, the bishops and the theologians focused on the issue of the sacrifice of the Mass and its relationship to the last supper and above all to the cross of Jesus. After much discussion, the following approach was made:[9]

> This sacrifice [at the last supper] was to re-present the bloody sacrifice which he accomplished on the cross once and for all. (Ch. 1)

> In the divine sacrifice that is offered in the Mass, the same Christ who offered himself once in a bloody manner on the altar of the cross is present and is offered in an unbloody manner. Therefore, the holy council teaches that this sacrifice is truly propitiatory. (Ch. 2)

> For by this oblation [the Mass] the Lord is appeased, he grants grace and the gift of repentance, and he pardons wrongdoings and sins, even grave ones. For it is one and the same victim: he who now makes the offering through the ministry of priests and he who then offered himself on the cross; the only difference is the manner of the offering. The benefits of this oblation (the bloody one, that is) are received in abundance through this unbloody oblation. (Ch. 2)

The Council of Trent reaffirmed the once-and-for-all and therefore complete propitiatory nature of Jesus' "sacrifice" on the cross. This alone should have allayed all the fears of Jean Calvin. None of the arguments which he adduces correspond to this approach of the Council of Trent. In the Mass, we have a ''modal'' difference: the cross is bloody, the Mass is unbloody, but the propitiatory sacrifice is only that of Jesus. The Church, the priest, the Mass itself adds absolutely nothing to this once-and-for-all propitiatory act of Jesus. If one were to say that the Mass added anything, it would simply be a modality, that is, the same sacrifice is not reoffered, but only re-presented, in an unbloody manner.

Betz reminds us, however: ''This interpretation should have been able to refute Luther's protest. Actually, however, the Tridentine clarification came several years too late. It could no longer effect a reversal of the split.''[10] There remained a lingering doubt among the Protestant Churches that the Mass was some sort of ''sacrifice'' in its own right. Private Masses, that is, Masses celebrated by the priest with only a server or with no server at all, continued to be fostered, and stipends were offered for Masses, which were to be celebrated to benefit some specific intention. Theologians, after the reformation, continued to argue about the ''essence'' of a sacrifice and among the Roman Catholics there were many divergent opinions on this matter. The Council of Trent did not really clarify the difference between ''bloody'' and ''unbloody,'' leaving this to theologians. But there was a clear statement that Jesus alone offered a total and perfect propitiatory sacrifice.

3. LATER THEOLOGY ON THE SACRIFICE OF THE MASS

From the writings of the reformers and the documents of the Council of Trent, four hundred years have gone by, and there has been much written on the subject of the ''sacrifice of the Mass.'' The Lima document of the World Council of Churches, using some traditional expressions, carefully remarks:

> The eucharist is the great sacrifice of praise by which the Church speaks on behalf of the whole creation. For the world which God has reconciled is present at every eucharist: in the bread and wine, in the persons of the faithful, and in the prayers they offer for themselves and for all people. Christ unites the faithful with himself and includes their prayers within his own intercession so that the faithful are transfigured and their prayers accepted. This sacrifice of praise is possible only through Christ, with him and in him.[11]

The WCC document uses the term "sacrifice of praise" which was not a cause of difficulty at the time of the reformation. In this understanding of the eucharist as a sacrifice of praise all Christian Churches are, for the most part, in accord.

When it comes to the "propitiatory" sacrifice, the WCC document carefully states:

> The eucharist is the sacrament of the unique sacrifice of Christ, who ever lives to make intercession for us.[12]

In its marginal commentary the same document clarifies this section:

> It is in the light of the significance of the eucharist as intercession that references to the eucharist in Catholic theology as "propitiatory sacrifice" may be understood. The understanding is that there is only one expiation, that of the unique sacrifice of the cross, made actual in the eucharist and presented before the Father in the intercession of Christ and of the Church for all humanity.
>
> In the light of the biblical conception of memorial, all churches might want to review the old controversies about "sacrifice" and deepen their understanding of the reasons why other traditions than their own have either used or rejected this term.[13]

The phrase that the WCC document uses which may prove to be of greatest value is "sacrament of the unique sacrifice of Christ." This bringing together of "sacrifice" and "sacrament" which for several centuries had been kept apart by Roman Catholic theologians is, in my view, the real key to a Protestant-Catholic reconciliation on this matter. To say the least, the issue of sacrifice has been the most controverted issue on the eucharist as far as Protestant-Catholic discussion is concerned.

Ways of moving out of the controverted situation have been diverse. One might, for instance, consider the issue of sacrifice more carefully from an Old Testament perspective, thus contextualizing the sacrifice of Jesus within a Jewish framework. The research of such scholars as R. De Vaux,[14] R. Daly,[15] E. J. Kilmartin,[16] and R. Rendtorff[17] has moved in this direction, providing us with insightful details regarding the milieu in which first of all the life, death and resurrection of Jesus himself was interpreted in the New Testament, and then secondly with a framework in which the eucharist initially, though somewhat cautiously, was likewise interpreted in the New Testament. A different way of moving beyond the controversy has been a restudy of the patristic period and its manifold discussion on sacrifice and eucharist. The name of Johannes Betz[18] stands out eminently in this kind of research, and more recently R. Daly[19] has also combed this field up to the Alexandrian period of Clement and Origen. Once again there is a richness of insight provided by such scholarship, which makes ever more evident the common basis of eucharistic thought for both the later Roman Catholic and the Protestant eucharistic theologies.

I would like to move in a different direction in the following pages, not that what I say runs contradictory to the above orientations or conclusions. Rather, the following must be seen merely as another item which might contribute to the overall resolution of the differences between the Catholic and Protestant discussion. It would seem that the new situation, in which the humanness of Jesus is seen as the primordial sacrament, must necessarily affect not only our eucharistic theology generally, but also the central aspects of such eucharistic theology, of which the issue of sacrifice is one. What, then, might the connection between Jesus as the primordial sacrament and the eucharist as sacrifice be? Methodologically, the researchers into the biblical notion of sacrifice have carefully drawn the Jewish understanding of sacrifice. Old Testament sacrifice, as it is generally described, is fulfilled and perfected in the sacrifice of Jesus. One might reach beyond the Old Testament to the entire milieu of the semitic world, considering sacrifice in non-semitic religions as well, and focusing on those essentials which constitute the very reality of sacrifice. Again, this reality of sacrifice is seen as perfected in the sacrifice of Jesus. Helpful as all this is, it might be equally illuminating to begin with the life, death and resurrection of Jesus as *the* sacrifice, and indeed the *the only* sacrifice. This is particularly important to the Catholic-Protestant controversy in which the issue of expiation is never absent, and in which also, as we have seen in detail, only in Jesus is there expiation of sin. We have but one savior, namely, the Lord himself. It was the question whether the Mass, of itself, could be considered an expiatory sacrifice, minor in importance when compared to the sacrifice of Jesus, indeed, but complementary to and fulfilling of Jesus' sacrifice. Catholic and Protestant teaching came out negatively to this question. Moreover, this expiatory sacrifice of Jesus has been seen throughout Christianity as the sole source of expiation for all men and women, no matter when they lived, no matter which religion, if any, they participated in. "Outside of Jesus there is no salvation" is at the heart of the Christian faith. The expiatory value of all other sacrifices is nil.

When one researches on Jewish, Old Testament understanding of sacrifice, on sacrifice generally within human history, with the theological understanding of the one and only sacrifice of Jesus, then it is not a question of some sacrifice being fulfilled in and perfected by *the* sacrifice of Jesus. This theological understanding of the sacrifice of Jesus emasculates and invalidates any and all apparently competitive sacrifices, as well as any and all preparatory and consequent sacrifices, that is, sacrifice which is preparatory in the Old Testament and Christian sacrifice which is consequent. An understanding of Jesus as *the* sacrifice demands that the very meaning of sacrifice be radically redefined.

It is precisely here that Jesus' humanness as the primordial sacrament offers an extremely helpful approach, since everything else which we have attached the name "sacrifice" to during human history is or at least might be a "sacrament" of that *one* and *only* sacrifice. To some degree Old Testament sacrifice, in all of its manifestations, can be considered revelatory of the sacrifice of Jesus, or can sacramentalize this same sacrifice. Sacraments, as is basically true of all signs and symbols, do two things: they both manifest and camouflage the reality of which they are a sacrament. This allows that some "sacrifices" in the historic past sacramentalize in a very thin way the reality of the one and only sacrifice, while other "sacrifices" of the past sacramentalize that one and only sacrifice in a far richer way.

Our concern, however, is much more with the eucharist, and once more the humanness of Jesus as the primordial sacrament is helpful, since the eucharist is a sacrament of *the* sacrament. It is a derived sacrament. However, since *the* sacrament (Jesus himself) is also in his life, death and risen life *the one* and *only* sacrifice, the eucharist is a sacrament of that sacrifice, and only in and through eucharistic sacramentality can one see anything sacrificial in the eucharist. The very term "the sacrifice of the Mass" requires so much nuancing and explaining, so that the *one* and *only* expiatory sacrifice of Jesus might be maintained in all its rigor; this indicates that that phrase might better be replaced by another phrase, such as the one suggested, namely, a sacrament of the sacrifice of Jesus. Daly concludes his appendix on the eucharist as sacrifice stating: "We have therefore seminally present two later (and from the time of the Reformation) highly controversial developments in eucharistic theology: the idea that the eucharist is a sacrifice which can be offered only by a priest specially ordained for that purpose, and the idea that this sacrifice offered by the priest is a fully real, cultic sacrifice.''[20] Daly finds this in the writings of Hippolytus, as supplanting a notion of Christian sacrifice, i.e., the self-dedication of a Christian to the Lord, either in martyrdom or in day-to-day living. The understanding of the eucharist as a sacrament of *the* sacrament and *the* sacrifice implies that the only priest who offers a sacrifice is Jesus himself in his humanness, and the visible ''priest'' at the eucharistic celebration is rather, and one might say merely, a sacrament of *the one* priest. Moreover, ''the idea that this sacrifice offered by the priest is a fully real cultic sacrifice'' is likewise eliminated since there is only *one* fully real, cultic sacrifice, namely, that of the Lord, and the eucharist is a sacrament of that one sacrifice.

It seems to me that the controversy which has separated Catholic and Protestant for so long over this issue of ''sacrifice'' is basically terminated, were one to accept this kind of sacramentality. One might argue that this is not the line of argumentation found in the Fathers of the Church, either as regards the eucharist, priesthood, or, as alluded to above, the ''sacrifice'' of the Christian life, and the immediate answer to the objection is that the objection is quite true. This approach to sacramentality is startlingly new to our age. The Fathers of the Church, the theologians of scholasticism, the theologians at the time of the reformation, at the Council of Trent, and all during the post-reformation period did not argue from the sacramental primordiality of Jesus' humanness. But if we, today, honestly argue from such sacramental primordiality, then our sacramental theology, and more specifically our eucharistic theology, is indeed going to change and change radically, since the root of eucharistic sacramentality is now established in the humanness of Jesus.

I think it is important to realize today that the theologians and bishops at the Council of Trent maintained precisely what the reformers of the sixteenth century were stating as regards the expiatory sacrifice of Jesus. I think that it is important to realize that in some counter-Reformation Catholic theology this one and only expiatory sacrifice of Jesus was at times compromised by a theology of the ''sacrifice'' of the Church, and to some degree even in the way in which the phrase ''sacrifice of the Mass'' was theologically interpreted. Finally, I believe that a major breakthrough has arisen in our time with the sacramental primordiality of Jesus' humanness, precisely in the way we might theologize today on the very reality of "sacrifice." It is for all of these reasons that I have spent so much time on this theme.

In many ways this approach clearly moves along the same lines as that expressed in the report of an Anglican/Roman Catholic study group:

> In examining the interpretation of biblical data embodied in the traditional teaching of both our Churches, we have seen how the Eucharist has been understood as a "re-presentation" of the one sacrifice of Christ, through the re-enactment of the words and actions of the Upper Room, which make the reconciling work of Christ present and effective for us, and through us for all men. Through the eucharistic mystery celebrated by the Church in the Spirit, the sacrifice of the Cross, achieved "once and for all," is brought to mind in the "memorial" of Christ and thus made *sacramentally* present, so that its saving power may be communicated to us.[21]

4. SUMMARY ON THE EUCHARIST AS SACRIFICE

Not all the issues on the question of sacrifice, and more particularly the sacrifice of the Mass, have been treated in this chapter, but we could summarize the material we considered as follows:

1. The reformers of the sixteenth century took issue with the phrase and the theology which was preached and taught at that time regarding the sacrifice of the Mass. However, the issue of the sacrifice of the Mass was simply one instance of a deeper problem, namely, the question of the relationship between grace and good works.

2. The reformers, on the basis of what they were then hearing from preachers and theologians, complained that the way in which the sacrifice of the Mass was being explained totally undermined the once and for all propitiatory sacrifice of Jesus. The issue was christological not eucharistic.

3. The Council of Trent maintained, officially, that there was only one propitiatory sacrifice, namely, that of Jesus. This teaching was at the heart of the Christian faith.

4. The council also maintained that everything done by men or women, even the disposing or preparatory "good works," were ultimately done because of God's grace.

5. The council maintained that men and women cooperated with God's grace by using their own free will and were not simply passive or of no account. However, because of sin all men and women were totally incapable of doing anything to bring about reconciliation and justification.

6. As far as the Mass is concerned, the council maintained that the one sacrifice of Jesus was offered by himself as priest in a bloody manner on Calvary; this same sacrifice is re-presented in an unbloody manner at the celebration of Mass. The council did not further clarify this bloody/unbloody modality.

7. The issue of the sacrifice of the Mass, however, remained one of the most divisive elements in the eucharistic theologies between Protestant and Catholic for almost four hundred years after the reformation and the Council of Trent.

8. Contemporary restudy of the entire issue as well as the efforts of ecumenical dialogue on the eucharist has pointed out a way in which the issue might be resolved, namely, the Mass is a sacrament of the one sacrifice of Jesus.

9. Jesus as the primordial sacrament furthers this very line of thought since it grounds the sacramentalizing of the eucharist in Jesus' humanness which includes the sacrifice of his life, death and resurrection.

10. The key issue in this matter of the relationship between the sacrificial work of Jesus and the eucharist as "sacrament." The eucharist is a sacrament of the one sacrifice. This says, today, much more and in a much better way, the thrust of the Tridentine formulation: bloody/unbloody.

This chapter has dealt with only one topic which the reformers and the Council of Trent discussed: namely, the relationship of the eucharist to the sacrifice of Jesus. This may seem to be a digression, but if, today, we are going to have some accord on the eucharist ecumenically, the issue of "sacrifice" must be considered.

In many ways, however, this discussion enhances the themes of this book. Trent required the sacrament of baptism or at least its *votum* in the process of justification. This makes baptism the ritual beginning of the process of true justification, and with the eucharist as the sacrament of the one sacrifice of Jesus through which all men and women have been justified, the theological relationship of baptism/eucharist is once again underscored. Such an approach also emphasizes that Jesus is the primordial sacrament, since by his sacrifice he brought about the salvation of the world. In other words, Jesus is the sacrament of God's justifying and saving love. Such a sacrament makes sense because there is a community called Church which responds to this sacramental message and reality of Jesus. In this way the Church is the basic sacrament, and only on this foundation do we celebrate baptism and eucharist.

Discussion Questions

1. What was the main difficulty of the reformers when they opposed the term and the theology of the sacrifice of the Mass?
2. Why is the issue of the sacrifice of the Mass a christological issue and not really a eucharistic issue?
3. What were the main points of the decree of the Council of Trent as regards justification?
4. How does the Council of Trent deal with the question of the sacrifice of the Mass?
5. How does the contemporary expression, a sacrament of the sacrifice of Jesus, help this controversy between Protestant and Catholic?
6. How does the understanding of the primordial sacrament of Jesus' humanity help this controversy?

13

The Eucharist,
An Integral Part of
Christian Initiation

Since the eucharist is such a multi-faceted reality and mystery, one can only approach it in terms of a variety of aspects: from the historical aspect; from the aspect of sacrifice; from the aspect of real presence. We have done this to some degree. Let us now focus on the eucharist as part of the rite of initiation, which is another very important aspect of eucharistic theology.

The current celebration of the liturgy in the Latin rite, as revised by the post Vatican II committee, exhibits a number of contacts with baptism, contacts which have been part and parcel of eucharistic celebration for centuries within the Christian era.

First of all, we call the first part of the Mass the Mass of the Catechumens. This name is still used to some extent, although liturgically it is called the liturgy of the Word. Originally, the Word liturgy did *not* develop from the rite of instructing catechumens; rather, a Word-liturgy was originally borrowed from the Jewish synagogue service and was more or less a time of reflection by the community on the Word of God and a time of instruction on this same Word. Between 100 and 200 we have the rise of the catechumenate and little by little some of the Sunday's liturgies, especially during the Lenten period, were focused on the catechumens. As this practice increased geographically and liturgically, this first part of the liturgy was given the name the "Mass of the Catechumens," and they were not allowed to stay for the "Mass of the Eucharist."

In the Sundays of Lent we still see, in the liturgy, particularly in the choice of the readings, a connection with this practice of instructing the catechumens during this section of the eucharistic celebration.

Secondly, in so many eucharistic celebrations, Sundays and major feasts, the creed is professed. The creeds originate in the various baptismal liturgies of the Church in the first three centuries. These baptismal creeds were part of the prayer formulas of the baptismal ritual, and as we saw above in some of the early baptismal liturgies they were really the "form" of baptism. It was the deacon or presbyter who asked: "Do you believe in God the Father?" etc. and the first immersion took place. Again he asked: "Do you believe in Jesus Christ?" etc. and the second immersion took place. Finally, he said: "Do you believe in the Holy Spirit?" etc. and the last immersion took place. Our profession of these creeds today in the eucharistic liturgy is an indication of the connection between baptism and eucharist.

Again, we have the "Prayers of the Faithful." These are really the prayers of the baptized, and they are meant as such. The baptized community gathers together and shares its hopes and needs with one another and with the Lord.

At times the beginning of the eucharistic liturgy takes place with the "asperges" or "sprinkling rite." From the prayers which are said, the connection with baptism is quite evident. This symbolic connection through the use of water is likewise seen in the presence of the holy water fonts at the doors of the churches.

The kiss of peace has baptismal overtones, since in the early church as we saw above this was generally reserved for the baptized and not given to the catechumens.

At the reception of the eucharist we have that beautiful passage from the gospel of John: "Behold the Lamb of God," etc. which is taken from the baptismal chapter of that gospel, with John the Baptist proclaiming the true Baptist, Jesus, who baptizes in water and the Spirit.

Other less obvious connections between baptism and eucharist are to be found in the eucharistic prayers. The point of all this is to show that (a) there is a close relationship between baptism and eucharist and that (b) this relationship has developed over the centuries because the eucharist was connected to the ritual of baptism as part of the rite of initiation. In the historical material on baptism, we saw the rather long list of early rituals which joined baptism and eucharist. We also spoke of the Eastern Churches' practice down to the present day of uniting baptism and eucharist. We referred to the RCIA and its flow of baptism-confirmation-eucharist. All these liturgical indications underscore the notion that the entire flow of these sacramental rituals has been the ''rite of initiation'' and not simply a baptismal ritual alone.

Theologically, however, there are also telling indications of this inter-involvement. We speak of baptism as an initiation. Krister Stendahl, in the Lutheran/Catholic dialogue on baptism, notes as we saw:

> I would take my point of departure in the fact that baptism in the NT and in the early church is always an act of *initiation,* and that this in fact should be the point of departure. Such an act is capable of many interpretations, but the force of initiation is primary. One cannot understand baptism by combining the elements of purification, with the elements of death/resurrection, with the elements of receiving the Spirit, with the incorporation in the Body of Christ, etc. One must begin with the fact that in all cases the practice of baptism is the rite by which initiation takes place.[1]

Undoubtedly, what Stendahl says is deserving of our consideration even though we might wish to enlarge upon his thought and therefore modify it in some degree.

Stendahl, for instance, does not make use of the contemporary approach that Jesus, in his humanity, is *the primordial sacrament.* Nor does he consider the Church itself as a basic sacrament. Were he to do so, then it would not be baptism itself which would be the point of departure for *initiation;* rather, it would be Jesus himself and secondly the Church. Jesus is *the sacrament of initiation.* The Church is in a subsequent and derivative way *the second sacrament of initiation.* Only on the basis of these two primordial, basic and fundamental sacraments would one turn to the sacrament of baptism. This would be the first modification one might make in Stendahl's position, and it is clearly a very substantial modification.

Secondly, one cannot simply say ''initiation'' and not further delineate what is meant by ''initiation.'' The first question which comes to mind when one hears the term ''initiation'' is: Initiation into what? The *into what* is of major importance here, since without it there is no clear understanding of the ''force of initiation'' or the meaning of the ''rite of initiation.''

From a study of the history of baptism, we see quite clearly that there was an "initiation" into the Jesus community (at first, when separation from the Jewish religious world was not that clear) and into the Christian community, when Christianity appeared to be a separate religious movement in the world. The Christians welcomed someone into their community and all that was theirs as a Christian community was now shared with these newly baptized.

Since it was the eucharistic celebration that centered the community in a liturgical way, the newly baptized were immediately brought to the eucharistic table and there with their new brothers and sisters shared the table of the Lord. The Christian community did not simply share with these newly baptized some tangential aspects of the Christian life. Rather, they indicated that all that they had, spiritually, was held in common. There was not another stage of initiation into an inner circle of eucharistic members.

If Stendahl is correct in connecting the baptismal rite with the notion of initiation, and in many respects he is correct in this, then the conclusion can only be that the newly baptized are welcome to eucharistic fellowship, since this is so central a part of that *to which* they have been initiated.

In the ecumenical world of today, the Roman Catholic Church has made some major strides in this matter. In the case of the Eastern Churches, the Roman Catholic Church has declared a sort of open *communicatio in sacris*, providing there is sufficient need. This includes the Latins receiving from the Orthodox and the welcome of the Orthodox to the Latin eucharist.[2]

In the case of the Protestant Churches, there are indeed times when the Protestant, who believes in the real presence and has need for eucharistic fellowship and who cannot under the circumstances receive from his or her own minister, may receive from the Catholic eucharistic table. The fundamental reason for this eucharistic hospitality is the mutual acceptance of baptism. Through baptism, one is accepted by the Lord and one comes to believe in and accept the Lord as one's savior.[3]

As is well known, the mutual acceptance of baptism by the various Christian churches is still an ongoing process. The Lima Document indicates that the issue of infant baptism remains a very difficult question between some of the Christian Churches. On the other hand, the Lima Document indicates a wide consensus on the matter of baptism by large areas of the Christian community.

Somewhere along the line, in the ecumenical discussion, the distinction between "sign of unity attained" and "sign of unity or a means of unity still to be attained" was formulated as regards ecumenical eucharist. The distinction has been employed at very high level ecumenical discussion on the issue of intercommunion between various Christian Churches. It is certainly not important to find out exactly when and where this distinction was first made and thereby first entered into the theological discussion. Rather, one should note that it is theologically more problematical than helpful, precisely in the relationship of baptism and eucharist.

The distinction indicates that one, through baptism, might not be fully "initiated" into the Christian community, and accordingly that baptism is not really the rite of Christian initiation, but rather a preliminary stage along the process, much like the scrutinies in the RCIA. Baptism might admit one to the vestibule, but not really into the house of God. There is still another initiation which the distinction does not identify in which one attains the unity of faith. Only with this second initiation (whatever it might be) is one able to enter into eucharistic fellowship. But if this is so, then Protestants should not be allowed under any circumstances to receive the eucharist at a Roman Catholic service. Such a total ban is not the present practice of the Roman Catholic Church, and a Protestant can receive who meets the requirements noted above, namely, (1) baptism, which is understood and not mentioned except in the case of the term "Protestant;" (2) belief in the real presence of Jesus in the eucharist, and this does not mean acceptance of transubstantiation; (3) a need to receive the eucharist, and this is not to be understood as "viaticum" or a near death situation; (4) a freely made request for eucharist; and (5) the inability to go to one's own minister under the circumstances. Given these conditions, the local ordinary can allow a Protestant to receive at the Roman Catholic liturgy. Evidently, if the above distinction holds any validity, this is adequate for "unity of faith attained." What is of interest to theologians are the issues not mentioned. The Protestant does not have to accept the pope as pope; he or she does not have to accept seven sacraments; he or she does not have to accept the authority of the Roman Catholic magisterium; and the list could go on.

Evidently, if the above distinction between the eucharist as a sign of "unity achieved" and "unity to be attained" would be taken seriously, Protestants meeting the above criteria, according to current Roman Catholic policy, have indeed reached "unity achieved" status. If that is true, then one must concede that the majority of mainstream Protestants, as far as Catholic policy is concerned, do indeed have "an attained unity of faith." A further interest to theologians are those faith areas which are not required of Protestants to receive the eucharist in the Roman Catholic Church, e.g., acceptance of papal supremacy.

One might say: But there has to be a belief in the real presence of Jesus in the eucharist. However, if one clearly understands baptism as part of the baptism-eucharist axis, then the acceptance of baptism in the Christian Church is already the acceptance of faith in the eucharist, since the two are essentially tied together, in history and in theology and in liturgy. There is no intermediate step between baptism and eucharist which marks "faith attained" and is another "initiation" toward eucharistic fellowship.

In the Roman Catholic Church today there is indeed a regulation that Protestants cannot indiscriminately receive from the Catholic eucharist; there is not "open eucharist" on the part of the Roman Catholic Church. Theological reasons for this are difficult to sustain if mutual acceptance of baptism is acknowledged. One can only say that it is an issue of Church law, but not of theological prohibition. Many Church laws are in effect which govern all churches, and were these laws to be altered, one's theology would not have to change. In other words, Church law and theology are not co-terminous, although there are of course many areas in which the two do overlap. In this matter of eucharistic exclusion, theology and law, it seems, do not overlap.

The interrelationship between baptism-eucharist has not only the flow of first baptism and then eucharist, so that the water-bath "flows" into the eucharistic fellowship. There is as well a retrospective aspect: eucharist-baptism, in the sense that with each eucharist we reaffirm our baptism and all that it implies. In many ways this is why one says that we believe "in baptism for the remission of sins," on the one hand, and, on the other, that the sacrament of the eucharist is *the* sacrament of reconciliation or remission of sins. Baptism is the sacrament of faith and yet at the eucharist we celebrate the "mystery of faith." Baptism gives us the Spirit of Jesus whereby we cry out "Abba! Father." The eucharist is the sacrament of his real presence, which is a presence in the Spirit of Jesus. The eucharist flows back into baptism.

The Christian rite of initiation is baptism-(confirmation)-eucharist. Such a sacramental process is based on the Church as a fundamental sacrament, since the Church is the community of baptized in which Jesus is really present both as "substantially present" and as "propitiatory sacrifice." Yet the Church itself is only such a sacrament of Jesus because Jesus, in his humanity, is the primordial sacrament. The theology of both baptism and eucharist is intimately conjoined to ecclesiology and even more fundamentally to christology. Indeed, we cannot speak of the baptism-confirmation-eucharist process as the Christian sacrament of initiation, unless the Church itself was fundamentally a sacrament of initiation, and even more basically were it not that Jesus is *the* sacrament of initiation, and entry into the life of Jesus is *the* process of initiation.

Furthermore, this insight into the baptism-eucharist rite of initiation raises questions regarding the "flow" of the other sacraments. It indicates that *age* cannot be the dominant factor in determining the "time" of confirmation. It indicates that first reception of the sacrament of reconciliation fits poorly into the separation of baptism and eucharist. How often does one find a discussion on first reconciliation, without really discussing all the issues involved in the baptism-eucharist relationship. How often does one discuss the "time" of confirmation, without including the issues of the baptism-eucharist interrelationship.

As regards the sacraments, we are indeed in a very favorable position today: we know more than any of our predecessors ever dreamed of the early history of these sacraments. Our horizons as regards the development of sacramental theology and the development of liturgy are broader and more comprehensive than all those which preceded it. Secondly, we have the theological understanding of Jesus as the primordial sacrament and the Church as a basic sacrament. Never before was a sacramental theology developed from such a basis. This, too, helps us see the sacraments in a richer and more profound way than a "two-sacrament" or a "seven-sacrament" theology. There is, today, a more intimate ecclesiological and christological base for our sacramental thought and our sacramental liturgy.

One cannot simply dismiss these two points in any summary way, since those who were enjoined to revise the sacramental rituals in the Roman Catholic Church after the Second Vatican Council both knew of these vistas and brought them to bear on the formulation of the new rituals. In other words, the new rituals clearly bespeak a profound understanding of history as regards sacramental theology and liturgy and bespeak a deep appreciation of Jesus as primordial sacrament and the Church as a fundamental sacrament.

It is precisely the reaffirmation of these two aspects which has given rise today in our Roman Catholic Church to a greater appreciation of the sacrament of initiation, which is primordially found in Christ, secondarily in the Church itself, and ritually in the connection of baptism-eucharist as *the ritual sacrament of ecclesial initiation.*

Notes

Introduction

1. World Council of Churches, *Baptism, Eucharist and Ministry,* Geneva: WCC, 1983. Cf. also Bryan D. Spinks, "Vivid Signs of the Gift of the Spirit? The Lima Text on Baptism and Some Recent English Language Baptismal Liturgies," *Worship,* v. 60, n. 3, May 1986, pp. 232–246.

2. Cf. Empie, Paul C. and Murphy, T. Austin, eds. *Lutherans and Catholics in Dialogue,* vols. I–VII, Minneapolis: Augsburg Publishing House, 1965–1985.

3. Bibliography dealing with a contemporary understanding of sacraments is currently quite extensive. No listings of these general works are included in this present volume. Bibliographical data will be limited to the three sacraments under consideration.

1. Holy Baptism: The Teaching of the Roman Catholic Church

1. Cf. John E. Steely, "The Lord's Supper: Theory and Practice among Baptists," *Southwestern Journal of Theology,* vol. 28, n. 2, 1986 (a volume dedicated to Roman Catholic/Southern Baptist Dialogue on the topic of Grace, 1982–1984), p. 91:
"Nomenclature can be misleading in this case as well as elsewhere, but a brief word about the names employed for this solemn rite of Christian believers will be helpful at this point. Baptists prefer, for a variety of reasons, not to speak of *sacraments* but rather of *ordinances,* of which there are only two, baptism and the Lord's Supper. The view generally prevailing among Baptists (though not universally held) is that the word 'sacrament' carries with it the idea of an automatic bestowal of grace—*ex opere operato*—or even a

234

sort of magical operation upon the recipient, apart from and independent of that person's will or intention. It may be fair to say that a Baptist invests the word 'sacrament' with more meaning than does a Catholic—but rejects it precisely because of that content!

"The word 'ordinance' on the other hand is understood to place the emphasis upon the Lord's commandment; it is something that Christ has ordained for his people. This is the term used not only for the Lord's Supper but for baptism as well. In both cases the word 'ordinance' intends two emphases: first, that it is something commanded by the Lord, and second, that in the performance of either of these there is a clear *intention of obedience* on the part of the church and of the individual."

In this passage we see that a Baptist professor of Historical Theology corroborates what is mentioned in the text.

2. Cf. *Baptism, Eucharist and Ministry,* pp. 2–7.

3. Cf. *Lumen Gentium* (Nov. 21, 1964) n. 1, n. 9, n. 48; *Gaudium et Spes* (Dec. 7, 1965) n. 45; equivalently, *Sacrosanctum Concilium* (Dec. 4, 1963) n. 2.

4. Cf. K. Rahner, *Kirche und Sakramente* (Freiburg i. Br.: Herder, 1961); E. Schillebeeckx, O.P., *Christ the Sacrament of the Encounter with God,* trans. Cornelius Ernst, O.P. (N.Y.: Sheed and Ward, 1963) pp. 13 ff.; Raphael Schulte, "Die Einzelsakramente als Ausgliederung des Wurzelsakraments," *Mysterium Salutis,* vol. 4/2 ed. J. Feiner and M. Loehrer (Einsiedeln: Benziger, 1973) pp. 46–155.

5. L. Lercher, *Institutiones Theologicae Dogmaticae,* vol. IV/2 (Innsbruck: Felicianus Rauch, 1948) pp. 113–114.

6. Francisco a.P. Solá, S.J., "De Sacramentis initiationis christianae," *Sacrae Theologiae Summa,* Biblioteca de Autores Cristianos (Madrid: La Editorial Católica, 1962) p. 128.

7. Ibid. pp. 132–138.

8. Cf. Jean Galot, *La Nature du charactère sacramentel: étude théologique médiévale,* 2nd ed. (Paris: Desclée de Brouwer, 1958).

9. Cf. J.N.D. Kelly, *Early Christian Creeds* (London: Adam & Charles Black, 1960) 2nd ed.

10. Cf. William A. Van Roo, S.J., "Infants Dying Without Baptism: A Survey of Recent Literature and Determination of the State of the Question," *Gregorianum,* vol. 35, 1954, pp. 406–473. Van Roo treats the views of Heris, Mulders, Boudes and Laurence, and then presents his own understanding of the state of the question at that time.

11. Cf. Brian O. McDermott, S.J., "The Theology of Original Sin: Recent Developments," *Theological Studies,* 1977, vol 38, pp. 478–512. This is only one of several such surveys, which McDermott alludes to in this article.

12. The translation is taken from *The Church Teaches: Documents of the Church in English Translation,* translated and prepared by J. F. Clarkson, S.J., et al. (St. Louis: B. Herder Book Co., 1955). This volume, as also a similar volume *The Teaching of the Catholic Church,* edited by Karl Rahner, S.J., transl. by Geoffrey Stevens (Cork: The Mercier Press, 1967), also *Enchiridion Symbolorum, Definitionum, Declarationum de Rebus Fidei et Morum,* edited by Denzinger et al. (Freiburg i. Br.: Herder, 1963) 32nd ed.—all of these volumes contain much more than the solemn teaching of the Roman Catholic Church. The latest Denzinger edition, the "Index Systematicus Rerum," attempts to give some sort of gradated value to the material gathered together. The other two volumes make no such effort.

13. Lercher in his manual of theology organizes the material on baptism around five theses and eight assertions. In all of this the author presents the following points as the solemn teaching of the Roman Catholic Church:

a. Baptism is a sacrament;
b. Baptism gives grace (the issues of validity and efficacy);
c. Baptism involves the use of water;
d. Baptism involves the trinitarian formula;
e. Baptism imprints a character;
f. Baptism is necessary for all (the issue of salvation).

All other topics are the common opinion of the theologians at the time of his writing. What this indicates, and Lercher is simply one case of this kind of theological writing, is that Catholic theologians do not simply repeat the statements of the Council of Trent verbatim; rather they organize the material in such a way that solemn teachings of the Church are distinguished from the theological opinions of scholars. The arrangements which I have made follow this pattern, but I have tried to state clearly what the "main issue" or "what was at stake" is all about.

2. Holy Baptism and the New Testament

1. A. Kavanagh, *The Shape of Baptism: The Rite of Christian Initiation* (New York: Pueblo, 1978) p. 25.
2. Cf. J. A. Fitzmyer, S.J., *The Gospel According to Luke* (I-IX) Anchor Bible Series (Garden City, N.Y.: Doubleday & Co, 1981) pp. 480–487.
3. Ibid. p. 481.
4. R. Brown, S.S., *The Gospel According to John,* Anchor Bible Series (Garden City, N.Y.: Doubleday, 1966) pp. 46ff.
5. Fitzmyer, op. cit., p. 482.
6. R. Brown, "The Johannine Sacramentary," *New Testament Essays* (Milwaukee: Bruce, 1965) pp. 64–66.
7. Ibid., p. 76.

8. Cf. E. Haenchen, *Die Apostelgeschichte* (Göttingen: Vandenhoeck & Ruprecht, 1965) pp. 244 ff., 314 ff.; W. Meeks, *The First Urban Christians* (New Haven, Conn.: Yale Univ. Press, 1983).

9. Feine-Behm-Kümmel, *Einleitung in das Neue Testament (Heidelberg: Quelle & Meyer, 1965) 14th ed.*

10. J. Jeremias, *Infant Baptism in the First Four Centuries,* trans. D. Cairns (London: SCM Press, 1960), p. 32. It should be noted that Jeremias is deliberately making a case for the connection between Jewish proselyte baptism and Christian baptism. His views as well as those of W. F. Flemington, *The New Testament Doctrine of Baptism* (London: S.P.C.K., 1957), have not gone unchallenged; nonetheless, there is a strong possibility that some connection between these two practices does exist.

11. J. Fitzmyer, *Pauline Theology* (Englewood Cliffs: Prentice-Hall, 1967) p. 66.

12. J. Fitzmyer, "The First Epistle of Peter," *Jerome Bibilical Commentary* (Englewood Cliffs: Prentice-Hall, 1968) p. 363.

13. Jeremias, op. cit., pp. 24–42; cf. also Reginald Fuller, "Christian Initiation in the New Testament," *Made Not Born* (Notre Dame: University of Notre Dame Press, 1976) pp. 7–31; W. D. Davies, *Paul and Rabbinic Judaism* (London: S.P.C.K., 1965) pp. 121ff.

14. Jeremias, op. cit.

15. Raphael Schulte, "Die Umkehr (metanoia) als Anfang und Form Christlichen Lebens," *Mysterium Salutis* (Zurich: Benziger, 1976) v. 5, pp. 136–137.

16. Rudolph Schnackenburg, "Baptism," *Sacramentum Verbi,* ed. J. Bauer (New York: Herder and Herder, 1970) vol. I, pp. 57ff. An older work by this same author remains valuable, *Baptism in the Thought of St. Paul,* trans. G. R. Beasley-Murray (Oxford: Basil Blackwell, 1964).

17. Fitzmyer, *The Gospel According to Luke,* p. 239.

18. K. Aland, *Did the Early Church Baptize Infants?* trans. G. R. Beasley-Murray (Philadelphia: Westminster, 1963); M. Barth, *Die Taufe—ein Sakrament?* (Zolikon-Zurich: Evangelischer Verlag, 1951); O. Cullmann, *Baptism in the New Testament,* trans. J. K. S. Reid (London: SCM Press, 1950); J. Jeremias, *The Origin of Infant Baptism,* trans. Dorothea M. Barton (London: SCM Press, 1963); Jeremias, *Infant Baptism in the First Four Centuries,* trans. D. Cairns (London: SCM Press, 1960).

19. R. Brown, "One Baptism for the Remission of Sins—New Testament Roots," *Lutherans and Catholics in Dialogue,* vol. II, ed. C. Empie and William W. Baum (Washington: NCWC, 1966) p. 15.

20. R. Schnackenburg, *Das Johannesevangelium,* (Freiburg: Herder, 1965) p. 383.

21. Brown, "One Baptism for the Remission of Sins," p. 20.

22. B. Neunheuser, *Baptism and Confirmation,* trans. J. J. Hughes (New York: Herder and Herder, 1964), offers a good and fairly detailed overview of this history. In the next chapter we will consider later scholars who have refined Neunheuser's work. Bibliographical data can be found there.

23. Kavanagh, op. cit.; cf. especially his bibliography on pp. 205–215.

3. Holy Baptism and the Early Church

1. Cf. B. Neunheuser, *Baptism and Confirmation;* R. Schulte, "Die Umkehr (Metanoia) als Anfang und Form christlichen Lebens," *loc cit.;* T. A. Marsh, *Gift of Community: Baptism and Confirmation* (Wilmington, Del.: Michael Glazier, 1984); E. C. Whitaker, *Documents of the Baptismal Liturgy* (London: SPCK, 1970); A. Kavanagh, *The Shape of Baptism: The Rite of Christian Initiation, ibid, Made Not Born* (Notre Dame: University of Notre Dame Press, 1976).

2. Translation is from J. Quasten, *Patrology,* vol. 1 (Westminster, Md.: Newman Press, 1951) p. 31.

3. Translation is from Quasten, *op. cit.,* p. 214.

4. Translation is from B. S. Easton, *The Apostolic Tradition of Hippolytus* (N.Y.: The Macmillan Co., 1934) pp. 42–48.

5. Translation is from E. C. Whitaker, *op cit.,* p. 68.

6. Translation is from L. McCauley and A. Stephenson, *The Works of Saint Cyril of Jerusalem,* v. 2 (Washington, D.C., The Catholic University of America Press, 1970) pp. 153–172 *passim.*

7. St. Bonaventure, *Sent.* IV, d. 3, p. 1, a. 1, q. 3.

8. St. Thomas Aquinas, *Sent.* IV, d. 6, q. 1, a. 3, sol. 2 and 3.

9. Cf. Neunheuser, *op. cit.,* pp. 206ff. for a discussion of the scholastic approach to baptism as remedial.

10. St. Bonaventure, *Sent.* IV, d. 3, p. 1, a. 1, q. 3.

4. Holy Baptism and Contemporary Theology

1. Cf. *Presbyterorum Ordines,* n. 2.

2. Cf. *Ordo paenitentiae,* "Praenotanda," nn. 1–6.

3. Cf. R. Bultmann, *The Gospel of John: A Commentary,* trans. G. R. Beasley-Murray, et al. (Philadelphia: Westminster, 1971) pp. 32ff.

4. C. Schütz, "Die Mysterien des "öffentlichen Lebens und Wirkens Jesu," *Mysterium Salutis,* v. 3/2, p. 61.

5. K. Osborne, *New Being* (The Hague: Mirtinus Nijhoff, 1969) p. 100.

6. Ibid., p. 101.

7. This union developed slowly, from a theological standpoint: first there seems to have been a Spirit-christology and then the form which we find

in Chalcedonian christology. Cf. the lengthy history on this in A. Grillmeier, *Christ in Christian Tradition,* trans. J. Bowden (Atlanta: John Knox Press, 1975).

8. C. Schutz, "Die Mysterien," p. 62. In all of this section, Schutz focuses on the humanity of Jesus.

9. D. Wiederkehr, "Entwurf einer systematischen Christologie," *Mysterium Salutis,* v. 3/1, p. 532.

10. *Baptism, Eucharist and Ministry,* nn. 2–7.

11. Schulte, "Die Umkehr," p. 179.

12. N. Mitchell, "Dissolution of the Rite of Christian Initiation," *Made Not Born,* p. 54.

13. K. Stendahl, "The Focal Point of the New Testament Baptismal Teachings," *One Baptism for the Remission of Sins,* p. 24.

14. Schulte, op. cit., p. 157.

15. P. Fransen, "Das Neue Sein des Menschen," *Mysterium Salutis,* v. 4/2, p. 922.

16. K. Stofft, "An Ecumenical Agenda for the Future," *Ecumenical Trends* 7 (1978) p. 3.

17. M. J. Hatchett, *Commentary on the American Prayer Book* (New York: Seabury Press, 1981) pp. 260ff.

18. *The Book of Common Prayer* (New York: Seabury Press, 1979) p. 298.

19. Philip H. Pfatteicher and Carlos R. Messerli, *Manual on the Liturgy: Liturgy Book of Worship* (Minneapolis: Augsburg, 1979) pp. 167ff. Cf. also *Lutheran Book of Worship* (Minneapolis: Augsburg, 1979) pp. 121ff.

20. *Manual on the Liturgy,* p. 198. Cf. also K. Watkins, "Baptism and Christian Identity: A Presbyterian Approach," *Worship* v. 60 n. 1, 1986, pp. 55–63.

5. The New Ritual of Baptism and Jesus

1. *The Rites* (New York: Pueblo Publishing Co., 1972) pp. 13–181.

2. *Rite of Receiving Baptized Christians into the Full Communion of the Catholic Church* (Washington D.C.: USCC, 1983) no. 895.

3. J. Dunning, *New Wine, New Wineskins* (New York: William H. Sadlier, 1981) pp. 20ff.

6. Confirmation and the Teaching of the Church

1. Solá, op. cit., p. 191.

2. Translation is from *The Church Teaches,* p. 274.

3. It may be of interest to note that in the manual of Lercher, the material is arranged into five theses and five assertions. In all of this arrangement,

Lercher states that only the following are the solemn teachings of the Church *(de fide definita catholica):*

a. Confirmation is a sacrament;
b. Confirmation imprints a character;
c. Confirmation gives grace;
d. Confirmation is given only to those baptized *(doctrina catholica).*

All other issues are the common theological opinions, prevalent at the time of his writing. Again, this indicates that theologians simply do not repeat the statements of the Council of Trent verbatim, but organize them and indicate which are the solemn teaching of the Church.

7. Confirmation and Its Historical and Theological Considerations

1. W. Bausch, *A New Look at the Sacraments* (Notre Dame: Fides, 1977) p. 91.

2. L. Ligier, S.J., *La Confirmacion: Sense conjoncture oecumenique hier* (Paris: Beauchesne, 1973) p. 208.

3. Cf. S. Regli, "Firmsakrament und christliche Entfaltung" *Mysterium Salutis,* v. 5, pp. 318–319; H. Küng, *Was ist Firmung?* (Einsiedeln: Benziger, 1976), pp. 30 ff.; ibid., "Die Firmung als Vollendung der Taufe," *Theologische Quartalschrift,* v. 154 (1974) pp. 26–47.

4. Regli, op. cit. p. 312.

5. Neunheuser, op. cit., p. 232.

6. Ibid. p. 233.

7. A. Benning, *Gabe des Geistes: Zur Theologie und Katechese des Firmsakraments* (Kevalaer: Butzen & Brecker, 1972) p. 22.

8. Regli, op. cit., pp. 304–305.

9. Cf. D. Gregory Dix, *The Theology of Confirmation in Relation to Baptism* (London: Dacre Press, 1946); George T. Montague, *The Spirit and His Gifts: The Biblical Background of Spirit-Baptism, Tongue-Speaking and Prophecy* (New York: Paulist Press, 1974); L. S. Thornton, *Confirmation: Its Place in the Baptismal Ministry* (Westminster: Dacre Press, 1954); E. Haenchen, *Die Apostelgeschichte;* J. Munck, *The Acts of the Apostles,* Anchor Bible Series (Garden City, N.Y.: Doubleday and Co., 1967); Geoffrey W. H. Lampe, *The Seal of the Spirit* (London: S.P.C.K., 1967).

10. Munck, op cit. pp. 73ff.

11. Ernst Käsemann, "Die Johannesjünger in Ephesus," *Exegetische Versuche und Besinnungen* (Göttingen: Vandenhoeck & Ruprecht, 1967) pp. 158–167.

12. J. D. G. Dunn, *Baptism in the Holy Spirit* (Naperville: A. R. Allenson, 1970) pp. 65ff.

13. Haenchen, op. cit., pp. 256–259.

14. Lampe, op. cit., pp. 64ff.

15. J. Fitzmyer, "Acts of the Apostles," *Jerome Biblical Commentary* (Englewood Cliffs, N.J.: Prentice-Hall, 1968) p. 185.

16. Montague, op. cit., pp. 8ff.

17. Thornton, op. cit., pp. 73ff.

18. *Didache*, 7; English trans. in Whitaker, op cit., p. 1.

19. *Barnabas and the Didache, The Apostolic Fathers*, trans. R. A. Kraft (New York: Nelson, 1965).

20. Justin, *The First Apology*, nn. 61–62, trans. in Whitaker, op. cit., p. 2.

21. Hermas, *The Shepherd, The Apostolic Fathers*, trans. G. F. Snyder (Camden, N.J.: Thomas Nelson & Sons, 1968).

22. Clement of Alexandria, *Christ the Educator*, trans. S. P. Wood, (New York: Fathers of the Church, Inc., 1954) I, 6, 25; I, 6, 32; III, 11, 59.

23. Hippolytus, *The Apostolic Tradition*, cc. 16–23, trans. in Whitaker, op. cit., pp. 3–7.

24. Whitaker, op cit., p. 6.

25. Origen, *Commentary on the Romans*, v. 9; cf. *Texte zur Geschichte der Taufe*, ed. H. Kraft (Berlin: Walter de Groyter, 1969) p. 26.

26. Tertullian, *De Baptismo*, cc. 6–8, trans. in Whitaker, op. cit., p. 9.

27. Tertullian, *De Carne Resurrectionis*, 8, trans. in Whitaker, op. cit., p. 9.

28. For a detailed description of this controversy cf. Neunheuser, op. cit., pp. 92ff.

29. Cyril of Jerusalem, *Mystagogical Catechesis*, n. 2–3, trans. in Whitaker op. cit., p. 26. Cf. also L. Mitchell, *Baptismal Anointing* (London: S.P.C.K., 1966). This latter is undoubtedly the most thorough study to date on the subject of these baptismal anointings.

30. Ambrose, *De Sacramentis*, B 3, nn. 4–5, trans. in Whitaker, op. cit., p. 120.

31. N. Mitchell, op. cit., p. 52.

32. Ibid., p. 55.

33. Ligier, op. cit., p. 120.

34. Ibid., p. 122.

35. This characterization of Kavanagh's opinion is from F. Quinn, "Confirmation Reconsidered: Rite and Meaning," *Worship*, v. 59 (1985) n. 4, p. 354; cf. Kavanagh, "Confirmation: A Suggestion from Structure," *Worship*, v. 58 (1984) pp. 386–395.

36. T. Marsh, *Gift of Community: Baptism and Confirmation*, p. 53.

37. Quinn. op. cit., pp. 354–370.

38. Neunheuser, op. cit., p. 247.

39. D. Winzen, *Kommentar zur Deutschen Thomas-Ausgabe,* v. 29, p. 530, cited in Neunheuser, op. cit., pp. 251–252.

40. Ligier, op. cit., p. 246.

41. J. Jeremias, *New Testament Theology,* trans. J. Bowden, (New York: Charles Scribner's Sons, 1971) pp. 76–85.

42. Haenchen, op. cit., pp. 130ff.

43. H. Küng, *The Church,* trans. Ray and Rosaleen Ockenden (New York: Sheed and Ward, 1967) p. 173.

44. *Lumen Gentium,* 8.

45. Ibid. 11.

46. Regli, op. cit., p. 323.

47. *Book of Common Prayer, p. 412.*

48. Hatchett, op. cit., p. 271.

49. *Manual on the Liturgy,* p. 339.

50. Ibid., p. 340.

51. *Lutheran Book of Worship,* p. 198.

8. Eucharist and the Teaching of the Church

1. Translation is from *The Church Teaches,* pp. 286–288, 290, 295–296.

2. Since the eucharist is such a sensitive and vital area for Roman Catholic thought, let me add here the theses as presented by Joseph A. de Aldama, S.J., who wrote in the BAC edition *Sacrae Theologiae Summa,* one of the finest and last of the manuals.

1. Jesus Christ at the Last Supper gave his body and blood under the appearance of bread and wine to his apostles for their reception. *(De fide divina et catholica definita)*

2. Christ at the Last Supper offered his body and blood under the appearance of bread and wine to God the Father. (It seems to be *de fide divina et catholica definita.* Other theologians whom he cites maintain that this was not defined.)

3. Christ at the Last Supper gave to the apostles and their succesors both the mandate and the power to consecrate, offer and minister his own body and blood, just as he had done. *(De fide divina et catholica definita.* Contemporary biblical scholars would require that his judgment be seriously modified.)

4. Christ in the sermon on the bread of life promised what he fulfilled in the Last Supper, by giving to his apostles his body and blood. *(Communis et certa)*

5. The offering made by Melchizedek was a type of the eucharistic mystery. *(Doctrina catholica)*

6. The eucharist is that offering which the Lord had foretold through Malachi which would be offered in every place to his name, and which would be great among the nations. *(Doctrina catholica)*

7. In the eucharist the body and blood, truly, really and substantially, together with the soul and divinity of our Lord Jesus Christ, and therefore the total Christ, is contained. *(De fide divina catholica)*

8. In the eucharist the substance of bread and wine does not remain with the body and blood of Christ; there occurs that wonderful and singular conversion of the entire substance of the bread and of the entire substance of the wine into the body and blood; indeed this conversion the Catholic Church most aptly calls transubstantiation.

   It is here that Aldama makes some distinctions, which we noted above, namely, that the *fact* of transubstantiation is solemnly defined; the term transubstantiation is to be retained and is called a matter of *doctrina catholica.*

9. In the eucharist the appearances of bread and wine really and objectively remain the very same appearances which were in the substance of bread and wine prior to the consecration; they now remain without any subject. *(Saltem doctrina catholica)*

10. Christ in the eucharist is present totally under each species and totally under any part of them, whether this is done before the separation or after. *(De fide divina et catholica definita* as regards the issue that the total Christ is present under either form; that the total Christ is contained in only a portion of each of the species when the separation is made, Aldama says is the same. Before the separation, it is only *doctrina catholica.)*

11. In the Mass a true and proper sacrifice is offered to God. *(De fide divina et catholica definita)*

12. The sacrifice of the Mass essentially is a representation and renewal of the sacrifice of the cross. *(De fide divina et catholica definita)*

13. The victim at the sacrifice of the Mass is Christ himself. *(De fide divina et catholica definita)*

14. Christ is the main offerer in the sacrifice of the Mass. *(De fide divina et catholica definita)*

15. The representation of the sacrifice of the cross in the Mass is formally had in the consecration of each species; the sacrificial action of this sacrifice is to be placed essentially here. *(Doctrina catholica, with many Roman Catholic theologians in dispute)*

244 THE CHRISTIAN SACRAMENTS OF INITIATION

16. The sacrificial action of the Mass occurs formally in the fact that through the dual consecration the bloody separation of the body and blood is presented in an unbloody manner and therefore the same victim of the cross is offered and immolated by the same principal offerer through distinct signs of his death. *(Theological opinion)*

17. The Mass is a latreutic, eucharistic, propitiatory and impetratory sacrifice. *(De fide divina et catholica definita)*

18. The eucharist is a true sacrament of the new law and is permanent. (That it is a sacrament is *de fide divina et catholica definita;* the permanency of the sacrament is *doctrina communis.*)

19. The sacrament of the eucharist essentially and intrinsically remains under the appearances of bread and wine with the words of consecration morally continuing and therefore the body and blood are really present. *(Communior et probabilior)*

20. Sacramental communion brings about a union with Christ insofar as it increases grace and arouses charity through which this union is perfected. (An increase of grace is *de fide divina et catholica definita;* the rest is *doctrina catholica.*)

21. Through sacramental communion we are freed from our venial sins and preserved from mortal sins; our concupiscence is lessened. (Liberation from sin is *de fide divina et catholica definita;* the remainder is *doctrina catholica.*)

22. The sacrament of the eucharist is sacramentally for those who receive it a pledge of eternal life. *(De fide divina et catholic definita)*

23. In sacramental communion the mutual union of the members of the Church is increased. *(De fide divina et catholica definita)*

24. The sacrament of the eucharist is not necessary by necessity of means, neither actually nor in desire, to obtain salvation; it is however necessary because of a widely defined moral necessity to remain for a long time in the state of grace. (That the eucharist is not necessary for salvation is *de fide divina et catholica definita;* the remainder is theological opinion.)

If one looks carefully at all the theses above, one notes that there are a large number which are not truly "official" or "solemn" Church teachings. This is perfectly legitimate for such authors as Aldama, who are trying to present a total "theology of eucharist," not simply the "official teaching." In doing this, they need to include many theological opinions. This is why Aldama continually tries to clarify what is really *de fide definita* and what is simply *common* doctrine. It might also be recalled that at the time of Aldama a certain Thomistic approach was "common," but other approaches were acceptable and respectable in the Church.

9. The Eucharist in the New Testament

1. Cf. among other works J. A. Jungmann, *The Mass of the Roman Rite: Its Origins and Development (Missarum Solemnia)*, trans. F. A. Brunner, 2 vols. (New York: Benziger, 1951–1955); A.-G. Martimort (ed.), *The Eucharist*, A. Flanery and V. Ryan, eds. (New York: Herder and Herder, 1973); L. Bouyer, *Eucharist*, trans. C. U. Quinn (Notre Dame, Ind.: University of Notre Dame Press, 1968); Theodor Klauser, *A Short History of the Western Liturgy*, trans. J. Halliburton (Oxford: Oxford University Press, 1981). Klauser provides a lengthy bibliography (pp. 175–231) which is quite helpful.

2. Cf. Jon Sobrino, *Christology at the Crossroads*, trans. J. Drury (Maryknoll, N.Y.: Orbis, 1982) pp. 365ff.; cf. also Leonardo Boff, *Jesus Christ Liberator*, trans. P. Hughes (Maryknoll, N.Y.: Orbis, 1978) pp. 100ff.

3. J. Jeremias, *The Eucharistic Words of Jesus*, pp. 96–100; cf. also J. Fitzmyer, *The Gospel according to Luke*, vol. 2, pp. 1386–1403.

4. Jeremias, ibid., p. 100.

5. Fitzmyer, ibid., p. 1395.

6. Howard Z. Cleveland, *Zondervan Pictorial Bible Dictionary* (Grand Rapids, Mich.: Zondervan Publishing House, 1963) p. 518.

7. Jeremias, *New Testament Theology*, p. 115.

8. Ibid.

9. Cf. L. Bouyer, op. cit.

10. Jeremias, *The Eucharistic Words of Jesus*, pp. 41–84.

11. This issue of the recognition of Jesus as *Kyrios* is connected with much of the material on the resurrection; among other works cf. F.-X Durwell, *La Résurrection de Jésus, Mystère de Salut* (Paris: Xavier Mappus, 1950); E. Dhanis (ed.), *Resurrexit: Actes du symposium international sur la Résurrection de Jésus* (Rome: Libreria Ediatrice Vaticana, 1974); C. F. Evans, *Resurrection and the New Testament* (London: SCM Press, 1970); R. Fuller, *The Formation of the Resurrection Narratives* (Philadelphia: Fortress Press, 1970); Xavier Leon-Dufour, S.J., *Resurrection and the Message of Jesus*, trans. G. Chapman (New York: Holt, Rinehart, Winston, 1974).

12. J. Betz, "Eucharistie als zentrales Mysterium," *Mysterium Salutis*, v. 4/2, p. 189.

13. J. Murphy-O'Connor, "Eucharist and Community in First Corinthians," *Worship*, v. 50 (1976) n. 5, pp. 370–385; v. 51 (1977) n. 1, pp. 56–69; reprinted in R. Kevin Seasoltz, *Living Bread, Saving Cup* (Collegeville, Minn.: The Liturgical Press, 1982). References are to this latter volume.

14. Op. cit., p. 16.

15. Ibid.
16. Ibid. p. 30.

10. Eucharist in the Early Church

1. J. Quasten, *Patrology* (Westminster, Md.: Newman Press, 1949) p. 31.

2. Cf. P. Drews, "Untersuchungen zur Didache," *Zeitschrift für die neutestamentliche Wissenschaft*, 5 (1904), pp. 53–79; M. Goguel, *L'Eucharistie des origénes a Justin Martyr* (Paris: 1910).

3. H. Lietzmann, *Messe und Herrenmahl* (Berlin: 1955).

4. W. Rordorf, "The *Didache*," *The Eucharist of the Early Christians*, trans. M. J. O'Connell (New York: Pueblo Publishing Co., 1978), pp. 1–23.

5. Translation is from D. J. Sheerin, *The Eucharist* (Wilmington, Del.: Michael Glazier, 1986) pp. 352–354. Sheerin has gathered together in this volume a number of excellent patristic sources on the eucharist.

6. Ibid. p. 284.

7. Ibid. pp. 33–37.

8. Cf. M. Jourjon, "Justin," *The Eucharist of the Early Christians*, pp. 71–85.

9. Ibid. p. 74.

10. Translation is from Sheerin, op. cit., pp. 355–356.

11. John Chrysostom, *In Hebr. hom.*, 17 3 (*PG* 63, 131). Other passages from John Chrysostom can be found in Sheerin, op. cit.

12. Betz, op. cit., p. 221.

13. Ibid., p. 267.

11. The Eucharistic Question of the Middle Ages and Beyond

1. Cf. E. Doronzo, *Tractatus dogmaticus de eucharistia*, v. 2 (Milwaukee: Bruce, 1948); E. Schillebeeckx, *The Eucharist*, trans. N. D. Smith (New York: Sheed and Ward, 1968) pp. 25–68; Jean de Baciocchi, "Le mystère eucharistique dans les perspectives de la bible," *Nouvelle Revue de Théologie*, 77 (1955) pp. 561–580; various articles in *Irenikon*, 33 (1959); B. Neunheuser, *Eucharistie in Mittelalter und Neuzeit* (Freiburg: Herder, 1963).

2. Guitmund of Aversa, *De corporis et sanguinis Christi veritate in eucharistia*, *PL*, v. 149, 1467 B.

3. Denzinger, *Enchiridion Symbolorum*, 700.

4. Betz, op. cit., p. 234 notes that at this time there was no clearly defined meaning of the word "substance," even though from this period onward "substance" came to be a key word for the eucharistic mystery: "Die Substanz

wurde von da an der Schlusselbegriff fur das Verständnis des Mysteriums. Aber man hatte zunächst noch gar keinen genauen und befriedigenden Begriff von der Substanz, nur eine vage Vorstellung und Spur.''

5. Denzinger, op. cit., 784; cf. also 782.

6. Ibid., 802.

7. Ibid., 860.

8. Ibid., 1151.

9. Ibid., 1321.

10. Ibid., 1352.

11. Cf. Jedin, *A History of the Council of Trent,* v. 2, pp. 179ff.

12. Denzinger, op. cit., 1642.

13. Ibid., 1651.

14. Ibid., 1652.

15. K. Rahner, ''Die Gegenwart Christi im Sakrament des Herren-mahles,'' *Schriften zür Theologie,* v. 4 (Einsiedeln: Benziger, 1964) p. 369.

16. *Concilii Tridentini Actorum Pars Septima,* v. 7 of *Concilium Tridentinum,* edited by Gorresgesellschaft (Freiburg: Herder, 1919) p. 184. This will be referred to henceforth by *CT.*

17. Ibid. p. 188.

18. E. Schillebeeckx, op. cit., p. 48.

19. Paul VI, *Mysterium Fidei,* Engl. text published by NCWC (Huntington, Ind.: Our Sunday Visitor Inc., 1965) n. 61.

20. Doronzo, op. cit., p. 267.

21. J. Piccirelli, *De Catholico Intellectu Dogmatis Transsubstantionis* (Naples: M. D'Auria, 1912) p. 40.

22. Ibid., p. 41.

23. Ibid., p. 41.

24. De Aldama, op. cit., pp. 275–276.

25. Ibid., p. 276.

26. Schillebeeckx, op. cit., pp. 372ff.

27. Rahner, op. cit., p. 372.

28. Denzinger, op. cit., 1642.

29. Cf. Betz, op. cit., p. 252: ''Auch wenn die Konzilsväter als Kinder ihrer Zeit die Transsubstantiation nur in aristotelischen Denkvorstellungen gedacht haben, so ist doch diese philosophische Substruktur ihres Denkens nicht mitkanonisiert.''

30. C. Vollert, ''Transubstantiation,'' *New Catholic Encyclopedia* (New York: McGraw-Hill, 1967) v. 14, p. 260.

31. E. Gutwenger, ''Transubstantiation,'' *Sacramentum Mundi,* v. 6, p. 293.

32. Neunheuser, *Eucharistie in Mittelalter und Neuzeit,* p. 63.

33. Cf. Schillebeeckx, op. cit., pp. 95–96.

34. For a detailed account of this theological discussion, cf. R. G. Cipolla, "Selvaggi Revisited: Transubstantiation and Contemporary Science," *Theological Studies*, v. 35 (1974) pp. 667–691.

35. C. Vollert, "Current Theology: The Eucharist: Controversy on Transubstantiation," *Theological Studies*, v. 22 (1961) pp. 391–425.

36. Cf. L. Swidler, *The Eucharist in Ecumenical Dialogue* (New York: Paulist Press, 1976) for a mutli-dimensional ecumenical approach to the eucharist by theologians of various denominations and Churches.

37. Paul VI, *Mysterium Fidei*, 41.

38. Ibid., 41–45.

39. Ibid. 45.

40. Cf. Regis Duffy, *Real Presence: Worship, Sacraments and Commitment* (San Francisco: Harper & Row, 1982).

41. Cf. a history of this eucharistic devotion in N. Mitchell, *Cult and Controversy: The Worship of the Eucharist Outside Mass* (New York: Pueblo Publishing Co., 1982).

12. The Eucharistic Question of the Reformation and Beyond

1. Cf. K. Osborne, "Ecumenical Eucharist," *Journal of Ecumenical Studies*, v. 6 (1969) pp. 598–619; also J. Betz, "Der Opfercharakter des Abendmahls in interkonfessionellen Dialog," *Theologie im Wandel* (Munich: Erich Wewel Verlag, 1967), p. 469–491.

2. John Calvin, *Institutes of the Christian Religion*, trans. F. L. Battles (Philadelphia: Westminster, Press, 1960) vol. II, pp. 1429–1437.

3. Martin Luther, *Die Bekenntnisschriften der evangelisch-lutherischen Kirche*, (Göttingen: Vandenhoeck & Ruprecht, 1959) p. 419; translated and edited by T. G. Tappert, *The Book of Concord* (Philadelphia: Muhlenberg Press, 1959) p. 294.

4. *Die Bekenntnisschriften und Kirchenordnungen der nach Gottes Wort reformierten Kirche* (Zurich: Evangelischer Verlag A.G. Zollikon, 1938) p. 168.

5. Cf. Jedin, *A History of the Council of Trent*.

6. Denzinger, op. cit., 1521.

7. The Thomistic school generally held to instrumental causality of the sacraments. Not all instrumental causality, as propounded by theologians, caused difficulty; only those theologians who made the instrumental causality of the sacraments something in addition to the causality of Jesus' own sacrifice should be regarded as contrary to Christian teaching.

8. A. Harnack, cited in Jedin, op. cit., v. II, p. 310.

9. Denzinger, op. cit., 1740–1743.

10. Betz, op. cit., p. 476.

11. *Baptism, Eucharist and Ministry,* 4.

12. Ibid., 8.

13. Ibid. "Commentary 8."

14. R. De Vaux, *Ancient Israel: Its Life and Institutions,* trans. J. McHugh (New York: McGraw-Hill, 1965).

15. R. Daly, *Christian Sacrifice* (Washington, D.C.: The Catholic University of America Press, 1978).

16. E. J. Kilmartin, "Eucharist as Sacrifice," *New Catholic Encyclopedia,* v. 5 (New York: McGraw-Hill, 1967).

17. R. Rendtorff, *Studien zur Geschichte des Opfers im Alten Israel,* WMANT v. 24 (Neukirchen: 1967).

18. J. Betz, "Eucharistie als zentrales Mysterium," loc. cit., pp. 185–313.

19. Cf. Daly, op. cit. It should be admitted that I find the orientation of this book somewhat at odds with my own. Daly is quite taken with Origen's theme of the sacrifice of the Christian, which in many ways might go against the once and for all aspect of Jesus' own sacrifice.

20. Daly, op. cit., p. 508.

21. "The Ecclesial Nature of the Eucharist," *A/RC Documents,* III, a Report by the Joint Study Group (Washington, D.C.: USCC, 1976). Italics are mine. Cf. also the section, "The Eucharist as Sacrifice," *The Eucharist as Sacrifice: Lutherans and Catholics in Dialogue,* pp. 181–191; cf. also the wording on eucharist and sacrifice in "The Canterbury Statement," *A/RC Documents* III, p. 78.

13. The Eucharist, An Integral Part of Christian Initiation

1. K. Stendahl, "The Focal Point of the New Testament Baptismal Teachings," *Lutherans and Catholics in Dialogue,* vol. II, "One Baptism for the Remission of Sins," ed. Paul C. Empie and William W. Baum (Washington D.C.: NCWC 1966) p. 24.

2. Cf. *Vatican II; The Conciliar and Post Conciliar Documents,* ed. Austin Flannery, O.P., *Decree on Ecumenism,* n. 15; *Ad Totam Ecclesiam* (May 14, 1967) from the Secretariat for Promotion of Christian Unity, nn. 39–54.

3. Cf. ibid., *Ad Totam Ecclesiam,* nn. 55–63; also from the same secretariat, *Dan ces dernier temps* (Jan. 7, 1970); also from the same source: *In quibus rerum circumstantiis* (June 1, 1972); *Dopo le publicazione* (Oct. 17, 1973).